Microsoft SharePo
2010 Development
with Visual Studio
2010: Expert
Cookbook

Develop, debug, and deploy business solutions for
SharePoint applications using Visual Studio 2010

Balaji Kithiganahalli

[PACKT]
PUBLISHING

BIRMINGHAM - MUMBAI

Microsoft SharePoint 2010 Development with Visual Studio 2010: Expert Cookbook

First published: September 2011

Production Reference: 1190911

Published by Packt Publishing Ltd.
Livery Place
35 Livery Street
Birmingham B3 2PB, UK.

ISBN 978-1-84968-458-3

www.packtpub.com

Cover Image by Sandeep Babu (sandyjb@gmail.com)

Credits

Author

Balaji Kithiganahalli

Reviewers

Wei Chung, Low
Michael Nemtsev
Doug Ortiz

Acquisition Editor

Dhwani Devater

Development Editor

Hithesh Uchil

Technical Editor

Prashant Macha

Project Coordinator

Shubhanjan Chatterjee

Proofreader

Lisa Brady

Indexer

Tejal Daruwale

Graphics

Nilesh Mohite

Production Coordinator

Melwyn Dsa

Cover Work

Melwyn Dsa

About the Author

Balaji Kithiganahalli has been a computer nerd since 1995. He has a Master's degree in Systems Engineering and is currently serving as CEO and partner for Integrate, LLC. His company specializes in systems integration and custom software development. He has over 15 years of software development and architectural experience. He has consulted with several government and multi-national clients.

He is a technology agnostic who used to mainly work on J2EE related technologies. Since 2003, he is mainly involved in implementing SharePoint and .NET technologies. He is currently architecting SharePoint 2010 implementation for a very large government organization in Atlanta, GA.

When not working, he enjoys going for bike rides with his kids and reading books about other technologies. He currently lives in Atlanta, GA with his beautiful wife and two kids.

Acknowledgement

Every journey begins with a first step; this is true in my case as it is my first book. This journey of mine would not have been successful if it was not for the support of my family and many of my friends. I am truly blessed with such wonderful family and friends.

First and foremost, I'd like to thank my mom, dad, and brother for their wonderful support and encouragement in every step of the way and providing moral support when needed. I would also like to thank my lovely wife Vanishree and kids Veda and Amit for their patience, support, and understanding without which I would have never been able to complete this book. Next, I would like to thank my technical reviewers. You guys did an awesome job. Your insight and input has increased the overall value of this book.

I would also like to thank my publisher Packt Publishing, and the many fine people such as Dhwani, Shubhanjan, Hithesh, and Prashant for their valuable input and patience. You guys ROCK! I guess I owe you guys a beer when you are here in Atlanta.

Writing a book is a lot of work and is time-consuming. Even though I am the only author on this book, there are many people who are involved in making this book a finished product for the readers. While I may not come in contact with many of these folks, I would like to thank them and certainly appreciate their work and effort.

About the Reviewers

Wei Chung, Low a Technical Lead in BizTalk and .NET and a MCT, MCPD, MCITP, MCTS, MCSD.NET, works with ResMed (NYSE: RMD), at its Kuala Lumpur, Malaysia campus. He is also a member of PMI, certified as a PMP. He started working on Microsoft .NET in his early career and has been involved in development, consultation, and corporate training in the area here of business intelligence, system integration, and virtualization. He previously worked for the Bursa Malaysia (formerly Kuala Lumpur Stock Exchange) and Shell IT International, which provided him with rich integration experience across different platforms.

He strongly believes that great system implementation delivers precious value to business, and the integration of various systems across different platforms shall always be a part of it. Just like how people from different cultures and diversities are used to living together in most of the major cities, in harmony.

Doug Ortiz is an independent consultant whose skillset encompasses multiple platforms such as .Net, SharePoint, Office, and SQL server.

He possesses a Master's degree in Relational Databases and has over 20 years of experience in Information Technology. Of those years of experience, half are within .Net and SharePoint. His roles have ranged from Architecture, Implementation, Administration, Disaster Recovery, Migrations, Development, and Automation of Information Systems; in and outside of SharePoint.

He is the founder of Illustris, LLC and can be reached at: dougortiz@illustris.org.

Interesting aspects of his profession:

- ▶ Doug has experience in integrating multiple platforms and products with the purpose of sharing data.
- ▶ He has improved, salvaged, and architected projects by utilizing unique and innovative techniques.

His hobbies include Yoga and Scuba Diving.

I would like to thank my wonderful wife Mila for all her help and support as well as Maria and Nikolay.

I would also like to thank everyone at Packt Publishing for their encouragement and guidance.

Michael Nemtsev is an ex-Microsoft MVP in .NET/C# and SharePoint Server 2010 and has held that status between the years 2005 and 2011.

Michael's expertize are in Enterprise Integration and Platform and Collaboration areas and currently he is working as a Senior Consultant at Microsoft in Sydney, Australia helping clients to improve business collaboration with SharePoint 2010 and Office365.

www.PacktPub.com

Support files, eBooks, discount offers, and more

You might want to visit `www.PacktPub.com` for support files and downloads related to your book.

Did you know that Packt offers eBook versions of every book published, with PDF and ePub files available? You can upgrade to the eBook version at `www.PacktPub.com` and as a print book customer, you are entitled to a discount on the eBook copy. Get in touch with us at `service@packtpub.com` for more details.

At `www.PacktPub.com`, you can also read a collection of free technical articles, sign up for a range of free newsletters, and receive exclusive discounts and offers on Packt books and eBooks.

`http://PacktLib.PacktPub.com`

Do you need instant solutions to your IT questions? PacktLib is Packt's online digital book library. Here, you can access, read, and search across Packt's entire library of books.

Why Subscribe?

- ▶ Fully searchable across every book published by Packt
- ▶ Copy and paste, print and bookmark content
- ▶ On demand and accessible via web browser

Free Access for Packt account holders

If you have an account with Packt at `www.PacktPub.com`, you can use this to access PacktLib today and view nine entirely free books. Simply use your login credentials for immediate access.

Instant Updates on New Packt Books

Get notified! Find out when new books are published by following `@PacktEnterprise` on Twitter, or the *Packt Enterprise* Facebook page.

Table of Contents

Preface

Microsoft SharePoint 2010 is the best-in-class platform for content management and collaboration. With Visual Studio, developers have an end-to-end business solutions development IDE. To leverage this powerful combination of tools it is necessary to understand the different building blocks of SharePoint. This book will provide necessary concepts and present ways to develop complex business solutions and take them further.

SharePoint 2010 Development with Visual Studio 2010 Expert Cookbook is an instructional guide for developing, debugging and deploying applications for SharePoint 2010 environment using Visual Studio 2010. The cookbook approach helps you to dip into any recipe that interests you or you can also read it from cover to cover if you want to get hands on with the complete application development cycle.

With this book you will learn to develop event handlers, workflows, content types, web parts, client object model applications, and web services for SharePoint 2010 in an instructional manner. You will discover the less known facts behind debugging feature receivers, deployment of web parts, utilizing free toolkits to enhance the development and debugging experience.

You will learn the newer development approach called Visual Web Parts and how to develop and deploy Silverlight applications that can be used with Silverlight web parts. You will also explore the SandBoxed deployment model and its usage. You will create your own web services for SharePoint and learn more about the Client Object Model introduced in SharePoint 2010. All in all, you will develop SharePoint solutions in an instructional manner that eases the learning process.

What this book covers

Chapter 1, List and Event Receivers: Event Receivers are used for responding to events raised by SharePoint on lists, features, list items, and so on. This chapter not only provides an overview of the event receivers that can be developed using Visual Studio 2010, but also guides you through the step-by-step process of creating them and applying them to real world scenarios.

Chapter 2, Workflows: In this chapter, you will learn about sequential workflows, site workflows, and deploying custom initiation forms with workflows using ASPX pages and InfoPath forms. You will also learn to create custom InfoPath task forms with the workflows.

Chapter 3, Advanced Workflows: In this chapter, you will learn Advanced Workflow topics such as creating custom activity for both sandboxed and non-sandboxed environments. You will not only learn how to create state machine workflows but also to model them. This chapter also guides you through the process of creating a Pluggable workflow service. Last but not least, this chapter also guides you through the process of changing workflow statuses.

Chapter 4, List Definitions and Content Types: In this chapter, we will discover the world of content types. We will use object models to create content types, add new columns, document templates, and workflows to content types using Visual Studio 2010. This chapter also guides you through the process of creating external content types that are linked to external data source such as the SQL Server database. In the end of the chapter, we will also learn how to create list definitions using Visual Studio.

Chapter 5, Web Parts: In this chapter, we will discover visual web parts, code-only web parts, AJAX enabled web parts, and Silverlight web parts. The chapter also provides details on connectable web parts and adding configuration properties to web parts. This chapter also provides detailed information on versioning and deployment of web parts.

Chapter 6, Web Services and REST: In this chapter, we will learn about using REST services to extract data from SharePoint. We will create client applications that make use of REST to extract data from SharePoint. We will also learn to create custom SharePoint WCF web services.

Chapter 7, Working with Client Object Model: SharePoint 2010 introduced the new Client Object Model which can be used to create client applications that use SharePoint as a backend data store. In this chapter, we will learn all the three client object models such as the managed object model, the JavaScript object model, and the Silverlight object model. We will also learn the exception handling techniques and asynchronous calling of these object models.

What you need for this book

This book presents a series of projects that demonstrates the features of SharePoint 2010 and Visual Studio 2010. In order to gain hands on experience of these features, it is recommended that you have a 64-bit Windows development machine with lots of memory. *Chapter 1, List and Event Receivers* of this book provides the list of software and links that you can refer to set up your development environment. If you do not have a license for this software, you can always get the trial version from the Microsoft website.

Alternatively, you can read through this book without working through the projects. There are plenty of screenshots that provide a good sense of how these solutions work. This is not a suitable approach for beginner programmers.

Who this book is for

This book is for .NET developers to understand the building blocks of SharePoint 2010. Although the book can be used by beginners, it is recommended that the readers have an understanding of the previous versions of SharePoint. Developing SharePoint solutions requires solid understanding of ASP.NET architecture. The book assumes that the reader is familiar with ASP.NET technology and development concepts.

Conventions

In this book, you will find a number of styles of text that distinguish between different kinds of information. Here are some examples of these styles, and an explanation of their meaning.

Code words in text are shown as follows: "We can include other contexts through the use of the include directive."

A block of code is set as follows:

```
private string GetInitiationData()
    {
       return this.txtCreditAmount.Text;
    }
```

Any command-line input or output is written as follows:

```
Add-SPSolution -LiteralPath <Location of your wsp>

Install-SPSolution -Identity <WSPName> -WebApplication <URLname>

Enable-SPFeature FeatureFolderName -Url <URLName>
```

New terms and **important words** are shown in bold. Words that you see on the screen, in menus or dialog boxes for example, appear in the text like this: "Select **File** | **New** | **Project**. The new project wizard dialog box as shown will be displayed (Make sure to select **.NET Framework 3.5** in the top drop-down box)".

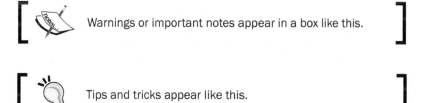

Warnings or important notes appear in a box like this.

Tips and tricks appear like this.

Reader feedback

Feedback from our readers is always welcome. Let us know what you think about this book—what you liked or may have disliked. Reader feedback is important for us to develop titles that you really get the most out of.

To send us general feedback, simply send an e-mail to feedback@packtpub.com, and mention the book title via the subject of your message.

If there is a book that you need and would like to see us publish, please send us a note in the **SUGGEST A TITLE** form on www.packtpub.com or e-mail suggest@packtpub.com.

If there is a topic that you have expertise in and you are interested in either writing or contributing to a book, see our author guide on www.packtpub.com/authors.

Customer support

Now that you are the proud owner of a Packt book, we have a number of things to help you to get the most from your purchase.

Downloading the example code for this book

You can download the example code files for all Packt books you have purchased from your account at http://www.PacktPub.com. If you purchased this book elsewhere, you can visit http://www.PacktPub.com/support and register to have the files e-mailed directly to you.

Errata

Although we have taken every care to ensure the accuracy of our content, mistakes do happen. If you find a mistake in one of our books—maybe a mistake in the text or the code—we would be grateful if you would report this to us. By doing so, you can save other readers from frustration and help us improve subsequent versions of this book. If you find any errata, please report them by visiting http://www.packtpub.com/support, selecting your book, clicking on the **errata submission form** link, and entering the details of your errata. Once your errata are verified, your submission will be accepted and the errata will be uploaded on our website, or added to any list of existing errata, under the Errata section of that title. Any existing errata can be viewed by selecting your title from http://www.packtpub.com/support.

Piracy

Piracy of copyright material on the Internet is an ongoing problem across all media. At Packt, we take the protection of our copyright and licenses very seriously. If you come across any illegal copies of our works, in any form, on the Internet, please provide us with the location address or website name immediately so that we can pursue a remedy.

Please contact us at `copyright@packtpub.com` with a link to the suspected pirated material.

We appreciate your help in protecting our authors, and our ability to bring you valuable content.

Questions

You can contact us at `questions@packtpub.com` if you are having a problem with any aspect of the book, and we will do our best to address it.

1
Lists and Event Receivers

In this chapter, we will cover:

- ▶ Validating data when an item is added to a list
- ▶ Adding a custom error message to the Event Receiver
- ▶ Adding an Application Page to an Event Receiver
- ▶ Working with List Event Receiver
- ▶ Deploying Event Receivers
- ▶ Creating a Feature Receiver
- ▶ Debugging a Feature Receiver
- ▶ Debugging Feature Installed events

Introduction

SharePoint 2010 has a very robust event handling capability that can be used for custom pre and post list event processing. When you create your custom event receivers, you are writing event handlers for different events that SharePoint fires due to an action. The main events triggered by SharePoint can be classified as follows:

- ▶ List Events
- ▶ List Item Events
- ▶ List Email Events
- ▶ Web Events
- ▶ List Workflow Events
- ▶ Feature Events

The preceding events are triggered by SharePoint when changes, creations, or deletions happen on different objects like Lists, Sites, Site Collections, List Items, and so on.

All the events listed previously can be further classified as, **Synchronous and Asynchronous** events. **Synchronous** events are those that are fired before an action takes place (for example, the `ItemAdding` event or the `ItemDeleting` event on a List Item). **Synchronous** events are executed on the same thread as the code, before sending the response to the browser. **Asynchronous** events are those that take place after the action has happened for example, the **FeatureActivated** event or **FeatureInstalled** event on Features.

For example, a Synchronous event `ItemAdded` on list item can be used to verify the data that is being added to a list before it gets added. This way you have control over the data that gets added and if needed, you can cancel the data getting added to the list. You cannot cancel an **Asynchronous** event. Asynchronous events are used for business process flow like sending an e-mail after the item gets added to the list.

Typical scenarios that include creating event handlers are as follows:

 ▸ Custom data validation so you can avoid adding an item to the list if data validation fails

 ▸ Sending a custom e-mail when an item is added to a list

 ▸ Logging to external database for audit purposes and so on

The custom event receiver you write will be packaged as a solution file (with .wsp extension) to deploy to SharePoint event host. Every event receiver is bound to some SharePoint object which is also its host. Site, Web, List, Features, and so on are some of the examples of the hosts. In the previous versions of the Visual Studio, there were no out-of-the-box templates that supported SharePoint development. You had to manually create your manifest files and `feature.xml` files and use `MakeCab.exe` for creating your solution files to deploy. The other alternative was to use open source tools like WSPBuilder for making life a little easier. However, this is not the case with Visual Studio 2010. There are templates available for Event Receivers, Workflows, List Definitions, Visual Web Parts, and many more. We will work with many of them in the subsequent chapters.

 Do not use event handlers for long running processes. Use Workflows for that purpose. We will handle Workflows in *Chapter 2, Workflows.*

Feature receivers like List Event Receivers are handlers that you write when certain events happen from Features. In the Feature Event Receivers, you can write custom handlers when events like **Feature Installation, Feature Activation, Feature Deactivation,** or **Feature Uninstall** happens.

Feature Event Receivers are used when you, as a programmer, needs to create entries in `web.config` for database access or if you are a product vendor, then activate license files, and so on when a Feature is installed or activated. You can also use event receivers for clean-up activities like removing an entry from `web.config` or delete a list, and so on when a Feature is removed or deactivated.

Validating data when an item is added to a list

In this recipe, we will learn how to create a custom event handler for the `ItemAdding` synchronous event. We will validate the data that is being added to the contact list. We will validate the format of the phone number and e-mail address. The phone number should be of U.S. format. It must consist of three numeric characters, optionally enclosed in parenthesis, followed by a set of three numeric characters, and a set of four numeric characters. The e-mail should follow the standard e-mail notation. We will not allow users to enter some garbage information in these fields. If the data fails, our custom validation will cancel the event so that the data is not inserted into the list.

Getting ready

You should have a fully functional development machine with SharePoint 2010 installed and configured. You also need Visual Studio 2010 IDE installed on the same development machine. The following is the baseline software that is needed to set up the development machine:

- Windows 64-bit compliant OS (like Windows 7 or Windows 2008 R2 server)
- NET Framework 4.0 (Visual Studio 2010 will install Framework 4.0 whereas SharePoint 2010 requires .NET Framework 3.5)
- Visual Studio 2010 with or without Service Pack 1
- Expression Blend (optional, but would be helpful in following on Silverlight example)
- SQL Server 2008 or SQL Server 2008 R2 (express version is also okay)
- SharePoint Designer (optional)
- SharePoint Server 2010
- Microsoft Office 2010 (InfoPath forms)

You can refer to step-by-step installation instructions of SharePoint on MSDN (`http://msdn.microsoft.com/en-us/library/ee554869.aspx`). You can also refer to *Microsoft 2010 SharePoint Administration Cookbook* by Peter Serzo published by Packt Publishing for initial configuration tasks. Peter provides detailed, step-by-step instructions on enabling Developer Dashboard, configuring Secure Store, and so on, which we will be using in the coming chapters. As a developer, it is good to have an understanding of SharePoint Administration as well.

Create a list from the SharePoint user interface called **Contacts** of template Contacts. The following screenshot shows the end result:

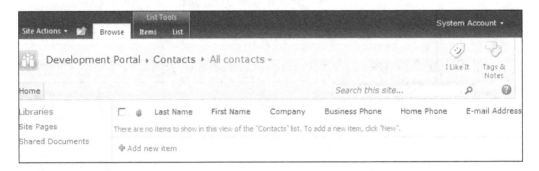

How to do it...

1. Launch your Visual Studio 2010 IDE as an administrator (right-click the shortcut and select **Run as administrator**).

2. Select **File | New | Project**. The new project wizard dialog box as shown will be displayed (Make sure to select **.NET Framework 3.5** in the top drop-down box):

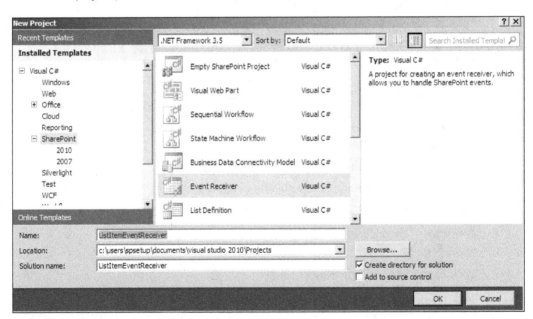

3. Select **Event Receiver** under **Visual C# | SharePoint | 2010** node from **Installed Templates** section on the left-hand side.

4. Name the project **ListItemEventReceiver** and provide a directory location where you want to save the project and click on **OK** to proceed to the next step in the wizard.

5. By default, Visual Studio selects the SharePoint site available on the machine. Select **Deploy as a Farm Solution** and click on **Next** to proceed to the next step in the wizard:

6. In here, make sure to select **List Item Events** from the drop-down for **What type of event receiver do you want?** and select **Contacts** for **What item should be the event source?**. Select the **An Item is being added** checkbox in the **Handle the following events** list box. The following screenshot indicates the selection:

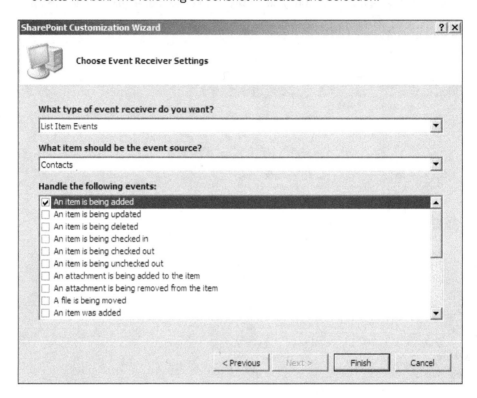

7. Click on **Finish** and Visual Studio adds in the necessary files and opens up the `EventReceiver1.cs`. This is the code file in which you are going to write your custom event handler.

8. Add the code necessary to validate the phone numbers and e-mail address of the list. Your code should look as follows:

```
using System;
using System.Security.Permissions;
using Microsoft.SharePoint;
using Microsoft.SharePoint.Security;
using Microsoft.SharePoint.Utilities;
using Microsoft.SharePoint.Workflow;
using System.Text.RegularExpressions;

namespace ListItemEventReceiver.EventReceiver1
{
```

```csharp
/// <summary>
/// List Item Events
/// </summary>
public class EventReceiver1 : SPItemEventReceiver
{
    /// <summary>
    /// An item is being added.
    /// </summary>
    public override void ItemAdding(SPItemEventProperties
    properties)
    {
        base.ItemAdding(properties);

        string sWorkPhone = properties.AfterProperties
        ["WorkPhone"].ToString();

        string sEmail = properties.AfterProperties["Email"].
        ToString();

        if (!string.IsNullOrEmpty(sWorkPhone))
        {
            if (!System.Text.RegularExpressions.Regex.
            IsMatch(sWorkPhone, @"^[01]?[- .]?(\([2-9]\
            d{2}\)|[2-9]\d{2})[- .]?\d{3}[- .]?\d{4}$"))
            {
                properties.Cancel = true;
            }
        }

        if (!string.IsNullOrEmpty(sEmail))
        {
            if (!System.Text.RegularExpressions.Regex.
            IsMatch(sEmail, @"^(?("")("".+?""@)|(([0-9a-zA-
            Z]((\.(?!\.))|[-!#\$%&'\*\+/=\?\^`\{\}\|~\
            w])*)(?<=[0-9a-zA-Z])@))(?(\[)(\[(\d{1,3}\.){3}\
            d{1,3}\])|(([0-9a-zA-Z][-\w]*[0-9a-zA-Z]\.)+[a-zA-
            Z]{2,6}))$"))
            {
                properties.Cancel = true;
            }
        }

    }


}
}
```

9. Build and execute the solution by pressing *F5* or from menu **Debug | Start Debugging**. This should bring up the default browser with the local site that you provided in the project creation wizard.

10. From your contacts list, select **Add new Item** to add a new item to the contact list. Here, we will deliberately enter a bad phone format for the **Business Phone** field as shown in the following screenshot to verify our list event handler:

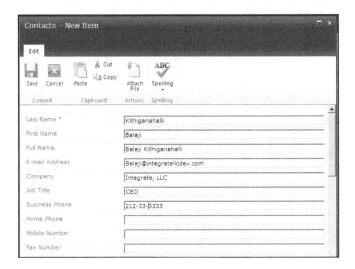

11. Click on the **Save** button on the toolbar, this will invoke the event handler and throws an error as shown in the next screenshot. If you notice, the error page indicates that an event receiver cancelled the request:

12. Close the error dialog and enter a new contact, but this time using the proper phone and e-mail format. The contact gets added without any problem as follows:

How it works...

When Visual Studio created the `EventReceiver` solution, it created a project item called **EventReceiver1**. This project item is a folder with two files `Elements.xml` and `EventReceiver1.cs`. The file `EventReceiver1.cs` is used to write our custom event handler code.

Elements.xml is the configuration file for our event receiver. It contains properties such as `Name`, `Type`, and `ListTemplateId`. Property `Type` indicates the event that we are handling. In this case we are handling `ItemAdding` event. In our solution, we associated our event receiver with the contacts list in the wizard. That information can be seen from the value associated with `ListTemplateId` attribute as shown in the next code snippet. The `ListTemplatId` of `105` corresponds to the contacts template. For the complete list of template IDs refer to MSDN at: `http://msdn.microsoft.com/en-us/library/microsoft.sharepoint.splisttemplatetype.aspx`.

If we deploy this solution to our website then any lists that are created using this template as the base will have our event receiver associated. Our code will get executed whenever SharePoint triggers the `ItemAdding` event for this `ListTemplateId`.

```xml
<?xml version="1.0" encoding="utf-8"?>
<Elements xmlns="http://schemas.microsoft.com/sharepoint/">
  <Receivers ListTemplateId="105">
    <Receiver>
      <Name>EventReceiver1ItemAdding</Name>
      <Type>ItemAdding</Type>
      <Assembly>$SharePoint.Project.AssemblyFullName$</Assembly>
      <Class>ListItemEventReceiver.EventReceiver1.EventReceiver1</Class>
      <SequenceNumber>10000</SequenceNumber>
    </Receiver>
  </Receivers>
</Elements>
```

Assembly element has some funny looking string. This is called the **Visual Studio** substitution token. When we build the package, these tokens are substituted by the actual value. In our case, the full assembly name will be added at this location. Class element just provides the fully qualified class name including the namespace.

In the `Elements.xml`, the `SequenceNumber` element has a special task. If there is multiple event receivers for the same list and if all are handling the same `ItemAdding` event like ours then SharePoint refers to this sequence number to determine the order of execution of the handlers. There is a missing element named **Synchronization**—that is an optional item not shown. It refers to execution of the event. You can set this to execute an event asynchronously or synchronously. But this element does not apply to a synchronous event like `ItemAdding`. Do not set this property in the `Elements.xml` file for synchronous events. You can set this property for asynchronous events like `ItemAdded` to run synchronously.

Visual Studio also added another project item called **Features**. This is another folder which contains a feature called **Feature1**. **Features** are the way to deploy customizations like Event Receivers, Visual Web Parts, Workflows, and so on to a SharePoint environment. If you have a large custom code that makes changes for example to site templates and creates various lists and so on, by using Features, you can package this code together and deploy this code across all the web front ends of your SharePoint farm in one go. This reduces the complexity of going to each and every location of your site template to add your customizations. Some of the capabilities that Features provide in SharePoint are as follows:

▶ Scoping—determines whether the custom code should run on Web Application, Site Collection, or on a Site.

▶ Pluggable behavior for installing and uninstalling the custom code

▶ Easy way to activate or deactivate the custom code to run

Using Features reduces the inconsistencies and versioning discrepancies across the web farm. In our case, it helps us deploy our custom Event Receiver. If you double-click on the **Feature1.feature** in Visual Studio, you can see as shown in the following screenshot that our Event Receiver is an item inside this feature. Here you can make modifications to the Feature's **Title**, **Scope,** and **Description**. We can deploy this feature across different sites and also on different farms.

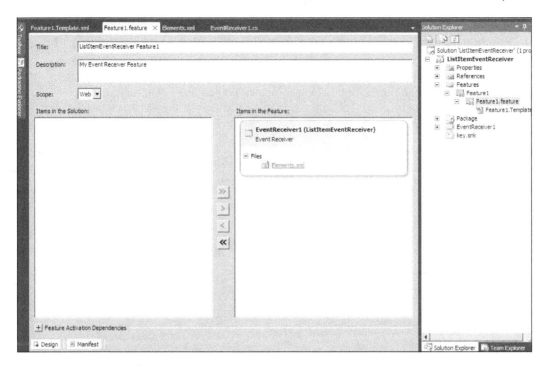

When we built and ran our solution, Visual Studio automatically created a package with an extension WSP and deployed it to our test site and activated it. When we stopped debugging the solution, Visual Studio deactivated this feature, uninstalled it, and did all the necessary clean-up work.

WSP extension files are SharePoint solution files. This is basically a CAB file with one or more features. Each of these features can refer to one or more items like Event Receivers, List Definitions, Web Parts, Workflows, and so on.

There's more...

Document libraries or form libraries in SharePoint are lists but with different content types. We will learn about content types in *Chapter 4, List Definitions and Content Types*. The recipe we learnt in here will work with any kind of list template. But some list templates populate different values in `BeforeProperties` and `AfterProperties`. For more information on `AfterProperties` and `BeforeProperties`, refer to MSDN (`http://msdn.microsoft.com/en-us/library/microsoft.sharepoint.spitemeventproperties_members.aspx`).

More information – Event Receivers base class

Event Receivers you create in Visual Studio inherits from particular SharePoint event receiver class that corresponds to the object to which you are writing the handler. For example, in the recipe we inherited our handler from `SPItemEventReceiver`. If we were to write an event handler for the List events, we would have inherited our class from `SPListEventReceiver`. The following table shows the complete list of the Event Receivers class that are used to inherit the event handlers.

List Item events	SPItemEventReceiver
Web events	`SPWebEventReceiver`
List events	`SPListEventReceiver`
Workflow events	`SPWorkflowEventReceiver`
List Email events	`SPEmailEventReceiver`

The entire event receivers except for Feature Event Receivers and List Email Event Receivers are derived from a base class called `SPEventReceiverBase`. `FeatureReceivers` are derived from a base class called `SPFeatureReceiver` and Email Event Receiver is derived from a base class called `System.Object`.

Not all event hosts will support all the event types. Say for example, the list event type `ListAdding` makes sense from the site or web level perspective. It does not make sense at the list level. Whereas `FieldAdding` event makes lots of sense for List even though both of these event types have the same base class. For a full list of hosts for event types and their supported events, refer to MSDN at: `http://msdn.microsoft.com/en-us/library/gg749858.aspx`.

Debugging Event Receivers

To debug Event Receivers, like any other Visual Studio project, put a breakpoint on the line you want to break. In our example, put a breakpoint on the first line in the method `ItemAdding` in the file `EventReceiver1.cs` and press *F5* to debug the solution.

Debugging helps you understand your code better. You must build your code with debug configuration enabled for debugger to work. By default, Visual Studio starts with this configuration. When you use debugging, you should stop your code at a certain location and complete the following:

- ▶ Inspect it for data that is being used by the code
- ▶ Inspect it for exceptions that occur on conditions
- ▶ Test while you write your code
- ▶ Figure out any logical errors

When you press *F5*, Visual Studio automatically starts a w3wp.exe process and attaches the debugger to that process. W3wp.exe is an IIS worker process that handles all the requests for a particular application pool. The following screenshot shows the output window (you can open the output window from menu **View | Output**). Here you can see that the first line indicates the process that the debugger has attached to. It also provides the process ID (in this case it is **3616**—it may be different for you).

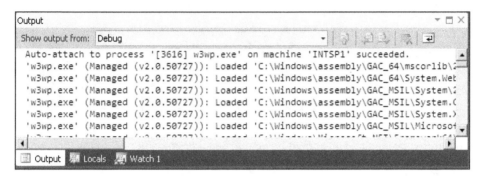

So whenever any requests arrive through this process, the debugger will be able to break at the line you have indicated and highlight the line as shown here. From here on, you can step into code by pressing *F11* or step over the code by pressing *F10*.

```
EventReceiverErrorPage.aspx.designer.cs  X  EventReceiver1.cs  X  EventReceiverErrorPage.aspx.cs  EventR
ListItemEventReceiver.EventReceiver1.EventReceiver1                                    ItemAdding(SPItemE
        /// </summary>
        public class EventReceiver1 : SPItemEventReceiver
        {
            /// <summary>
            /// An item is being added.
            /// </summary>
            public override void ItemAdding(SPItemEventProperties properties)
            {
                base.ItemAdding(properties);

                string sWorkPhone = properties.AfterProperties["WorkPhone"].ToString();

                string sEmail = properties.AfterProperties["Email"].ToString();
```

You can add watch on the variables in the code. But you cannot change the variable values while running.

Developer Dashboard

SharePoint 2010 offers Developer Dashboard which provides information that can help developers to debug a problem. By default, Developer Dashboard is not turned on. Turn it on by executing the following command. The following command sets a value on a property named `developer-dashboard` to `ondemand`:

```
Stsadm -o setproperty -pn developer-dashboard -pv ondemand
```

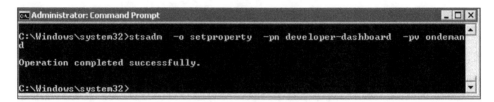

When you refresh your site, you should be able to see a green icon next to the login name on the right-hand side as shown. Clicking that will open the Developer Dashboard which provides information on all the calls SharePoint makes in order to open a page or to execute an event handler.

The following screenshot shows the Developer Dashboard on the initial opening page. If you look closely, you can see that it also provides information on how long certain methods took to process. It also provides information on SQL stored procedures or queries that were executed. You can click on each of these procedures and verify the data that is passed to the queries. Remember, Developer Dashboard does not provide information on how long the custom code took to execute, it provides information on the calls that the custom code made.

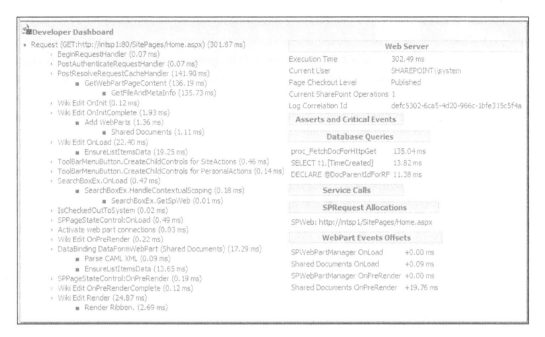

The **Log Correlation Id** helps you to dig through the ULS logs and find any corresponding problems related to the events that are shown in the Developer Dashboard. Using both the Developer Dashboard and ULS logs, you should be able to find any problem with your custom code.

See also

▸ *Chapter1, Adding a custom error message to the Event Receiver* recipe

▸ *Chapter1, Adding an Application Page to an Event Receiver* recipe

Adding a custom error message to the Event Receiver

When we created our Event Receiver in the previous recipe, we saw that if we cancelled the insertion of an item into a list (due to a data validation error), an ugly error message appeared indicating that an Event Receiver had cancelled the request. It is difficult for users to comprehend this error message, it does not indicate that the error is due to data validation and that there is nothing wrong with SharePoint. In this recipe, we will customize this error message that indicates what the error is.

Getting ready

The solution from the previous recipe is used for further modifications. You should complete the previous recipe successfully to follow this one.

How to do it...

1. If you have closed your Visual Studio IDE, launch it now as an administrator and open the solution file that we created in the previous recipe.

2. Open **EventReceiver1.cs** and add the following two lines of code just before the **properties.cancel = true** line in the `workphone` regular expression match "if statement":

    ```
    string sErrMsg = "Business Phone is not in correct format";
    properties.ErrorMessage = sErrMsg;
    ```

3. Do the same for the `Email` regular expression match `if statement`. Your `ItemAdding` method should look like the following code bundle:

    ```
    public override void ItemAdding(SPItemEventProperties properties)
        {
            base.ItemAdding(properties);

            string sWorkPhone = properties.AfterProperties
            ["WorkPhone"].ToString();

            string sEmail = properties.AfterProperties["Email"].
            ToString();

            if (!string.IsNullOrEmpty(sWorkPhone))
            {
                if (!System.Text.RegularExpressions.Regex.
    IsMatch(sWorkPhone, @"^[01]?[- .]?(\([2-9]\d{2}\)|[2-9]\d{2})[-
    .]?\d{3}[- .]?\d{4}$"))
                    {
                        string sErrMsg = "Business Phone is not in
                        correct format";
                        properties.ErrorMessage = sErrMsg;
                        properties.Cancel = true;
                    }
            }

            if (!string.IsNullOrEmpty(sEmail))
            {
                if (!System.Text.RegularExpressions.Regex.
    IsMatch(sEmail, @"^(?("")("".+?""@)|(([0-9a-zA-Z]((\.(?!\.))|[-
    ```

```
!#\$%&'\*\+/=\?\^`\{\}\|~\w])*)(?<=[0-9a-zA-Z])@))(?(\[)(\[(\
d{1,3}\.){3}\d{1,3}\])|(([0-9a-zA-Z][-\w]*[0-9a-zA-Z]\.)+[a-zA-
Z]{2,6}))$"))
                    {
                            string sErrMsg = "Email is not in correct
                            format";
                            properties.ErrorMessage = sErrMsg;
                            properties.Cancel = true;

                    }

            }

    }
```

4. When you build and run this solution, as done previously, you should be directed to the site that you provided in the solution creation wizard.

5. Enter a new contact with an improper phone format for the **Business Phone** field. You should see the same error screen as shown previously including a custom error message that you coded as shown here:

How it works...

The properties object that you use in the `ItemAdding` method has a property called **Error Message**. It is null by default. When SharePoint encounters a null value, it just uses the default error message. Adding a custom error message to this field will cause SharePoint to display your error message.

There's more...

If you want to just cancel the insertion of an item into the list to list without displaying the error page as done previously, just set the properties object's status property as shown in the following code. This will cancel the insert, but will not display the error page.

```
properties.Status = SPEventReceiverStatus.CancelNoError;
```

More information on `SPEventReceiverStatus` can be found on MSDN (`http://msdn.microsoft.com/en-us/library/microsoft.sharepoint.speventreceiverstatus.aspx`)

More information – How to get field names

In the Event Receiver we have used field name **WorkPhone** for the **Business Phone** and **Email** for the **Email Address** fields. How did I figure these names? In Visual Studio 2010 there is a new tool called **Add SharePoint Connection**. You can access it from menu **Tools | Add SharePoint Connection**

It will ask the URL to connect. Provide URL information for your site and it will list all the information pertaining to your site in a tree structure. This information is read-only and you cannot make any changes through the IDE. You can navigate to the **Contacts List** and to the fields as shown here:

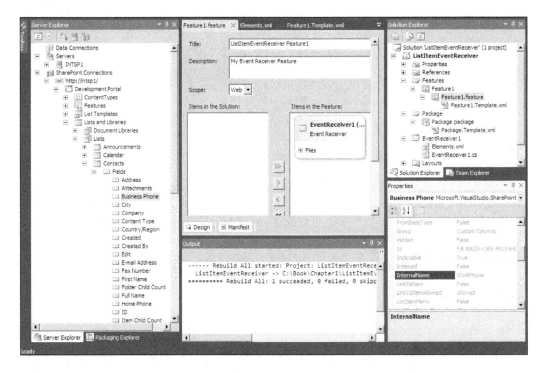

You can select the **Business Phone** field and in the **Properties** window look for **InternalName**. This is the field name that we used in the code to get the values. Just go through the different properties of the field in the properties window, and you will find some interesting properties like `Field ID` which is a GUID, whether the field is hidden or not, and so on.

See also

▸ *Adding an Application Page to an Event Receiver* recipe

Adding an Application Page to an Event Receiver

Well, we know how to write an Event Receiver, we know how to customize the error message that is displayed to the user but is there a way to customize the error page that is displayed? The answer is—YES. Visual Studio provides a very easy way to customize these error pages. In the following recipe, we will find out how it is done.

Getting ready

You should have successfully completed the previous two recipes to follow this.

How to do it...

1. If you have closed Visual Studio IDE, launch it as an administrator.

2. Open the previously created **ListItemEventReceiver** solution.

3. Right-click on the project and select **Add New Item** to add an **Application Page** as shown in the following screenshot:

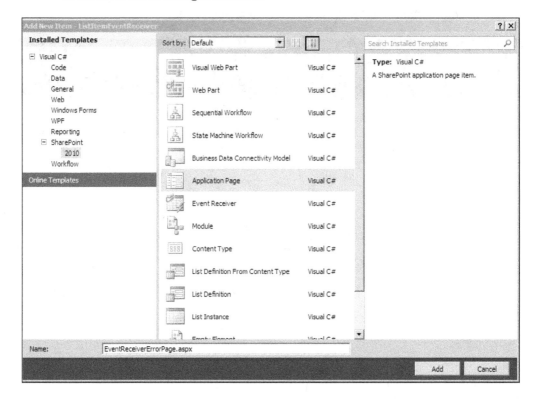

4. Name it `EventReceiverErrorPage.aspx` and click **Add**. This will generate an `.aspx` page underneath a folder called `Layouts`. This is a SharePoint mapped folder hence the green circular icon next to this folder. Underneath this mapped folder a subfolder with the same name as the project (in our case `ListItemEventReceiver`) is created and this is where you will find you're newly created **Application Page**.

5. Open up the `.aspx` page and add a label under the section:

    ```
    <asp:Content ID="Main" ContentPlaceHolderID="PlaceHolderMain"
    runat="server">
    ```

6. Change the ID of the label to `"lblErrMsg"` and clear out the `Text` attribute. Your ASPX mark-up should be as follows:

    ```
    <%@ Assembly Name="$SharePoint.Project.AssemblyFullName$" %>
    ```

```
<%@ Import Namespace="Microsoft.SharePoint.ApplicationPages" %>
<%@ Register Tagprefix="SharePoint" Namespace="Microsoft.
SharePoint.WebControls" Assembly="Microsoft.SharePoint,
Version=14.0.0.0, Culture=neutral, PublicKeyToken=71e9bce111e9429c
" %>
<%@ Register Tagprefix="Utilities" Namespace="Microsoft.
SharePoint.Utilities" Assembly="Microsoft.SharePoint,
Version=14.0.0.0, Culture=neutral, PublicKeyToken=71e9bce111e9429c
" %>
<%@ Register Tagprefix="asp" Namespace="System.Web.UI"
Assembly="System.Web.Extensions, Version=3.5.0.0, Culture=neutral,
PublicKeyToken=31bf3856ad364e35" %>
<%@ Import Namespace="Microsoft.SharePoint" %>
<%@ Assembly Name="Microsoft.Web.CommandUI, Version=14.0.0.0,
Culture=neutral, PublicKeyToken=71e9bce111e9429c" %>
<%@ Page Language="C#" AutoEventWireup="true" CodeBehind="EventRe
ceiverErrorPage.aspx.cs" Inherits="ListItemEventReceiver.Layouts.
ListItemEventReceiver.EventReceiverErrorPage" DynamicMasterPageFil
e="~masterurl/default.master" %>

<asp:Content ID="PageHead" ContentPlaceHolderID="PlaceHolderAdditi
onalPageHead" runat="server">

</asp:Content>

<asp:Content ID="Main" ContentPlaceHolderID="PlaceHolderMain"
runat="server">
    <asp:Label ID="lblErrMsg" runat="server" Text=""></asp:Label>
</asp:Content>

<asp:Content ID="PageTitle" ContentPlaceHolderID="PlaceHolderPageT
itle" runat="server">
Event Receiver Error
</asp:Content>

<asp:Content ID="PageTitleInTitleArea" ContentPlaceHolderID="Place
HolderPageTitleInTitleArea" runat="server" >
Event Receiver Error
</asp:Content>
```

7. Right-click anywhere on the ASPX page and select **View Code** to open the
   `EventReceiverErrorPage.apsx.cs` file in order to wire the label created
   previously to the error message. The code inside the `Page_Load` method should be
   as follows:

```
protected void Page_Load(object sender, EventArgs e)
  {
        string sErrMsg = Request.Params["ErrMsg"];
        lblErrMsg.Text = sErrMsg;
  }
```

8. Now we need to wire this page in our Event Receiver whenever there is an error. To do that, we will open `EventReceiver1.cs` file and add the following code after the line that says `properties.Cancel = true:`.

```
properties.Status = SPEventReceiverStatus.CancelWithRedirectUrl;
properties.RedirectUrl = string.Format("/_layouts/
ListItemEventReceiver/EventReceiverErrorPage.aspx?ErrMsg={0}",
sErrMsg);
```

9. Enter a new contact with an improper phone format for the **Business Phone** field. You should see your custom error screen and custom error message as follows:

Event Receiver Error   □ ✕

Business Phone is not in correct format

How it works...

As indicated in the previous recipe, the properties object can be set with different statuses. One such status is `CancelWithRedirectUrl`. This directs SharePoint to look at another property called `RedirectUrl`. This is the property where you set up your custom URL and send the error message to it as a query parameter.

When you added the Application Page to the project, we saw a mapped folder called **Layouts** getting added. Mapped folders are file system locations on the SharePoint server. The `Layouts` folder can be found at: "`\Program Files\Common Files\Microsoft Shared\ Web Server Extensions\14\TEMPLATE`". Generally this location is referred to as *Root*. Some SharePoint developers refer to this location as *Hive*. Any subfolders that are added underneath these mapped folders will be created on the disk on each of the SharePoint servers in the farm.

Whenever you create a web application in SharePoint, all these mapped folders are mapped for the web application. The layouts mapped folder is mapped as `_layouts` and CONTROLTEMPLATES as `_controltemplates` and so on. So all the site collections and sites in the web application can access these mapped folders through their relative paths. This is the reason why we qualified the link to our Application Page with `/_layouts/`.

There's more...

Visual Studio follows a good development model of creating subfolders underneath mapped folders when you need to add your custom resources. This way you do not overwrite any of the OOB SharePoint components with the same name. Also, do not try to change the files in the `Root`. This will affect the entire farm.

See also

▸ *Validating data when an item is added to a list* recipe

▸ *Adding a custom error message to the Event Receiver* recipe

▸ *Working with List Event Receiver* recipe

Working with List Event Receiver

Until now we worked with List Item Event Receivers. Let us take a look at List Event Receiver in this recipe. In this recipe, whenever a new list is created on the site, we need to log an audit entry into another list.

Getting ready

Create a custom list called `EventReceivers` using the SharePoint user interface.

How to do it...

1. If you have closed your Visual Studio IDE, launch it now as an administrator and create a new Event Receiver project. Name the project **ListEventReceiver**.

2. By default, Visual Studio selects the SharePoint site available on the machine. Select **Deploy as Sandboxed Solution** and click **Next** to proceed to the next step in the wizard.

3. In here, make sure to select **List Events** from the drop down for **What type of event receiver do you want?** Check **A List is being added** in the **Handle the following events** list box.

4. Click on **Finish** and Visual Studio adds in the necessary files and opens up the `EventReceiver1.cs`. This is the code file in which you are going to write your custom event handler.

5. Now add the code necessary to write an entry into the **EventReceivers** custom list that we created in the *Getting Ready* section of this recipe. Your code should be as follows:

```
using System;
using System.Security.Permissions;
using Microsoft.SharePoint;
using Microsoft.SharePoint.Security;
using Microsoft.SharePoint.Utilities;
using Microsoft.SharePoint.Workflow;
namespace ListEventReceiver.EventReceiver1
{
```

```
/// <summary>
/// List Events
/// </summary>
public class EventReceiver1 : SPListEventReceiver
{
    /// <summary>
    /// A list is being added.
    /// </summary>
    public override void ListAdding(SPListEventProperties
    properties)
    {
        AddMessage(ref properties, "Adding List");
base.ListAdding(properties);
    }

    private void AddMessage(ref SPListEventProperties
    properties, string sMessage)
    {
        using (SPWeb web = properties.Web as SPWeb)
        {
            SPList list = web.Lists["EventReceivers"];
            SPListItem li = list.AddItem();
            li["Title"] = properties.ListTitle;
            li["Message"] = sMessage + " - " + properties.
            ListId;
            li.Update();
            li = null;
            list = null;
        }

    }

}
}
```

6. Build and execute the solution by pressing *F5* or by navigating to menu **Debug | Start Debugging**. This should bring up the default browser with the local site that you provided in the project creation wizard.

7. Add a new list of custom list templates and call it **TestList**. You should be able to see an entry in the EventReceivers List as shown below. Your List ID, and the GUID may be different from what is shown in the following screenshot:

How it works...

It works in the same way as the List Item Event Receivers works, except for the fact that the List Event Receivers have a base class of `SPListEventReceiver`. You can compare the elements.`xml` file from the List Item Event Receiver (created in our first recipe) with this one. The only difference you will see is that it does not have a `ListTemplateId` attribute. This makes sense as this is applied to all lists in the site. The Event Receiver in this case is acting at the site level. That means, whenever you create a new list in the site where this is deployed, this event gets triggered.

There's more...

If you have noticed, `base.ItemAdding` method is called first in some cases and called last in some other. Where should we call this method and how do we know if it should be called first or last? The rule of thumb for calling this method is very simple. If you are going to cancel the event then call it in the end. If not, call it in the beginning. So for synchronous events like `ListAdding` or `ListItemAdding` events, where you are doing some data validations and will cancel the events, call it in the end.

See also

▶ *Deploying Event Receivers* recipe

Deploying Event Receivers

During the previous recipes, we saw Visual Studio automatically uploading a solution and activating it for our test purposes. The entire step-by-step process that Visual Studio does in order to deploy a solution to the site can be seen in the output window as shownin the following screenshot Development is all done and now we need to deploy this solution to production. Here are the step-by-step instructions on how we deploy solutions:

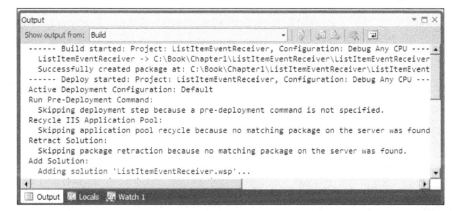

Getting ready

It is necessary to understand the concept of event receivers to follow through this recipe. It is advised to complete the previous recipes sucessfully.

How to do it...

1. If you have closed Visual Studio IDE, launch it as an administrator.

2. Open the previously created **ListItemEventReceiver** solution.

3. Open the project properties window by right-clicking the project and selecting **Properties**.

4. Select the **Build Tab** and set the **Configuration to Active (release)**.

5. Rebuild the solution from menu **Build | Rebuild**.

6. From the same build menu, select **Package** to make a package of this solution. This will generate a `.wsp` solution file in the `bin` folder of your solution as shown:

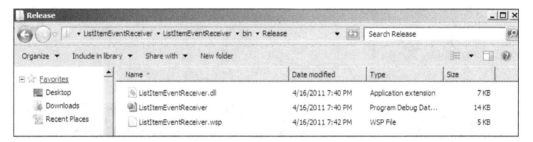

7. You can use the `stsadm` command to deploy this solution file to any site in the farm.

8. To add the solution to the solution store use the command:

   ```
   stsadm -o addsolution -filename ListItemEventReceiver.wsp
   ```

9. To deploy the solution use the command:

   ```
   stsadm -o deploysolution -name ListItemEventReceiver.wsp -local -
   allowgacdeployment
   ```

10. Now install the feature by using the command:

    ```
    stsadm -o installfeature -filename ListEventReceiver_Feature1\
    Feature.xml
    ```

11. You can navigate to **Manage Site Features** from **Site Action | Site Actions | Manage Site Features**. You should see your Feature deployed to the site but not activated as shown:

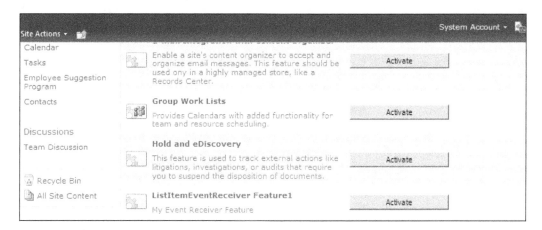

12. You can activate the feature by clicking the **Activate** button.

How it works...

When we built and packaged our solution, a `.wsp` solution file was created. This is nothing but a CAB file contaning feature file and the items that the feature is going to install. You can rename the `.wsp` file to a `.CAB` extension and open it through any ZIP file extractor. The following is a screenshot showing the contents of a `.wsp` file:

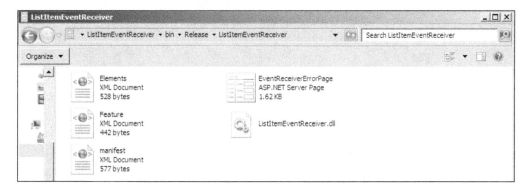

The `.wsp` file contains the DLL, Application Page, and three different XML documents. These XML documents provide the necessary information on where the resources need to be deployed. Open up the `manifest.xml` in notepad. You can see it lists the locations of the Application Page, Event Receiver DLL, and the Feature.

In SharePoint, a Feature is nothing but an XML file. The XML file is named `Feature.xml`. This XML contains the name, the ID, and the scope information of the feature. The name and the ID attributes of the Feature uniquely identifies the Feature. An ID is a GUID in the format "xxxxxxxx-xxxx-xxxx-xxxx-xxxxxxxxxxxx" where x is a hexadecimal number that can be from 0-9 and a-f. When you created the solution, Visual Studio automatically created this GUID. `Feature.xml` also includes the location of the Event Receiver's `Elements.xml`.

Scope indicates how the Feature needs to be scoped. You can scope a Feature in four ways:

1. **Farm Level**: This can be activated at a farm level. That is, all the web applications in the farm will have access to the feature.

2. **Site Level**: Can be activated at site collection level, meaning all the sites in the sites collection will have access to this feature.

3. **Web Level**: Can be activated for a specific website.

4. **Web Application Level**: Can be activated for all sites in the web application.

We already went through the `Elements.xml` in the previous recipe and it basically contains the information about the Event Receiver that we deployed.

There's more...

You can use `PowerShell` commands to install and activate features instead of `stsadm` commands. The corresponding `PowerShell` commands for the `STSADM` commands that we have used in this recipe are:

```
Add-SPSolution -LiteralPath <Location of your wsp>

Install-SPSolution -Identity <WSPName> -WebApplication <URLname>

Enable-SPFeature FeatureFolderName -Url <URLName>
```

See also

▶ *Creating a Feature Receiver* recipe

Creating a Feature Receiver

Feature Receiver as the name indicates is an event handler written to handle events triggered by Features. In this recipe, we will handle some of the Feature events and add a message to a custom list in our site.

Getting ready

Create a custom list from the SharePoint user interface called `FeatureEventReceiver`. By default, SharePoint adds a column called **Title**. Add a new column called **Message** to this list. The end result should look like the following:

How to do it...

1. Launch Visual Studio as an administrator.

2. Create an empty SharePoint project and name it **FeatureEventReceiver**.

3. Stick with the defaults and click on **Finish** on the **New Solution Wizard**. As this is an Empty SharePoint project, there are no items in the project.

4. Add a new Feature to this project by right-clicking on the **Features** folder. This should add a new feature called **Feature1** and should open the **Feature Designer** in the IDE.

5. Right-click this new feature to add an Event Receiver. This should add a code file named **Feature1.EventReceiver.cs**. Uncomment **FeatureActivated** and **FeatureDeactivating** methods. The project structure should look similar to the following screenshot:

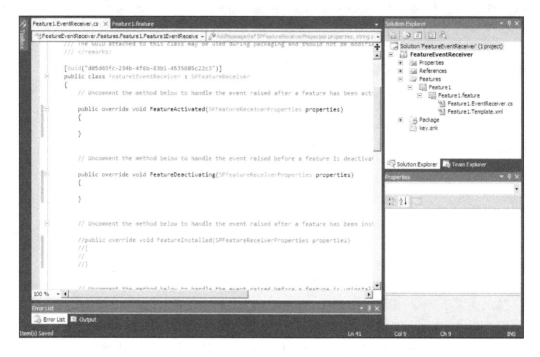

6. Add the following method to the class `Feature1EventReceiver`:

```
private void AddMessage(ref SPFeatureReceiverProperties
properties, string sMessage)
{

    using(SPWeb web = properties.Feature.Parent as SPWeb)
    {
        SPList list = web.Lists["FeatureEventReceiver"];
        SPListItem li = list.AddItem();
        li["Title"] = properties.Feature.Definition.
        DisplayName;
        li["Message"] = sMessage;
        li.Update();
        li = null;
        list = null;
    }
}
```

7. Call this method from the `FeatureActivated` and `FeatureDeactivating` methods. Your code should look like the following:

```
public override void FeatureActivated(SPFeatureReceiverProperties
properties)
        {
            AddMessage(ref properties, "Feature Activated");

        }

        public override void FeatureDeactivating
        (SPFeatureReceiverProperties properties)
        {
            AddMessage(ref properties, "Feature Deactivating");
        }
```

8. Put break points on both the `FeatureActivated` and `FeatureDeactivating` methods and build and run the solution. This will open the default browser with the site that was provided in the solution creation wizard. The debugger never stops at the break points that were set. Exit out of this site to close the debugger so that the Visual Studio can retract the solution as well.

9. Navigate to your site and open up the **FeatureEventReceiver** list where you should see two list items corresponding to **Feature Activated** and **Feature Deactivating** message as shown here, even though you could not see your code getting executed:

<h2>How it works...</h2>

From the code perspective, it is very simple. All we are doing is from the `Feature` properties, we get the reference to the site where Feature is being activated and deactivated. From this site reference, we will get the list object and add new items to it.

When we built and ran the solution, behind the scenes, Visual Studio packaged the solution as `.wsp` file and executed all the commands for activating the solution. The debugger has not yet attached to the process and hence cannot stop at the break point provided.

Visual Studio first builds the solutions and during this process also deploys the solution and activates it. The next step in the process is to run the solution, during which time the Visual Studio debugger attaches itself to the `w3wp.exe` process. At this time, the Feature is already installed and activated and there is no way for the debugger to stop at the break point indicated. Closing the browser does not indicate that the Feature will be deactivated either and hence the break point for `FeatureDeactivating` never gets executed.

See also

▸ *Debugging a Feature Receiver* recipe

Debugging a Feature Receiver

Debugging a Feature Receiver is a different process. It is not like debugging the List Item Event Receivers. As described in the previous recipe, Visual Studio does lots of work behind the scenes and so we are unable to hit the break points.

Apart from that, debugging Feature Receivers are dependent on events that we are trying to debug. In this recipe, we will follow through the process of debugging `FeatureActivated` and `FeatureDeactivating` events.

Getting ready

You should have successfully completed the *Creating a Feature Receiver* recipe.

How to do it...

1. Launch Visual Studio as an administrator and open the solution that was created in the previous recipe.

2. In the solution explorer, select the project and press *F4* to bring open the project properties window.

3. Set the **Active Deployment Configuration** to **No Activation** as shown here:

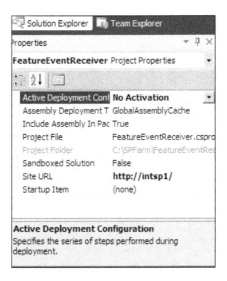

4. Put break points on both `FeatureActivated` and `FeatureDeactivating` methods and run the project.

5. This will bring up the site in the default browser. Navigate to **Site Actions | Site Settings | Site Actions | Manage** site features. This should bring up the page as shown in the following screenshot and you should be able to see your `Feature` installed, but not activated.

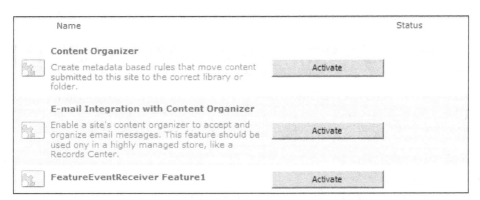

6. Clicking the **Activate** button should invoke the debugger now.

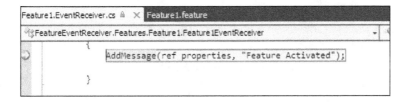

7. Similarly, clicking the **Deactivate** button should invoke the debugger to hit the break point on the `FeatureDeactivating` method.

How it works...

By default Visual Studio sets up for Activation of the features. This makes sense as all the different SharePoint projects make use of Features and for test purposes it is very necessary to activate it and execute the solution. So every time a developer creates a SharePoint project, they do not need to remember to set this flag.

This does create a problem for Feature Receivers though. Hence we set the flag to **No Activation** and there by Visual Studio just installs the solution without activating it.

There's more...

That's right, now we know how to debug Feature Receivers events like **Feature Activated** and **Feature Deactivating**. Is there a similar flag that we can set in Visual Studio to **Debug Feature Installed** and **Feature Uninstalled**? No, there are no flags that you can set to make debugger stop on the break points on **Feature Installed** and the **Feature Uninstalling** methods.

See also

▸ *Creating a Feature Receiver* recipe

▸ *Debugging Feature Installed Events* recipe

Debugging Feature Installed Events

The commands for installing the features are part of the deployment process in Visual Studio. There are no flags or properties that you can set to debug this event in the Feature Receiver. In this recipe, we will guide you through the step-by-step process to accomplish this task.

Getting ready

You should have successfully completed *Debugging a Feature Receiver* recipe.

How to do it...

1. Launch Visual Studio as an administrator and open the solution that was created in the previous recipe.
2. Retract the solution if it was already deployed to a site.

3. Uncomment the **FeatureInstalled** method and press *F9* to put in a break point.

4. Build the solution and package it.

5. From the command prompt use `stsadm` to add solution to solution store and deploy it as described in the recipe *Deploying the Event Receivers*. Follow the steps 8 and 9 in that recipe to deploy the solution.

6. In the Visual Studio, go to project properties from menu **Project |**
   FeatureEventReceiver Properties.

7. In the **Debug** tab, set the external program to `Program Files\Common Files\`
   `Microsoft Shared\Web Server Extensions\14\BIN\STSADM.exe`.

8. Enter the command line arguments in the same tab as follows:

   `-o installfeature -name FeatureEventReceiver_Feature1 -force`

   ❑ Your debug tab should be similar to the one shown in the following screenshot:

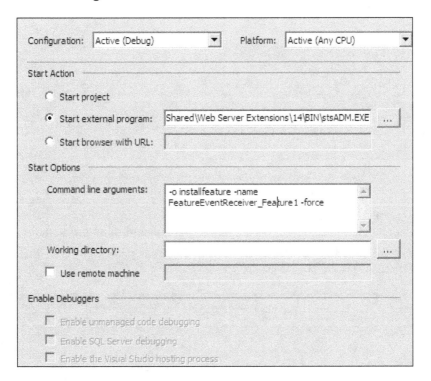

9. In the window, open the **SharePoint** tab. Create a new **Active Deployment Configuration** and name it **Empty Configuration** as shown here and click **OK**.

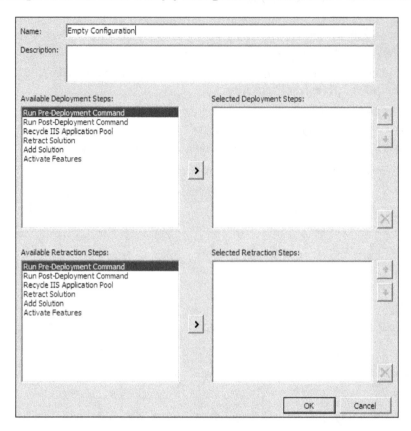

10. Select the new configuration in the **Active Deployment Configuration** drop-down.

11. When you press *F5*, the debugger stops at the break point on `FeatureInstalled` method as shown in the following screenshot:

```
// Uncomment the method below to handle the event raised after a feature has been installed.

public override void FeatureInstalled(SPFeatureReceiverProperties properties)
{
    string s = "Hello World";
}
```

How it works...

In here, we are manually attaching an external process to the Visual Studio debugger. In our case, STSADM.exe is our external program. We did the preliminary work of adding the solution to the solution store and deploying the solution. We bypassed the entire deployment process that Visual Studio uses, so we can debug our Feature Receiver.

By default, Visual Studio provides two configurations: the **Default** configuration and the **No Activation** configuration. You cannot edit those configurations. None of these configurations are good for our purpose here. What we needed was a configuration that just deploys the solution without installing it. So we created an empty configuration and resorted to a manual process to debug this solution.

There's more...

Use the same process as used previously to debug the uninstalled event in the Feature Receiver. In step 8, substitute command line arguments as follows:

```
-o uninstallfeature –filename FeatureEventReceiver_Feature1\Feature.xml
```

See also

▶ *Debugging a Feature Receiver* recipe

2
Workflows

In this chapter, we will cover:

- ▶ Creating a sequential workflow
- ▶ Creating a site workflow with initiation form
- ▶ Deploying an InfoPath form with a workflow
- ▶ Creating a task from the workflow
- ▶ Creating a custom task form

Introduction

According to **Workflow Management Coalition** (http://www.WFMC.org) a standards organization that solely concentrates on processes, defines a workflow as follows:

The automation of a business process, in whole or part, during which documents, information or tasks are passed from one participant to another for action, according to a set of procedural rules.

In simple terms, it means a workflow is a system that manages the execution of a business process. Organizations implement workflows for many different reasons such as:

- ▶ Auditing and tracking
- ▶ Better efficiency
- ▶ Consistency
- ▶ Better customer support

Whatever may be the reason for workflow implementation; it is implemented by breaking up the business processes into small activities and executed in a logical order.

An activity in a workflow is the smallest piece or item that you execute. Take for instance a business process that manages employee time and expense reporting (T&E). In here, when employee submits the T&E, a notification is sent to the manager to make a decision regarding approval or rejection and when once that is complete, a notification is sent back to the employee. Each of these steps that happen in the business process is considered an activity. There are three types of activities:

1. Standard activities.
2. Control flow activities.
3. Container activities.

Standard activities are those that perform some tasks like sending an e-mail or executing a .NET code or creating a task and so on. **Control flow activities** are those that are used as decision points. Examples of control flow activities are `if-else`, `while` loop, and so on. These activities require you to provide rules for decision-making purposes. These rules can be defined declaratively or code based. The declarative rules are stored in an XML file with `.rules` extension. **Container activities** are those that can host other activities and create a composite activity. Examples of container activities are sequence activity, conditioned activities groups, and so on. Remember some control flow activities are container activities too.

SharePoint 2010 workflows are based on **Windows Workflow Foundation** (**WF**). WF is part of .NET 3.5 Framework. Using WF you can build many workflow enabled applications that do not need to interact with SharePoint at all. Your applications can also host other workflows and execute them. In this scenario, your application has to manage the lifecycle of the hosted workflows. Since workflows can be long running processes, and a system reboot or reset should not terminate the workflow process, hosts can persist the status of the workflow instance as it sees fit like may be in a database or in XML storage. The applications that host workflows are called **host applications**. Host applications can provide custom communication and other services that can make your hosted workflows interact with external applications in an efficient manner. Hosts have workflow runtime engines and some runtime services that help the workflow activities to perform their function.

SharePoint is a host application. It provides a runtime engine for workflows to execute. It has runtime services like persistence service, which stores the status of the workflow instance to a content database. There is a communication service that manages the communication of tasks on a SharePoint workflow. Tasks are the way SharePoint communicates with the users. There is a transaction service as well that manages the transactional scenarios in the workflow like rolling back to a previous state in case of an exception. SharePoint also provides a timer service and a tracking service that store the history of the workflow instance in a history list. The timer service helps in automatically rehydrating the workflow from idle state after some lapse of time. In our example, of T&E if a manager does not respond to a task within five business days, we can code a delay activity that wakes up after the inactivity and sends an alert to the manager of the impending task.

WF supports two types of workflows—state machine, and sequential workflows. SharePoint based on WF supports both of these types. In sequential workflows, the activities are placed in a logical order with an explicit start and an explicit end. The activities are executed sequentially one after the other like a flow chart. There is no going back to the previous step in a sequential workflow. Sequential workflows are better suited to automated processes that do not need human interaction like moving documents from one library to another or in an order entry process after the user submits the order, the system can automatically do the credit check, inventory check and send a notification to the fulfillment department. They can also be used in a situation where you want the users to follow a certain pattern. State machine workflows are explained in *Chapter 3, Advanced Workflows*. Visual Studio 2010 provides templates to develop both state machine and sequential workflows for SharePoint 2010. To define a workflow, we create a project and add activities to the workflow designer surface to construct our logical flow.

In SharePoint, the workflow definitions can be associated with lists or document libraries, content types, and sites. When associated with lists or document libraries, the workflow acts on the item in it. You can manually start the workflow, or start automatically when a new item is created or modified. Since site workflows do not have any items to act upon, it has to be started by an external event like clicking on the link to start the workflow or an external application starting it via code.

When workflows are associated with a content type, workflows can be started on any item that contains this content type irrespective of the list or libraries that the item belongs to. We will learn more about content types in *Chapter 4, List Definitions and Content Types*.

Site workflows are new to SharePoint 2010. There are no dependencies on lists or libraries in these kinds of workflows. These exists at the site level and can act on all the lists and libraries associated in the site. These types of workflows are usually used in scheduling maintenance tasks or where workflows needs to interact with multiple items located in different lists of the same site.

Both state machine and sequential workflows can be associated with all three categories listed previously. Your business requirements will be the driving factor on what type of workflow that needs to be created and whether it needs to be site or list workflow. When associating, you can ask the user associating the workflow to provide information for the workflow. This can be configuration information like approval groups or database connection string and so on that are specific to the site or list to which the workflow is associated. This is done by providing a form so that users associating the workflow can input this information. This is called an **Association Form**. You can also present a form for user input on every instance of the workflow started. This form is called an **Initiation Form**. Initiation forms are generally used to get the input from users. This can also be used for overriding associated data for specific instances of the workflow. **Task Forms** are those that are presented to the users when the user is assigned a task. As stated before, tasks are the way SharePoint interacts with the user for the activities to progress.

Apart from providing a framework for developing custom workflows, SharePoint also provides many **out of the box** (**OOB**) workflows like the approval workflow, the three-state workflow, the collect feedback workflow, the disposition workflow, and others. The number of OOB workflows enabled depends on the version of SharePoint that is deployed. For more information on the OOB workflows, please refer to MSDN at: `http://office.microsoft.com/en-us/` `sharepoint-server-help/about-the-workflows-included-with-sharepoint-` `HA102420739.aspx`.

Creating a sequential workflow

In this recipe, we will learn how to create a sequential workflow. For this recipe, we will model a credit approval process. When a user adds an item to a list, we will let the workflow instantiate automatically on the inserted item and flow through the process of checking the user's requested credit line and approving it based on user's employment and credit history.

Getting ready

You should have a fully functional development machine with SharePoint 2010 installed and configured. You also need Visual Studio 2010 IDE installed on the same development machine. We are using a team site template for our examples.

Use the custom list template and create a list from the SharePoint user interface called **Credit Approval**. The following table provides information on fields and its properties:

Field Name	Data Type	Required
Credit Requested	Currency	Yes
Employment History	Choice (Choices - Good, Bad, and None Exists)	Yes
Credit History	Choice (Choices - Good, Bad, and None Exists)	Yes

The following screenshot shows the end result:

| | | Title | Credit Requested | Employment History | Credit History |

There are no items to show in this view of the "Credit Approval" list. To add a new item, click "New".

➕ Add new item

How to do it...

1. Launch your Visual Studio 2010 IDE as an administrator (right-click on the shortcut and select **Run as administrator**).

2. Select **File | New | Project**. The new project wizard dialog box as shown will be displayed (make sure to select **.NET Framework 3.5** in the top drop-down box).

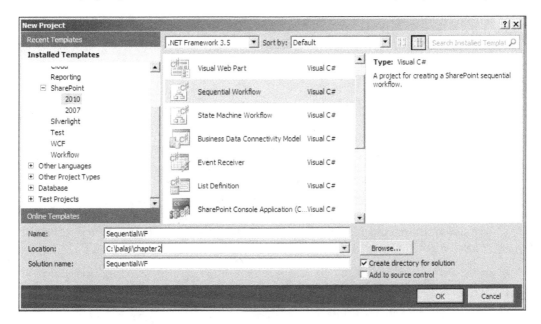

3. Select **Sequential Workflow** under **Visual C# | SharePoint | 2010** node from the **Installed Templates** section on the left-hand side.

4. Name the project **SequentialWF** and provide a directory location where you want to save the project and click on **OK** to proceed to the next step in the wizard.

5. By default, Visual Studio selects the SharePoint site available on the machine. Select **Deploy as Farm Solution** and click on **Next** to proceed to the next step in the wizard.

6. In here, provide a name for your workflow and make sure to select **List Workflow** for the workflow template type as shown in the following screenshot:

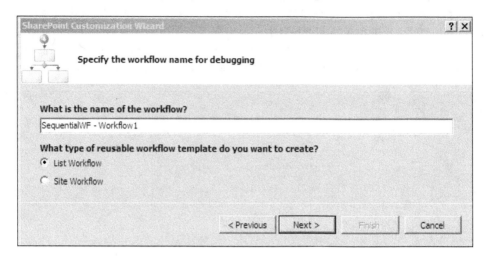

7. Click on **Next** and move on to select the list association and task list and history list selection window. Select **Credit Approval** list from the drop-down for **The library or list to associate your workflow with** and take default selections for the rest as shown in the following screenshot:

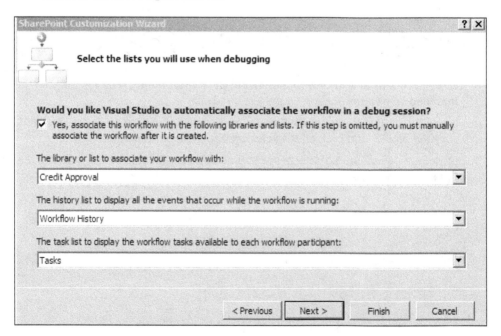

8. In the next window, keep the defaults for **How do you want the workflow to start?** as shown in the following screenshot:

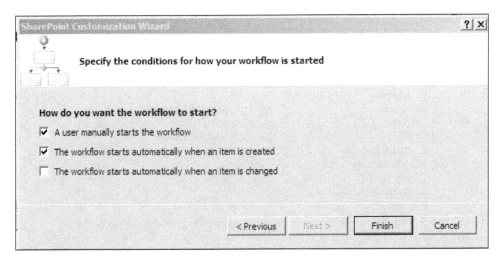

9. By selecting **Finish** the wizard and Visual Studio will generate the necessary files and by default they will open up the workflow designer surface with workflow start and workflow terminator. In between these two items, you should also see the onWorkflowActivated activity added.

10. We will build our workflow flowchart by starting off with **LogToHistoryListActivity**. The **LogToHistoryListActivity** is a SharePoint specific activity that can be found in the **Toolbox** under the **SharePoint Workflow** section as shown in the following screenshot:

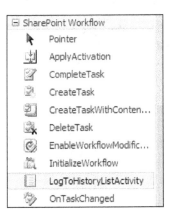

11. Add this activity below the `onWorkflowActivate` activity and change the name to **logWorkflowStarted** from the properties window. Also set the **HistoryDescription** property to **Workflow Started** as shown in the following screenshot:

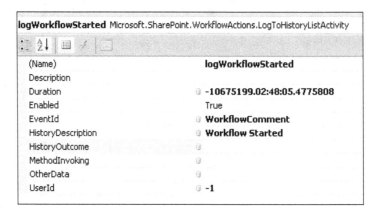

12. Drag an **IfElse** activity and drop it on the designer just below the **logWorkflowStarted** and name it **CheckEmploymentHistoryActivity**. The **IfElse** activity by default adds two branches. One of the branches follows when the condition evaluates to true and the other to false.

   ❑ Add **LogToHistoryListActivities** on both of these branches and name the one in the left as **GoodEmploymentHistoryBranch** and the one in the right as **BadEmploymentHistoryBranch**.

   ❑ Also change the names of the **LogToHistoryListActivities** underneath these branches. The one under **GoodEmploymentHistoryBranch** is called **logGoodEmploymentHistory** and other as **logBadEmploymentHistory**.

   ❑ Set the **HistoryDescription** property for **logGoodEmploymentHistory** to **Employment History is good** and for the other **Employment History is bad**.

The following screenshot shows the finished screen:

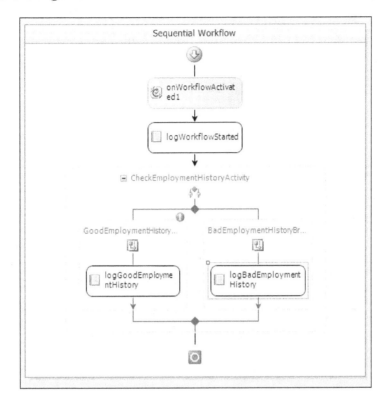

13. The exclamation mark on the branch is indicating that the condition evaluation to execute the branch is not set. This is a required action for an **IfElse** activity. Without this the **IfElse,** activity does not know which branch to execute. From the properties window of the branch, select the **Code Condition** and set the **Condition** property to **CheckEmploymentHistory** as shown in the following screenshot:

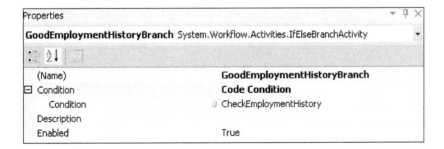

14. Follow the same routine and add another **IfElse** activity under the
GoodEmploymentHistoryBranch and name it **CheckCreditHistoryActivity** and
add **LogToHistoryListActivity** on both of the branches. Here too, set the condition
to **Code Condition** and the **Condition** property to **CheckCreditHistory**. The
HistoryDescription property on **GoodCreditHistoryBranch** should be set to **Credit
History is good** and for the other property set it to **Credit History is bad**. The
completed workflow flowchart should look as follows:

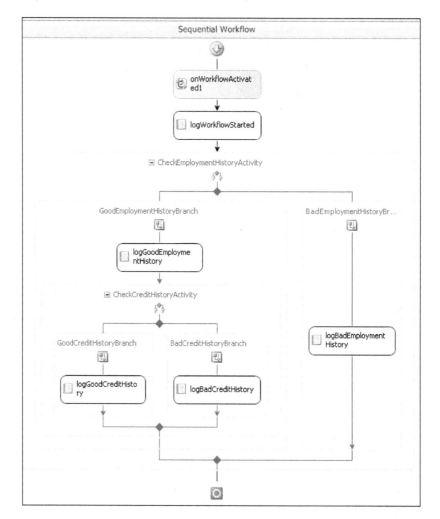

15. From the code view, add the code to verify the employment history. Since the workflow acts on the item that is inserted into the list, you can verify the item values in the workflow. Your code for `CheckEmploymentHistory` method should look like the following:

```
    private void CheckEmploymentHistory(object sender,
ConditionalEventArgs e)
        {
            string sEmpHistory = "";
            sEmpHistory = workflowProperties.Item["Employment
History"].ToString();

            if (sEmpHistory.Trim().ToLower() == "good")
                e.Result = true;
            else
                e.Result = false;
        }
```

16. Similarly, add the code to verify the credit history as well. Your code in the `CheckCreditHistory` method should be as follows:

```
private void CheckCreditHistory(object sender,
ConditionalEventArgs e)
        {
            string sCrdHistory = "";
            sCrdHistory = workflowProperties.Item["Credit
History"].ToString();

            if (sCrdHistory.Trim().ToLower() == "good")
                e.Result = true;
            else
                e.Result = false;
        }
```

17. Build and run the project by pressing *F5*. This should bring up the site that you provided during the project creation. The workflow is already associated with the list that we provided during the project creation. Add a new item to the list with all fields filled in as follows:

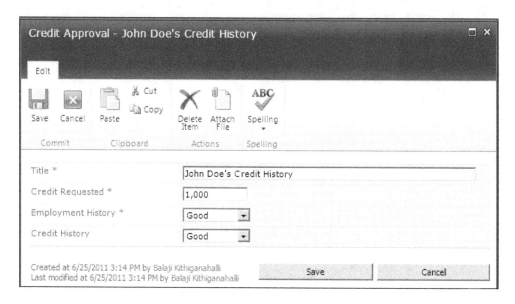

18. As soon as you save the item to the list, the workflow will get initiated and start an instance of it. Since there is no user interaction, the workflow completes and shows the status as shown in the following screenshot:

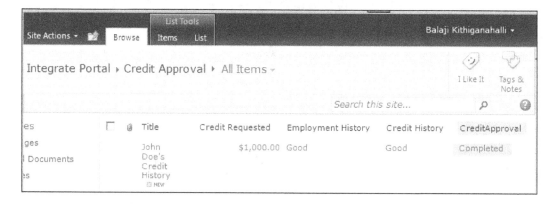

19. Click on the **Completed** status of the workflow to see the history list associated with the workflow. This should list all the history that we logged during the workflow process. The following screenshot shows the history list:

Workflow History

☐ View workflow reports
The following events have occurred in this workflow.

☐	Date Occurred	Event Type	☐ User ID	Description	Outcome
	6/25/2011 3:14 PM	Comment	System Account	Workflow Started	
	6/25/2011 3:14 PM	Comment	System Account	Employment History is Good	
	6/25/2011 3:14 PM	Comment	System Account	Credit History is Good	Credit is approved

20. Add more items to the list with different conditions of employment history and credit history to verify the other conditions of the workflow.

How it works...

Every SharePoint workflow project starts with an `onWorkflowActivated` activity. This activity is a mandatory activity and hence Visual Studio added it to the designer automatically. By default, this activity is bound to a variable called `workflowProperties` of type `SPWorkflowActivationProperties`. The `workflowProperties` provides information about the current workflow context, the item that initiated the workflow, the list to which this workflow belongs to, the originator user, and other information. SharePoint workflow runtime fills in all these values for us to make use of. For all the items that `workflowProperties` provide, refer to: `http://msdn.microsoft.com/en-us/library/microsoft.sharepoint.workflow.spworkflowactivationproperties.aspx`.

Using the `workflowProperties` we were able to get access to the list item that initiated the workflow and from this, we were able to access the item information in the code and create the conditions for the `IfElse` activities. The code is pretty simple such that it checks the values that were put in and makes decision on them.

The `logToHistoryListActivity` is a SharePoint specific activity that logs information to the history list. This activity behind the scenes calls the method `LogToHistoryList` from the `ISharePointService` interface, which is implemented in the assembly `Microsoft.SharePoint.Workflow.dll`. The following code shows the method signature for this method:

```
void LogToHistoryList(
  Guid workflowId,
  SPWorkflowHistoryEventType eventId,
  int userId,
  TimeSpan duration,
  string outcome,
  string description,
  string otherData
)
```

In this method, you can specify an event type like the one workflow started, a workflow comment, and others to group your comments to a specific category. For more information on event types that can be passed to this method, refer to MSDN at: `http://msdn.microsoft.com/en-us/library/microsoft.sharepoint.workflow.spworkflowhistoryeventtype.aspx`.

The `ISharePointService` interface enables activities to exchange data outside of the workflow instance. In this case, writing to the history list. There are other methods like `SendEmail`, `SetState` that are part of this interface as well. Refer to MSDN for more information at: `http://msdn.microsoft.com/en-us/library/microsoft.sharepoint.workflow.isharepointservice_members.aspx`.

In Visual Studio 2010, all the SharePoint project items like Event Receivers, workflow projects, or content types will have a similar structure such as having a feature, a folder for the project item, and so on. When our workflow project was created, Visual Studio added a feature folder with `Feature.xml` file and a `Workflow1` folder that contains the `Elements.xml`, `Workflow1.cs`, and `Worlflow1.designer.cs`. The last two files make up the activities of the workflow and the code associated with these activities. Like with Event Receivers, the `Elements.xml` file provides metadata information about the workflow to the SharePoint. You can name this file anything you want. But Visual Studio, always names it `Elements.xml` for all of the SharePoint templates when you first create the project. In here you set the attributes like the workflow name, the class file, and assembly that contains the code and so on. You can also set the association form, the initiation form, and the task form that are associated with the workflow. Since our workflow did not have any of these resources, we did not make any changes. All the attributes of the `Elements.xml` are as follows:

```
<Workflow
   Title="Text"
   Name="Text"
   CodeBesideAssembly="Text"
   CodeBesideClass="Text"
   Description="Text"
   Id="Text"
   EngineClass="Text"
   EngineAssembly="Text"
   AssociationUrl="Text"
   InstantiationUrl="Text"
   ModificationUrl="Text"
   StatusUrl="Text"
   TaskListContentTypeId="Text"  >
</Workflow>
```

For more information on the descriptions of all the elements of the workflow `Elements.xml` file, refer to MSDN at: `http://msdn.microsoft.com/en-us/library/aa543564.aspx`.

In the project creation wizard, we set our sequential workflow as a list workflow. This information can be found in the `.spdata` file located in the `Workflow1` folder. By default this file is hidden. To list this file in the project explorer, toggle the **Show All Files** menu item from **Project** menu. The `.spdata` file is a SharePoint project metadata information file. This is of XML format. You should not manually change this file as it may get overwritten by Visual Studio when you make changes to the project structure like adding and removing items to and from the project. This file is used during the packaging process. It contains information about the SharePoint project item that is in the solution. You can also verify that property from the properties window of the `Workflow1` folder. The other items that we set during the project creation wizard can also be verified in the properties window. You can see the history list and task list associated with the workflow. The target list property specifies the list that the workflow is associated with. This is only for debugging purposes. You can always associate the workflows to different lists after it is built and deployed. You do the association with the target list via SharePoint user interface or through object model code using Feature receivers. You can also associate it to a content type and deploy it. You will learn about content types and how to associate workflows with it in *Chapter 4*.

There's more...

When we build and deploy a workflow to a production environment, you have a couple of ways to associate the workflow with the content type, the list or with the site:

▸   Manually by using SharePoint user interface

▸   During activation of the feature via feature receiver

We will show you how to associate a workflow with a content type using a feature receiver in *Chapter 4*. It is the same process to associate a workflow with a list also. Here is the manual way to associate a workflow to a list.

1. Navigate to **List Settings** | **Workflow Settings** of the list to which you need to associate a workflow as shown in the following screenshot:

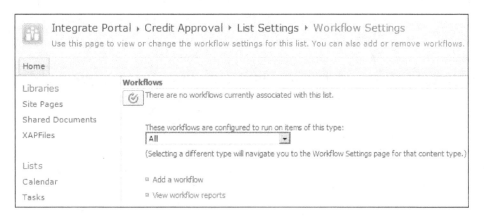

2. Click on the **Add Workflow** link to add a new workflow. The following screenshot shows the **Add Workflow** page:

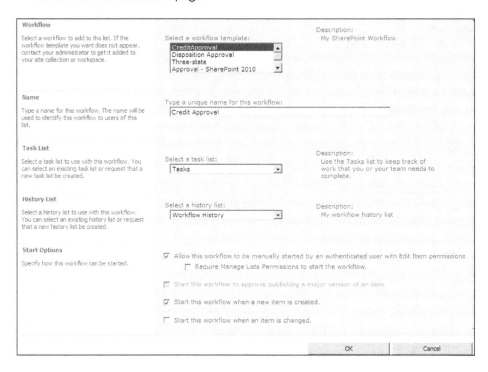

3. Provide a unique name to your workflow and select the supporting task list and history list. Start options provide the way to initiate the workflow.

See also

▶ *Creating a site workflow with an initiation form recipe*

Creating a site workflow with an initiation form

The previous recipe is a good example of a sequential workflow where there is no human interaction. If it were really dealing with a credit approval process on a credit application, this could have gone through the external applications to verify the credit history and employment history and made the decision. So to take advantage of this automation, let us create our own credit application approval system. In this recipe, we will create a site workflow to enact our credit application approval process. Since site workflows are not associated with any lists, there is no form that we can get out of the box for a user to input data and start the workflow. For this purpose, we will also incorporate an initiation form that upon submission will start the workflow.

To keep the workflow simple, the workflow will base its decision on the credit amount requested. If the credit amount is less than $1000.00 it will be automatically approved or if it is greater than that amount, it is rejected.

Getting ready

Since this recipe incorporates ideas from the previous recipe, you should have successfully completed the previous recipe.

How to do it...

1. Launch your Visual Studio 2010 IDE as an administrator (right-click the shortcut and select **Run as administrator**).

2. Select **File | New | Project** and select **Sequential Workflow** under **Visual C# | SharePoint | 2010** node from the **Installed Templates** section on the left-hand side.

3. Name the project **SiteWF** and provide a directory location where you want to save the project and click **OK** to proceed to the next step in the wizard.

4. By default, Visual Studio selects the SharePoint site available on the machine. Select **Deploy as Farm Solution** and click **Next** to proceed to the next step in the wizard.

5. In here, provide a name for your workflow and make sure to select **Site Workflow** for the workflow template type as shown in the following screenshot:

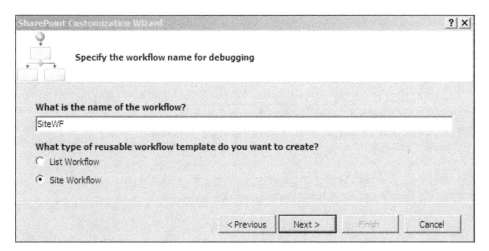

6. Click on **Next** and move on to select the task list and history list selection window. Take the defaults and proceed to the next step.

7. The only option for the site workflows will be to start the workflow manually. Select the default option provided and finish the wizard to create the project.

8. Similar to the *Creating the sequential workflow* recipe, place **LogToHistoryListActivity** and the **IfElse** activity and build our workflow flowchart. Name the code condition for the **IfElse** activity as `CheckCreditAmount`. The final result should be as shown in the following screenshot:

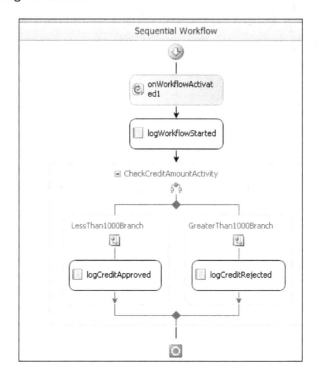

9. In the code file of the workflow, add the code for the method `CheckCreditAmount` so that the true condition is evaluated when the credit request amount is less than $1000.00. Your code should look like the following:

```
private void CheckCreditAmount(object sender,
ConditionalEventArgs e)
        {
            string sInitData =  workflowProperties.InitiationData;
            double initAmount = 0;

            double.TryParse(sInitData, out initAmount);

            if (initAmount <= 1000)
                e.Result = true;
            else
                e.Result = false;
        }
```

10. Right-click on the **Workflow1** folder and from the context menu, **Add** | **New Item** and select **Workflow Initiation Form** and name it `CreditApplication.aspx` as shown in the following screenshot:

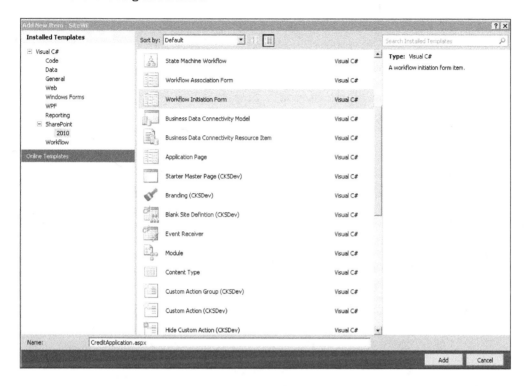

11. Visual Studio adds the code behind file along with the `.aspx` page. There is no designer support for building the user interface. Visual Studio by default also adds a couple of buttons for the **Start Workflow** and **Cancel** in the main content placeholder. Just before these buttons, add a label control and have the text property set to **Credit Amount Requested:** Add a textbox control and name it **txtCreditRequested**. Your `.aspx` markup should look like the following:

```
<asp:Content ID="Main" ContentPlaceHolderID="PlaceHolderMain"
runat="server">

<asp:Label ID="lblEnterCreditAmount" runat="server" Text="Credit
Amount Requested:"></asp:Label>
<asp:TextBox ID="txtCreditAmount" runat="server"></asp:TextBox>
<br />
    <asp:RequiredFieldValidator ID="rfCreditAmount" runat="server"
ErrorMessage="Credit Amount is Required" ControlToValidate="txtCre
ditAmount"></asp:RequiredFieldValidator>

<br />
```

```
<asp:Button ID="StartWorkflow" runat="server"
OnClick="StartWorkflow_Click" Text="Submit" />
          
    <asp:Button ID="Cancel" runat="server" OnClick="Cancel_Click"
Text="Cancel" />
</asp:Content>
```

12. Open the code behind file of the ASPX page and find the method
`GetInitiationData` and return the contents of `txtCreditAmount`
textbox from this method. Your code in the method should look as follows:

```
private string GetInitiationData()
        {
            return this.txtCreditAmount.Text;
        }
```

13. Build and run the project by pressing *F5*. This should bring up the site that was
provided in the project wizard. As there is no list associated with the workflow, the
main page of the site provided will be displayed. Navigate to **All Site Content | Site
Workflows | Start a New Workflow** and start the workflow by clicking on the name
of the workflow as shown in the following screenshot:

14. This will bring up the initiation form as shown in the following screenshot:

15. Enter the amount **1000** in the textbox and click on the **Start Workflow** button to kick
start the workflow. This will start the workflow. You should see the complete status
and you should be able to verify the history list for the statuses that the workflow
added during the execution.

How it works...

The workflow code and process flow is similar to the recipe *Creating a sequential workflow*. An initiation form provided the data that was needed to do the condition check. An initiation form is an ASPX page which is presented to the user to input the data necessary for the workflow. This form is presented for every instance of the workflow that is started. You can also provide an association form that is common to all the workflow instances. Adding an association form to a workflow is similar to initiation form. An `InfoPath` form can also be added. The deployment procedure for the InfoPath form is different compared to an ASPX page. Since an initiation form is an ASPX page, you can do all the things like adding validation controls, writing business logic in the code behind file, and so on. Designing the ASPX page using the designer is not supported. Since designing a properly formatted ASPX page without designer support is hard, InfoPath forms have taken a special role in creating workflow-related forms. We will learn about deploying InfoPath forms with workflows later in this chapter. In our recipe, we utilized the ASPX page due to the fact that Visual Studio provides the template to create it. InfoPath forms cannot be created with Visual Studio. Previous versions of Visual Studio provided that capability but it was removed from the current 2010 version.

Initiation forms are not just for site workflows. They are equally applicable to list workflows. In fact, they can be presented to all kinds of SharePoint workflows. Workflow manager manages these forms. Whenever an initiation form or association form is submitted, Workflow Manager passes the information from these forms to each instance of the workflow that is created and can be accessed from the Workflow properties collection. Workflow manager is responsible for filling in the property collection of the workflow instance. If there is no initiation data, then it passes an empty string.

Similar to application pages, initiation pages are also stored in the root layouts folder. Visual Studio deployment creates a folder in the same name as the project and a subfolder underneath it with the workflow folder name. In our recipe, this is `SiteWF` and `Workflow1` respectively. If you deploy this workflow, you can navigate to the root layouts folder to verify the initiation page. As stated in the previous recipe, `InstantiationUrl` is one of the attributes of the workflow element in the `Elements.xml` file. Visual Studio automatically updates this attribute with the proper URL of the initiation form. In case you want to change the name of the initiation page, this is the place to verify and make changes if needed.

The Initiation form template in Visual Studio also adds a default code that starts workflow. Workflow is started based on the workflow template ID which is passed to the form as a query string parameter to the initiation form from the workflow runtime. Since ours is a site workflow, only the workflow template ID is passed in the query string. If it were a list workflow, List ID and Item ID that initiated the workflow would have been passed to the initiation form.

On submission of the form, workflow is started programmatically by calling the `SPWorkflowManager` object's `StartWorkflow` method. `SPWorkflowManager` is at the site collection level and is the object responsible for managing the workflow templates and instances across the site collection. The `StartWorkflow` is an overloaded method and takes initiation data as one of the parameters. It is of `string` type. Here is where we passed in our Textbox contents. If you have multiple values to pass, construct a XML string and pass it to this parameter. For more information on `SPWorkflowManager` and `StartWorkflow` refer to MSDN at: `http://msdn.microsoft.com/en-us/library/microsoft.sharepoint.workflow.spworkflowmanager_members.aspx`.

There's more...

As we stated previously, InfoPath forms have become a preferred method for developing initiation, association, or task forms in SharePoint workflows. This is because InfoPath designer provides easier development and designer support to develop custom forms. InfoPath forms when used with SharePoint workflows, opens the form in a browser window. This is controlled by InfoPath form services in SharePoint. This is not available with the SharePoint foundation.

See also

> ▸ *Creating a sequential workflow recipe*
> ▸ *Deploying an InfoPath form with the workflow recipe*

Deploying an InfoPath form with the workflow

In this recipe, we will recreate the previous recipe to use InfoPath forms for initiation form.

Getting ready

This recipe assumes that you are familiar with creating InfoPath forms using InfoPath designer 2010. Your SharePoint server should be configured to use form services. Refer to MSDN at: `http://technet.microsoft.com/en-us/library/cc262263.aspx` for more information on configuring the form services.

How to do it...

1. Using InfoPath designer, create a browser compatible form template.
2. Add a textbox control and name it **txtCreditRequested**. Also add a **Submit** button.

3. Go to the Submit Options of the button and add a new data connection to submit to the **Hosting environment** as shown in the following screenshot:

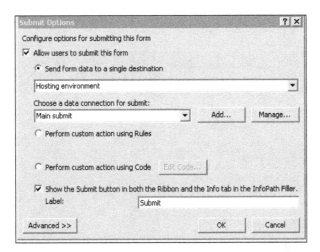

4. From the **File** tab, click on the **Form options** button to open the options dialog box.

5. Uncheck the **Automatically determine security level (recommended)** and select **Domain (the form can access content from the domain in which it is located)** security as shown in the following screenshot:

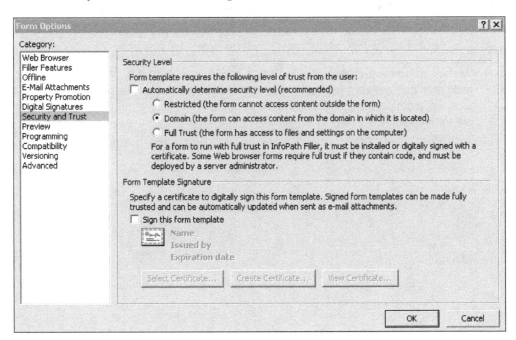

6. From the **File** tab, select **Publish** menu and click on **Network Location** to start the publishing wizard.

7. Provide the path and name of the template for the published form in the wizard's first step as shown in the following screenshot:

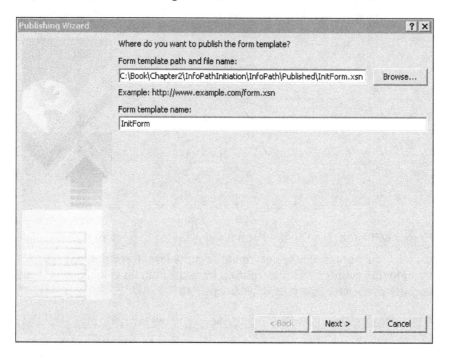

8. Make sure to delete the access path that is added by default by the designer in the next step of the wizard as it only applies to the forms that can be opened from a network location using the InfoPath client application. Ignore the warning and move on to the next step.

9. The final step of the wizard shows the summary of your selection in the previous steps as shown in the following screenshot:

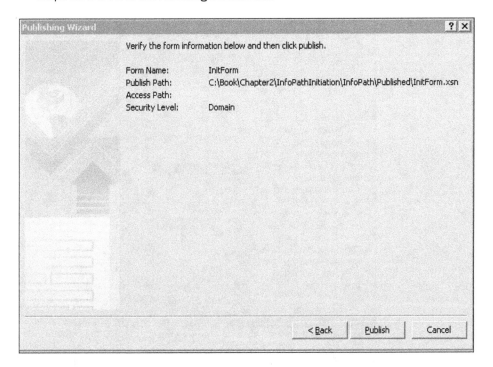

10. After we are done with publishing, from the **File** tab, select **Publish** and select the **Export Source files** option. Provide a location to store the source files of the InfoPath form. This will also save the **XSD** (**XML Schema Definition**) of the form. By default this is always named `myschema.xsd`. There are situations when you use controls like people picker on the form, the export option may also create another XSD file named `BuiltInActiveXControls.xsd`.

11. Open **Visual Studio Command Prompt (2010)** from **Start | All Programs | Microsoft Visual Studio 2010 | Visual Studio Tools** as an administrator as shown in the following screenshot:

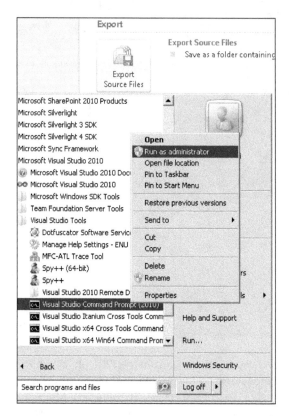

12. From the command prompt, navigate to the location where you saved the source files and type in the following command to generate the class file from the schema file using XSD tool:

```
Xsd.exe myschema.xsd /c /l:cs
```

13. This will generate the C# class file of the InfoPath form. By default this is named `myschema.cs`. To generate the VB.Net class file, change the switch `/l:cs` to `/l:vb`. In case you had `BuiltInActiveXControls.xsd` file, provide that too in the preceding command. The command in this case would be as follows:

```
Xsd.exe myschema.xsd BuiltInActiveXControls.xsd /c /l:cs
```

14. Add this C# class file to your workflow project. Also add a new module and name it IPForms to your workflow project. This module is used to upload the InfoPath forms that are associated with the workflow to the server.

15. Module is just a folder with two files `Sample.txt` and `Elements.xml`. The `Elements.xml` is used by the project feature to deploy the contents of the module. Delete the `Samples.txt` file as it is just a placeholder to show that files can be deployed using modules. Visual Studio automatically makes the necessary changes to `Elements.xml` whenever you add and delete files from the module.

16. Add the published InfoPath form to this module and Visual Studio automatically updates the `Elements.xml` file in the module. The following code shows the `Elements.xml` file contents:

```xml
<?xml version="1.0" encoding="utf-8"?>
<Elements xmlns="http://schemas.microsoft.com/sharepoint/">
  <Module Name="IPForms">
    <File Path="IPForms\InitForm.xsn" Url="IPForms/InitForm.xsn" />
  </Module>
</Elements>
```

17. Open the feature that deploys the module and click the **Manifest** link as shown in the following screenshot:

18. Click the **Edit Options** link to open the manifest editor as shown in the following screenshot:

19. Open the manifest editor and add a new property `RegisterForms` and provide the path of your module that contains the InfoPath forms for the value of the property. This will register the forms in the module when the feature is activated. Your end result of the manifest changes should be similar to the following code:

```xml
<?xml version="1.0" encoding="utf-8" ?>
<Feature xmlns="http://schemas.microsoft.com/sharepoint/">
  <Properties>
    <Property Key="GloballyAvailable" Value="true" />
    <Property Key="RegisterForms" Value="IPForms\*.xsn" />
  </Properties>
</Feature>
```

20. From the feature's property window, set the `Receiver Assembly` and `Receiver Class` properties to the following values:

    ```
    Receiver Assembly = Microsoft.Office.Workflow.Feature,
    Version=14.0.0.0, Culture=neutral, PublicKeyToken=71e9bce111e9429c
    Receiver Class = Microsoft.Office.Workflow.Feature.
    WorkflowFeatureReceiver
    ```

21. The `WorkflowFeatureReceiver` class processes the manifest file changes that we did in the previous step. This class will manage the registration of the InfoPath files for use with `Workflow`. Until now we created the form and we created the necessary source files that can be used in the workflow and also we made changes to the feature to register the forms for workflow. The last step is to associate this form with the workflow. To do this, we will open the `Elements.xml` file of the workflow and add the **URN** (**Uniform Resource Name**) of the InfoPath form.

22. To get the URN of the InfoPath Form, go to **File** tab in the **InfoPath Designer** of your form and click the button **Form template properties**. This should bring up the form properties as shown in the following screenshot. From this window, copy the ID element of the form. The URN may be different for you than what is shown:

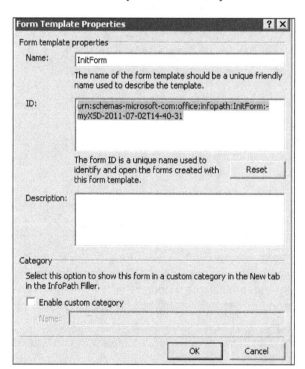

23. Open the `Elements.xml` file of the workflow and add the `Instantiation_FormURN` property under `MetaData` element and also make changes to `InstantiationUrl` property. `InstantiationUrl` refers to an ASPX page that hosts the InfoPath form. Your `elements.xml` file should look like following:

```xml
<?xml version="1.0" encoding="utf-8" ?>
<Elements xmlns="http://schemas.microsoft.com/sharepoint/">
  <Workflow
      Name="InfoPathInitiation - Workflow1"
      Description="My SharePoint Workflow"
      Id="d1b973a0-9f8b-4abd-befa-0113641cfb34"
      CodeBesideClass="InfoPathInitiation.Workflow1.Workflow1"
      CodeBesideAssembly="$assemblyname$"
      InstantiationUrl="_layouts/IniWrkflIP.aspx">
    <Categories/>
    <MetaData>
      <AssociationCategories>Site</AssociationCategories>
      <Instantiation_FormURN>urn:schemas-microsoft-com:office:
infopath:InitForm:-myXSD-2011-07-02T14-40-31</Instantiation_
FormURN>
      <StatusPageUrl>_layouts/WrkStat.aspx</StatusPageUrl>
    </MetaData>
  </Workflow>
</Elements>
```

24. Now on to the workflow code, where we will use the `XmlSerializer` to deserialize the string initiation data (in the XML format) from our form to `.NET` object. The `myFields` object is in the `myschema.cs` file that we created via the XSD tool. Make changes to the `CheckCreditAmount` method as follows:

```csharp
private void CheckCreditAmount(object sender,
ConditionalEventArgs e)
        {

            string sInitData = workflowProperties.InitiationData;

            XmlSerializer ser = new XmlSerializer(typeof(myFields)
);
            XmlTextReader reader = new XmlTextReader(
              new System.IO.StringReader(sInitData));
            myFields ipInitForm =
              (myFields)ser.Deserialize(reader);

            string sCreditRequested = ipInitForm.
txtCreditRequested;
            double initAmount = 0;
```

```
double.TryParse(sCreditRequested, out initAmount);

if (initAmount <= 1000)
    e.Result = true;
else
    e.Result = false;
}
```

25. Build and run the project and when you manually invoke the site workflow, you should see the InfoPath form as shown in the following screenshot:

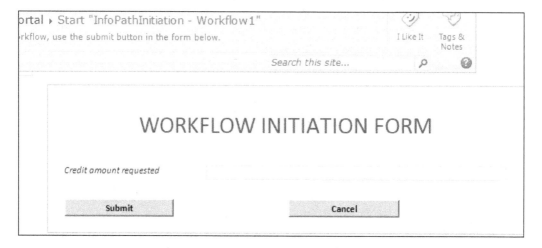

How it works...

As usual, we get the initiation data from the `WorkflowProperties` object like we did in the previous recipe. The difference in here is that we get XML string for the initiation data as InfoPath forms are XML files. To read values from this XML string, we cast the string into a `.NET` class that was generated from the form's schema definition file. This is the reason why we used the XSD generator to create the `.NET` class for our initiation form. The XSD generator when created the `.NET` class from the schema file, each of the control in the form is mapped to a property. Hence we can just use the dot notation to read the values of the form's controls. The `XmlSerializer` is used in the `CheckCreditAmount` method to cast the XML string to the `.NET` class.

To make use of the InfoPath forms in the workflow, we need to deploy it to the form server of the SharePoint and make it workflow enabled. This is the reason, why we used a feature to deploy our InfoPath form. Just using feature would not deploy it to the forms server. We need to instruct the feature to do that task, for this purpose, we made use of the event receiver. We made use of the built-in event receiver `Microsoft.Office.Workflow.Feature.WorkflowFeatureReceiver` for this task.

Apart from deploying InfoPath forms to the form server, we need to hook this form to the workflow so it opens it at the initiation stage. Since InfoPath forms are XML files, it needs to be hosted on some page. SharePoint provides `IniWrkflIP.aspx` that resides in the `_layout` root directory in the SharePoint server. This ASPX page can host InfoPath forms. Apart from that we need to notify the workflow what form to open. This is done providing the form's URN (Uniform Resource Name). We made these changes to the workflow's `Elements.xml` file.

If you have managed code with your InfoPath forms, the procedure is exactly the same. Just add the compiled DLL with the published InfoPath form to the module and proceed with the rest of the steps.

See also

▸ *Creating a sequential workflow recipe*

▸ *Creating a site workflow with an initiation form recipe*

▸ *Creating a task from the workflow recipe*

Creating a task from the workflow

So far we created workflows that run automatically without stopping for user input in the middle of the process. Initiation or association data come before the workflow is started. There are many situations where in the middle of the workflow process you may want input from a user to proceed further. To do this, we will create tasks in SharePoint.

In this recipe, we will create an **Employee Suggestion Program** (**ESP**) workflow, where employees of a company can provide suggestions on the betterment of the business processes that are in place in the company. For this, when an employee suggests a process improvement, a task is assigned to the department director to take a look at and decide on the value of the suggestion.

Getting ready

Create a custom list from the SharePoint UI called ESP. The following table lists all the attributes of the fields in the list:

Field Name	Data Type	Required
Title	Single line of text	Yes
Department Director	Person or group	Yes
Suggestion	Multiple lines of text	Yes

How to do it...

1. Create a sequential list workflow project named **ESPWF** and associate the workflow to ESP list created using Visual Studio 2010 new project wizard.

2. On the workflow designer surface, add **CreateTask** activity from the toolbox under the section SharePoint workflow below the **onWorkflowActivated1** activity as shown in the following screenshot:

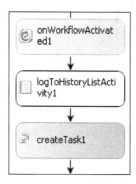

3. Set the **CorrelationToken** of this activity to **taskToken** and **OwnerActivityName** to **Workflow1**. The properties window of **CreateTask** activity is shown in the following screenshot:

Properties	
createTask1 Microsoft.SharePoint.WorkflowActions.CreateTask	
(Name)	createTask1
⊟ CorrelationToken	taskToken
OwnerActivityName	Workflow1

4. Next, we need to set a binding variable to the **TaskId** property. We will bind this property to a new field named **taskId**. In order to do this, click on the yellow cylinder icon next to the property, as shown in the following screenshot:

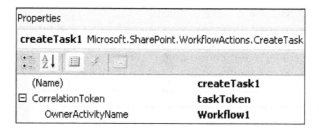

MethodName	CreateTask
⊞ SpecialPermissions	Activity=Workflow1,
⊞ TaskId	Activity=Workflow1,
⊞ TaskProperties	Activity=Workflow1,

5. This will bring up the variable binding window and select the tab **Bind to a new member** as shown in the following screenshot:

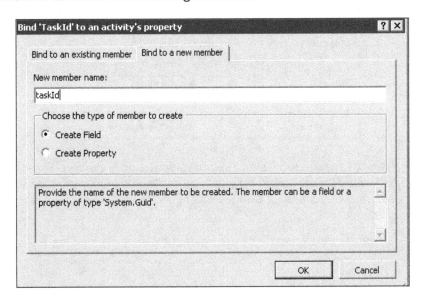

6. Repeat the process for **TaskProperties** as well. Name the variable as **taskProps**.

7. Right-click on the **CreateTask** activity and generate an event handler method as shown in the following screenshot:

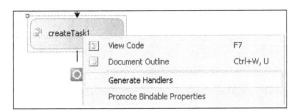

8   Visual Studio will add an event handler in the `Workflow1.cs` file. While in the code file, declare a new variable of type `bool` called `isTaskComplete` and set the default value to false.

9. From the workflow designer, add a `while` activity below the **CreateTask** activity and inside this `while` loop add an **onTaskChanged** activity.

10. Set the `while` loop condition property to `Declarative Rule Condition` and set the **ConditionName** and expression to **IsTaskCompleted** and the **!this. isTaskComplete** respectively. The following screenshot shows the end result:

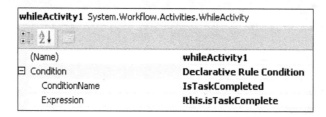

11. For **onTaskChanged** activity bind the **CorrelationToken** to the same thing as the one created for **CreateTask** activity. Also set the **TaskId** property to the same bind variable that we declared for **CreateTask** activity. The following screenshot shows the end result:

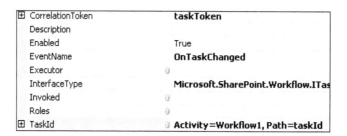

12. Bind the **AfterProperties** and the **BeforeProperties** property to new variables named **taskAfterProperties** and **taskBeforeProperties** using the variable binding window. Also create an event handler method for this activity.

13. To complete our workflow flowchart, add a **CompleteTask** below the `while loop` activity. Set the **CorrelationToken** and **TaskId** properties to the same ones as the **CreateTask** activity. Your finished workflow flowchart should look as shown in the following screenshot:

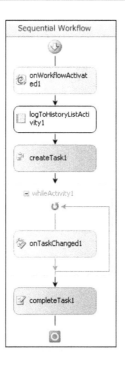

14. In the code file `Workflow1.cs`, add the following code to the `createTask1_` `MethodInvoking` and `onTaskChanged1_Invoked` methods.

```
private void createTask1_MethodInvoking(object sender,
EventArgs e)
        {
            taskId = Guid.NewGuid();
            string sDepartmentDirector = workflowProperties.
Item["Department Director"].ToString();
            SPFieldLookupValue fld = new SPFieldLookupValue
(sDepartmentDirector);
            taskProps.AssignedTo = fld.LookupValue;
            taskProps.Title = "Review Employee Suggestion";
            taskProps.DueDate = DateTime.Today.AddDays(7);
            taskProps.SendEmailNotification = true;
        }
private void onTaskChanged1_Invoked(object sender,
ExternalDataEventArgs e)
        {
            Guid statusFieldID = workflowProperties.TaskList.
Fields["Status"].Id;
            string taskStatus = taskAfterProperties.Extended
            Properties[statusFieldID].ToString();
```

```
        if (!string.IsNullOrEmpty(taskStatus) &&
        taskStatus == "Completed")
        {
            // If so, let the While Loop Activity know
            that we are done!
            this.isTaskComplete = true;
        }


    }
```

15. Build and run the application and this will open the site and list that the workflow is associated. Add a new item to the ESP list and the workflow should start automatically with a task created to the person provided in the list item. The following screenshot shows the task list of the workflow with task created:

16. Click on the **Review Employee Suggestion** title in the task list to open the task item. Edit this item to bring up the task edit form as shown in the following screenshot:

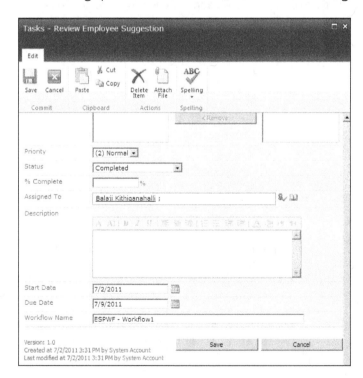

17. Set the **Status** field to **Completed** and save the form. This will complete the workflow as shown in the following screenshot:

Workflow Information			
Initiator: System Account		**Item:**	Use SharePoint
Started: 7/2/2011 3:31 PM		**Status:**	Completed
Last run: 7/2/2011 3:47 PM			

How it works...

Tasks are the way SharePoint workflows interact with the users. So if your workflows need input from users in the middle of the workflow process, you will create a task for that user and ask them to provide input through the task forms. This is exactly what we achieved in this recipe.

Since SharePoint workflows only interact via the tasks, Visual Studio provides a `CreateTask` activity which can be conveniently used to create a task for any person available on SharePoint. The `CreateTask` activity implements the `ITaskService` to create a task item in the task list associated with the workflow.

For every `CreateTask` activity it is necessary to create a correlation token. This should be unique for each task you reference in the workflow. Correlation tokens are unique string identifiers that are used by the workflow to map the items in the workflow to the hosting environment and workflow runtime. Workflows to maximize the resource usage will reuse objects in multiple instances of the workflow. That is, when SharePoint workflow is initiated, it verifies to see if any other instance is already running. Then if so, it tries to reuse some of the objects that were created during that instance. This helps in resource usage and also in performance. To correctly identify an instance to which any received messages need to be passed, the runtime environment needs to have a unique key to identify the workflow instance. This is accomplished by the correlation tokens.

Any other activities like `OnTaskChanged` and `CompleteTask` that refer to the same task should also set their `CorrelationToken` properties to the same as the one used in the `CreateTask` activity.

The `CreateTask` activity also has the task properties object of type `SPWorkflowTaskProperties`. This object is used to specify the task properties such as `AssignedTo`, `DueDate`, `Title`, and whether to send an e-mail notification to the assigned user when the task is created. For more information on `SPWorkflowTaskProperties` refer to MSDN at `http://msdn.microsoft.com/en-us/library/microsoft.sharepoint.workflow.spworkflowtaskproperties_members.aspx`.

We can always associate custom task forms in the workflow. If no custom forms are provided, a default task form is presented to the user to complete the task. This is what we did in this recipe and in the `OnTaskChanged` activity—we referred to this default form field to check the status set by the user to determine whether the task is completed or not. The information from the task form is available through the `AfterTaskProperties` object. The extended properties in this object stores key value pair of information based on the task form used. The `BeforeTaskProperties` is used to pass the information from the workflow to the task form.

There's more...

We made use of the `IfElse` activity and while activity from the general activities list. Out of 30 activities that are listed in the general activity list, not all of them can be used in the SharePoint workflow. The following table provides the activities that cannot be used in the SharePoint workflows:

Activity Name	Description
Compensate	This is used to undo in case of an error. None of the compensating activities can be used in SharePoint.
CompenstableSequence	This is used to execute a group of activities and is capable of compensating in case of an error.
CompenstableTransactionScope	Executes activities inside this sequentially under a transaction and compensates in case of an error.
InvokeWebService	Invokes a web service from the workflow.
InvokeWorkflow	Invokes another workflow from inside of the workflow.
Policy	A group of IfElse statements that make up a policy and are applied to a workflow item.
ReceiveActivity	Implements **Windows Communication Foundation** (**WCF**) service interfaces. This way a workflow can be exposed as a web service.
SendActivity	Implements WCF client side operations.
Suspend	Suspends the workflow execution.
Throw	Throws an exception.
TransactionScope	Groups the activities to work inside a transaction.
WebServiceInput	Used in enabling workflow to act as a web service.
WebServiceOutput	Used in enabling workflow to act as a web service.
WebServiceFault	Throws an exception to a web service

See also

▸ _Creating a custom task form_ recipe

Creating a custom task form

In the previous recipe, when the department director completes the task, we cannot determine whether he wants the suggestion implemented or rejected. We may have to find out using the comments field as there is no other field that provides a way for him to convey that information. If the workflow has to take action based on this input, the default form provided will not fit the situation. We may have to create a custom form and present it to the user to perform their tasks. You can use either the ASPX page or InfoPath form to create the custom task form. In this recipe, we will create a custom InfoPath task form.

Getting ready

This recipe is an extension of the previous recipe. Hence, a successful completion of the previous recipe will provide a good foundation for understanding this. This recipe also assumes that you have working knowledge of designing InfoPath forms.

How to do it...

1. Using InfoPath designer, create a form named `TaskEditForm.xsn` with a drop-down list control for status with values "Approved", "Rejected", and "Working". Add some textbox controls for the department director to enter comments on the suggestion and to show the title and suggestion information entered by the employee. The end result of the InfoPath screen is shown in the following screenshot:

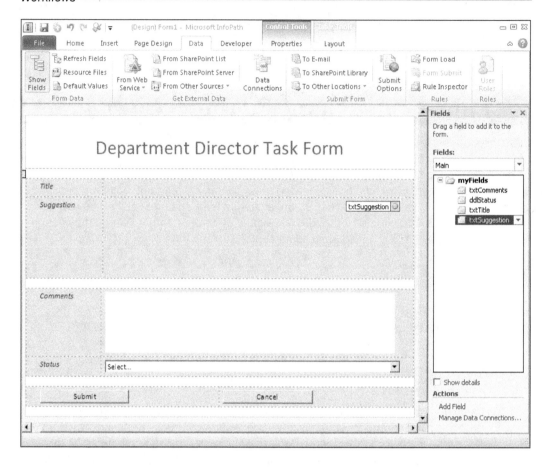

2. Create a new XML file called `ItemMetadata.xml`. The file name is case-sensitive and should be named `ItemMetadata.xml`. Add the following content to this file:

```xml
<?xml version="1.0" encoding="utf-8"?>
<z:row xmlns:z="#RowsetSchema"
ows_Title=""
ows_Suggestion=""
/>
```

3. Add a receive data connection to the InfoPath form with the previously created XML file and associate the `txtTitle` and `txtSuggestion` with `ows_Title` and `ows_Suggestion`.

4. Also create a submit data connection that submits the form to the hosting environment.

5. Follow the same procedure outlined in the recipe for creating the InfoPath initiation form to publish this form. Follow all the steps in that recipe from 3 to 9. For task forms there is no need to save the InfoPath source files and create the class file using XSD.exe as indicated in that recipe.

6. Open the **ESPWF** solution file that we created in the previous recipe. Add a new module to this project and name the module **IPForms**.

7. Remove the added Sample.txt file from the **IPForms** module and add the published InfoPath form. Visual Studio will automatically update the Elements.xml file under **IPForms**.

8. Add the property key **RegisterForms** to the feature manifest file and set the value to the path of **IPForms** module. Also set the feature's receiver assembly and class properties to the following values:

```
Receiver Assembly = Microsoft.Office.Workflow.Feature,
Version=14.0.0.0, Culture=neutral, PublicKeyToken=71e9bce111e9429c
 Receiver Class = Microsoft.Office.Workflow.Feature.
WorkflowFeatureReceiver
```

9. Modify the workflow Elements.xml file and add a new attribute TaskListContentTypeId to the workflow element and set the value to "0x010801 00C9C9515DE4E24001905074F980F93160".

10. Add a new element under the **MetaData** element to define the task types. Add the URN of your InfoPath form as the element's value. You can get the URN from the InfoPath form's template properties section. The following code shows the end result:

```
<Task0_FormURN>urn:schemas-microsoft-com:office:infopath:
TaskEditForm:-myXSD-2011-07-03T12-10-50</Task0_FormURN>
```

11. Make modification to the createTask1_MethodInvoking method in the workflow code to associate this form to the task. Your resulting code should be as follows:

```
private void createTask1_MethodInvoking(object sender,
EventArgs e)
        {
            taskId = Guid.NewGuid();
            string sDepartmentDirector = workflowProperties.
            Item["Department Director"].ToString();
            SPFieldLookupValue fld = new SPFieldLookupValue
            (sDepartmentDirector);
            taskProps.AssignedTo = fld.LookupValue;
            taskProps.Title = "Review Employee Suggestion";
            taskProps.DueDate = DateTime.Today.AddDays(7);
            taskProps.EmailBody = "An employee suggestion is
             received. Please review this";
            taskProps.SendEmailNotification = true;
            taskProps.ExtendedProperties["ows_Title"] =
            workflowProperties.Item["Title"].ToString();
```

```
taskProps.ExtendedProperties["ows_Suggestion"] =
workflowProperties.Item["Suggestion"].ToString();
taskProps.TaskType = 0;
}
```

12. Also make changes to the `onTaskChanged1_Invoked` method to check the status from the drop-down field from the InfoPath form. Your resulting code should be as follows:

```
private void onTaskChanged1_Invoked(object sender,
ExternalDataEventArgs e)
        {
            string taskStatus = taskAfterProperties.Extended
            Properties["ddlStatus"].ToString();
            if (!string.IsNullOrEmpty(taskStatus) &&
            (taskStatus == "Approved" || taskStatus =="Rejected"))
            {
                // If so, let the While Loop Activity know that
                we are done!
                this.isTaskComplete = true;
            }

        }
```

13. Build and run the project. Create a new item in your list and the workflow should automatically start on the insert of the new item and create a task for the person specified in the list item. When you click the task item, you should see the InfoPath form associated with the task edit as shown in the following screenshot:

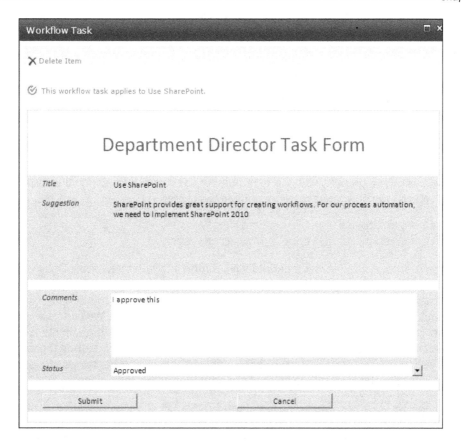

How it works...

The workflow is exactly the same as the previous recipe except for the fact that we are using the custom task edit form instead of the default form. Task edit forms can be created by either using ASPX pages or by using InfoPath forms. For using ASPX pages, you have to create a custom content type and associate the ASPX page with the content type. Instead of `CreateTask` activity, you will be using `CreateTaskWithContentType` activity for this purpose. This activity will create a task based on a specific content type. All the other procedures will remain the same. In case all the tasks in the workflow use the same form, you will only need to create one content type and can reuse it in all task creation activities. More information on content types is provided in *Chapter 4*. If your workflow is creating many types of tasks then using the ASPX page approach will end up creating many different content types. Managing all these content types in a huge workflow will become a daunting task. But if you are not running form services, then this is the only way to create custom task forms. You cannot use InfoPath forms as it depends on the form services in the SharePoint.

InfoPath forms provide a better alternative to task forms even though the deployment procedure is a little convoluted. You do not have to create all the content types for deploying InfoPath forms as task edit forms. This is due to the fact that InfoPath forms are hosted from an ASPX page. This page (`WrkTaskIP.aspx`) is located in the root `_layouts` folder. This page is also associated with a content type but is capable of hosting the InfoPath forms. Hence, we provide the default content type ID in the workflow `Elements.xml` file.

To associate different task forms for the tasks that we create in the workflow, we create task type elements in the `Elements.xml` file of the workflow. This stores the URN information of the form. We can use as many number here of these as we need. All we need to do is increment the number in the task type element. In the code during the creation of the task, we set the `TaskType` property with the right number to show the corresponding form. The following code shows how we can define multiple task types in `Elements.xml` file.

```
<Task0_FormURN>URN of form 1</Task0_FormURN>
<Task1_FormURN>URN of form 2</Task1_FormURN>
```

The `ItemMetadata.xml` file is a mandatory file for the InfoPath task forms. This is the way SharePoint workflow passes data to the task form. Since during the form load event, SharePoint always passes the data to the task form, it expects to see this file associated with the InfoPath task forms. If this is not provided, an exception is thrown. We can use this file and pass in any necessary information that we need to display on the task form. In our example we passed title and suggestion from the workflow item. This is done, by setting those values in the `TaskProperties ExtendedProperties` object. This `ExtendedProperties` object is a hashtable that contains key-value pairs of the data that needs to be passed.

Similar to how we pass the data to the task form via the `ExtendedProperties` object, SharePoint stores all the InfoPath elements data in the `ExtendedProperties` of the task `AfterProperties` object when the task form is submitted. We can use the name of the field defined in the InfoPath form to access the value of the field. This is the reason why we do not have to create the class file of the InfoPath form using the XSD tool.

> Do not use group elements in your schema when you are designing InfoPath task forms. The reason is SharePoint cannot associate these to the `ExtendedProperties` object. Always use flat structure in designing InfoPath task forms.

There's more...

When you create a task using the preceding method, any person with sufficient permission on the task list will be able to edit the task and complete the task. Tasks are not restricted to the person associated to the task via the `AssignedTo` property. This may not work in real-world workflows as you may need to audit the task completion time and the users for whatever reasons. If you need to restrict that only `AssignedTo` person be able to edit the task you have to set `SpecialPermissions` property on `CreateTask` activity.

The `SpecialPermissions` object is of `HybridDictionary` type and takes in username and permission type to be set. So in the `CreateTask` method invoking adds the following code to restrict the task edit by a `AssignedTo` user.

```
createTask1_TaskProperties1.AssignedTo = "domain\\user";
System.Collections.Specialized.HybridDictionary specialPermissions =
new System.Collections.Specialized.HybridDictionary();
specialPermissions.Add(createTask1_TaskProperties1.AssignedTo,
SPRoleType.Contributor);
createTask1.SpecialPermissions = specialPermissions;
```

Task delete

The person who can edit the task can also delete it. If you are not handling the deleted task event, your workflow can go haywire if the user deletes the task. There is no straightforward way to restrict the deletion of the task. One method to restrict deletion is to write an event handler on the task list and throw an error message whenever someone tries to delete the task. For more information on Event Receivers, refer to *Chapter 1*.

The other method is to add a listening activity to your workflow and listen to multiple events like the task changed and the task deleted events. Depending on your business requirements, you can send an e-mail or stop the workflow completely or just continue to the next step. The following screenshot shows how to add a listening activity and handle the `delete` event of the task:

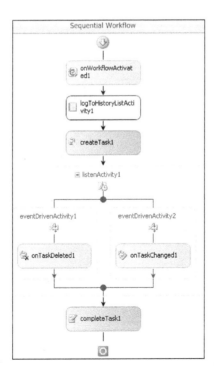

See also

▸ *Adding custom error message to Event Receiver* recipe in *Chapter 1*

▸ *Creating a custom content type using Object Model* recipe in *Chapter 4*

3
Advanced Workflows

In this chapter, we will cover:

- ▶ Creating a custom activity
- ▶ Creating a custom activity for Sandboxed solution
- ▶ Creating a state machine workflow
- ▶ Adding a custom workflow status
- ▶ Creating a pluggable workflow service

Introduction

In *Chapter 2, Workflows* we introduced sequential workflows that used out-of-the-box activities that are provided in Visual Studio 2010. Visual Studio 2010 provides 30 general workflow activities along with 26 Sharepoint specific activities. Not all of the 30 general workflow activities are supported in a SharePoint environment. The list of activities that are not supported in SharePoint environment is provided in *Chapter 2*. We have used many of the supported actvities in our recipes in *Chapter 2* and we will continue to use them in this chapter as well. There can be situations where we supported out-of-the-box acitvities which would not provide the complete solution that is required for your workflow problem. In these situations you can always create your own custom activity. In this chapter, we will show you how to create your own custom activity.

The development of custom activity is a very important subject especially when we have to model a domain-specific problem as an activity. By modeling a domain-specific functionality as an activity, you can use it with workflows created in SharePoint designer or Visual studio. Apart from that, you can reuse the same functionality in multiple workflows as well. In this chapter, apart from creating custom activity, we will learn about the differences that exist when creating activities that target only SharePoint designer workflows.

When we explained sequential workflows in *Chapter 2*, we said, there is no going back to the previous step if we needed to. This could pose a problem if there is a need in the business requirement such as requiring a feedback from the person who worked in the previous step or requiring a correction to the document from the person who worked on it previously and so on. Even though you can create these kinds of scenarios in the sequential workflow, it can become very complicated. This is one of the constraints of the sequential workflows.

On the contrary, state machine workflows do not have these constraints. They move from one state to another. You have control over what these states are and what event transitions them to another state. Since you cannot foresee the events that get triggered, there is no prescribed path for the workflow to take. When the workflow is in a state, it can perform a series of steps before moving to another state. State machine workflows have a beginning state but the end state is optional. If there is no end state then that workflow will run indefinitely. State machine workflows are mainly used in situations where human interactions are necessary. For example, a project submission process requires the user to submit the proposal for approval. The approver can send it back to the submitter for more information or approve the project. Here we do not know what the approver will do beforehand. He can raise the more information required event or `approved event` or he can raise the more information required event until he is satisfied with the end result of the project. This uncertainity of the user action and the back and forth nature of the process makes this a state machine workflow.

A pluggable workflow service (also referred to as local service) provides a mechanism for external systems to communicate with a workflow instance. For example, in our credit approval workflow from *Chapter 2*, if a workflow were to access an external system for credit verification, it has to send a request for a credit check and has to wait until the system responded with the result. What happens if the response takes hours or even days? We have to keep our workflow active until we get the response back, otherwise the workflow will never be able to move forward unless we model our workflow for manual input of this information. This is not a good use of the resources. This is not scalable in large volume scenarios. So what if we had a mechanism in which these external systems can raise an event and wake a workflow up when it is ready with the response? This is what we can achieve using a pluggable workflow service. In this chapter, we will learn how to create pluggable workflow service.

Creating a custom activity

In this recipe, we will create a custom activity that gets the manager information of a user. Usually, in a real world workflow, tasks get escalated to the user manager if a task does not get completed within the due date provided or may need the manager's approval for a document submitted and so on. To get the manager information, we have to retrieve the user profile information and query the manager information. There is a similar one available in SharePoint designer but is not available in Visual Studio. This activity can be used by both tools.

Getting ready

This recipe assumes that you have successfully configured the user profile synchronization on your SharePoint server. For more information on configuring user profile, refer to *Microsoft 2010 SharePoint Administration Cookbook* by Peter Serzo published by Packt publishing.

How to do it...

1. Create an empty SharePoint project named **GetManagerActivity** with the farm deployment option selected.

2. Add a new component class item as shown in the following screenshot and name it `GetManager.cs`:

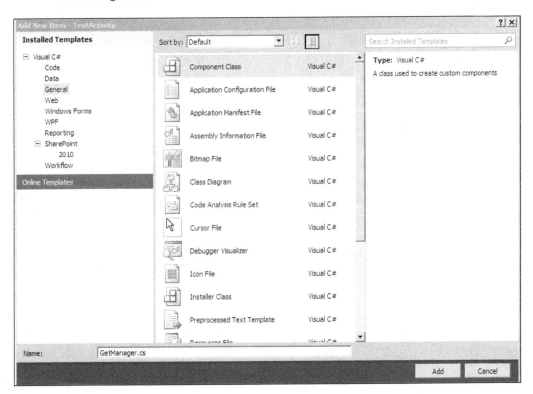

3. Visual Studio shows an error as shown in the following screenshot as soon as you add this class. Ignore the error for now.

Error loading workflow

An error occurred while loading the workflow. Please correct the following error and try reloading the document to view the workflow.

The designer could not be shown for this file because none of the classes within it can be designed. The designer inspected the following classes in the file: GetManager. The base class GetManager for the class needs to be an Activity.

4. Add references to `System.Web.dll`, `Microsoft.Office.Server.UserProfiles.dll`, and `Microsoft.Office.Server.dll`.

5. To correct the error we got in step three, open `GetManager.cs` class and add the following four `using` statements:

```
using Microsoft.SharePoint;
using System.Workflow.Activities;
using System.Workflow.ComponentModel;
using Microsoft.Office.Server.UserProfiles;
```

6. Change the base class of `GetManager` from `Component` to `Activity`. Delete the constructor that takes the `IContainer` parameter. This will correct the error that you saw earlier. Also override the `Execute` method of the `Activity` class.

7. Now we need to add `DependencyProperties` to this class. To add a `DependencyProperty` right-click and from the context menu select **Insert Snippet > Other > workflow > Add DependencyProperty – Property** as shown in the following screenshot:

```
namespace TestActivity
{
    public partial class GetManager : Activity
    {
        public GetManager()
        {
            InitializeComponent();
        }

        Insert Snippet: Other > workflow > |
    }
}
creating a dependency property in a Windows Workflow
```

Add DependencyProperty - EventHandler
Add DependencyProperty - Property

8. This will add the `DependencyProperty` code snippet and you can change the name, description, and type of the property. For our example, name this property `UserEmail` and of the type `string`. The following code shows the definition of the `UserEmail` property:

```
public static DependencyProperty UserEmailProperty =
DependencyProperty.Register("UserEmail", typeof(string),
typeof(GetManager));


        [Description("UserEmail")]
        [Category("UserEmail Category")]
        [Browsable(true)]
            [DesignerSerializationVisibility(DesignerSerialization
            Visibility.Visible)]
        public string UserEmail
        {
            get
            {
            return ((string)(base.GetValue(GetManager.
            UserEmailProperty)));
            }
            set
            {
             base.SetValue(GetManager.UserEmailProperty, value);
            }
        }
```

9. Follow the same preceding procedure and add two more dependency properties named `Manager` and `__Context`. The `Manager` is of type string and `__Context` is of type `WorkflowContext`.

10. Create a method named `RetrieveManagerFromUserEmail()` and add code to retrieve manager information for the given e-mail address from the user profile information of the user. Your code should be as follows:

```
private void RetrieveManagerFromUserEmail()
        {
            if (string.IsNullOrEmpty(this.UserEmail))
                this.Manager = "";

            SPSecurity.RunWithElevatedPrivileges(delegate()
            {
                using (SPSite site = new SPSite(this.__Context.Site.
                ID))
                {
                    using (SPWeb web = site.OpenWeb(this.__Context.
                    Web.ID))
```

```
                    {
                            SPUser user = web.AllUsers.
        GetByEmail(UserEmail);
                            if (user != null)
                            {
                                string manager = string.Empty;
                                SPServiceContext context =
        SPServiceContext.GetContext(site);
                                UserProfileManager profileManger = new
        UserProfileManager(context);

                                try
                                {
                                    UserProfile prof = profileManger.
        GetUserProfile(user.RawSid);
                                    manager = (prof[PropertyConstants.
        Manager].Value == null)
                                    ? "" : prof[PropertyConstants.
        Manager].Value.ToString(); //Get the manager
                                }
                                catch (Exception)
                                {
                                    manager = "Manager was not found";
                                }

                                this.Manager = manager;
                            }

                        }
                    }
                });

            }
```

11. Call this method from the `Execute` method. Your code in the `Execute` method should be as follows:

```
protected override ActivityExecutionStatus Execute(ActivityExecuti
onContext executionContext)
    {
        RetrieveManagerFromUserEmail();
        return ActivityExecutionStatus.Closed;
    }
```

12. Build and deploy this assembly to the **Global Assembly Cache** (**GAC**) by executing the following command from the Visual Studio command prompt:

```
Gacutil /I GetManagerActivity.dll
```

13. Add an `authorizedType` entry in the `web.config` file of your web application. The `authorizedType` entry contains the `publicKeyToken` of your assembly and can be obtained from the GAC itself. The entry should be as follows:

```
<authorizedType Assembly="GetManagerActivity, Version=1.0.0.0,
Culture=neutral, PublicKeyToken=ed3ef6151b74125b" Namespace="GetMa
nagerActivity" TypeName="*" Authorized="True" />
```

14. Create a XML file named `GetManager.ACTIONS`. This file provides metadata information for the SharePoint designer so it can recognize this as a custom action and display it under the **Actions** menu. The content of the `.ACTIONS` file is as follows:

```
<?xml version="1.0" encoding="utf-8" ?>
<WorkflowInfo Language="en-us">
  <Actions Sequential="then" Parallel="and">
    <Action Name="Get Manager for a User"
      ClassName="GetManagerActivity.GetManager"
      Assembly="GetManagerActivity, Version=1.0.0.0,Culture=neutral
,PublicKeyToken=ed3ef6151b74125b"
      Category="Chapter2 Actions"
      AppliesTo="all ">
      <RuleDesigner Sentence="Get Manager for %1 (Output to %2)">
        <FieldBind Field="UserEmail" Text="user email" Id="1"
DesignerType="TextBox" />
      <FieldBind Field="Manager" Text="Manager" Id="2" DesignerType=
"ParameterNames" />
      </RuleDesigner>
      <Parameters>
        <Parameter Name="__Context"
          Type="Microsoft.SharePoint.WorkflowActions.
          WorkflowContext,Microsoft.SharePoint.WorkflowActions"
          Direction="In" DesignerType="Hide" />
        <Parameter Name="Manager" Type="System.String, mscorlib"
Direction="Out" />
        <Parameter Name="UserEmail" Type="System.String, mscorlib"
Direction="In" />
      </Parameters>
    </Action>
  </Actions>
</WorkflowInfo>
```

15. Copy the `GetManager.ACTIONS` file to the SharePoint `ROOT\TEMPLATE\1033\Workflow` folder.

16. From the command prompt do an `iisreset` and open your SharePoint designer, connect to the website and create a new workflow.

17. From the **Actions** menu, you should be able to see our newly created action under the category specified in the `.ACTIONS` file. The following screenshot shows the custom activity in the **Action** menu:

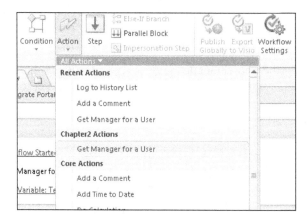

18. Insert the action to the workflow designer surface and you should be able to provide user e-mail as input and set a variable for receiving the manager's name. The following screenshot shows the custom action in SharePoint designer workflow editor:

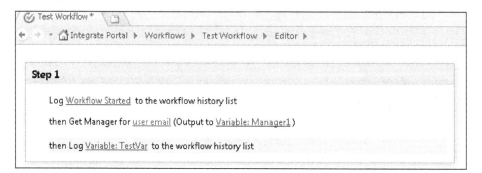

How it works...

Every workflow is basically an activity. The information here applies to a workflow as well. Thus, you can create a workflow and make that a custom activity that can be used inside other workflows. The one we created in this recipe is a simple activity that solves a domain-specific problem. In this activity, we want to get the manager's information for a given user's e-mail. The code is pretty straightforward; it uses the profile manager object of the user to get the manager information. User Profile synchronization services synchronize the user information with Active Directory or other LDAP-supported directories. The manager property is only available if your Active Directory has populated that information. For more information on User Profile synchronization, please refer to MSDN at: `http://technet.microsoft.com/en-us/library/gg188041.aspx`.

To input or to output values to or from a custom activity, you define properties. You can also provide these properties access in a designer user interface to bind to a certain variable. In the previous recipes we used some of these properties like task properties, correlation tokens and so on. We bound these properties to variables via the Visual Studio workflow designer. These designer binding properties are called dependency properties.

Dependency properties are similar to .NET properties that we define in a custom class except that it makes use of the shared repository of the workflow state. It is based on `DependencyObject` type. To define these dependency properties, we declare a static property of type `DependencyProperty` with the name of the property always appended by *Property*. This is registered to the actual implementation of the property and also provides information about the type that this property returns or takes in. The other attributes that decorate the property provide information to the designer window.

When you develop an activity that needs to be compatible with SharePoint designer, all the properties that you define in the activity should be dependency properties. This is a requirement. This is not required if you are just targeting Visual Studio 2010 workflows.

The other requirement of SharePoint designer is to have a mandatory dependency property `__Context`. This is of type `Microsoft.SharePoint.WorkfowActions.WorkfowContext`. It is populated automatically by the SharePoint designer with the context of the current workflow. This is not required if your custom activity is only for Visual Studio workflows.

Custom actions are deployed to GAC as it requires full trust and can be used by the SharePoint designer. When used in the SharePoint designer, it can be used farm wide that is on any web application or any site collection that you can connect to. Even though we used the manual approach to deploy, you can create a Visual Studio project that does that for you. Apart from that, since SharePoint only loads the authorized assemblies for security reasons, you also have to modify the `web.config` file of your web application to put `authorizedType` entry.

You will also have to provide metadata information of your custom activity so SharePoint designer can display the activity in the **Actions** menu. This is done by providing an `.ACTIONS` file for your custom activity. Again, this is not required if you are just targeting Visual Studio workflows, but is mandatory for SharePoint designer support.

You do not have to create a new .ACTIONS file for every custom activity that you develop; you can just append your metadata to an existing one. These action files are always stored at Template\workflow at the root of the locale that you are targeting. In our example, we were targeting the en-US culture and so you would deploy this file to the Root\ Template\1033\Workflow folder. If you want deploy to say English Australia, your locale ID would be 3081. For more information on the locale ID please refer to MSDN at: http://msdn.microsoft.com/en-us/goglobal/bb964664.

The .ACTIONS file always starts with the WorkflowInfo element with the language attribute that targets the culture to which you want to deploy. Below this element is the Actions element where you can define one or more actions. The Action element provides information about the custom activity like Name, ClassName, Assembly, Category, and AppliesTo. Valid values for AppliesTo are **list, doclib** and **all**, which target list, document library, and everything else respectively.

The Name attribute is used in the display of the activity in the **Actions** menu. Category helps in where the user can find this activity in **Actions** menu of the SharePoint designer.

Each Action element has a RuleDesigner element which defines the behavior of the activity in the SharePoint designer's workflow designer. The Sentence attribute of RuleDesigner defines the verbiage that is shown in the SharePoint designer activity display. The %1 in the sentence corresponds to the FieldBind element with ID equaling one and %2 corresponding to the FieldBind element with ID equaling two. The FieldBind elements describe the binding of the variables from the designer surface. You would define all the properties that are not set by the SharePoint designer automatically. Hence we have not defined __Context property in the FieldBind element. As indicated, this __Context property is automatically set by the SharePoint designer. The Parameters element defines each of the properties that the activity contains and their types. For more information on WorkflowInfo schema, refer to MSDN at: http://msdn.microsoft.com/en-us/ library/bb897626.aspx.

There's more...

The __Context property that we defined previously is only initialized automatically in SharePoint designer but not in Visual Studio workflows. If you want to use this activity in Visual Studio workflow, you have to manually create this context and set the property. To do so you can use the following code:

```
Microsoft.SharePoint.WorkflowActions.WorkflowContext _context = new
WorkflowContext();
_context.Initialize(workflowProperties);
getManager1.__Context = _context;
```

Workflow security

In this example, we used `SPSecurity.RunWithElevatedPrivileges` to get the profile information of the user. This is used to run the specific method with full control rights even if the user does not have full control.

Behind the scenes, `RunWithElevatedPrivileges` impersonates the identity of the current thread. In effect, this means that the delegate will run under the context of the application pool account if it is executed in a web page, and under `SPTimerV4` service if it is running under the context of the timer job. If the code is running in a user-initiated application like console application or windows application, the delegate will run under the context of the user who started the application (usually this is the default behavior).

When using in workflows, bear in mind that the workflow may start running under the W3WP process, but can continue executing under the `owstimer` (SPTimerV4) depending on what it is actually doing. In this case, a delegate executed using `RunWithElevatedPrivileges` would not necessarily yield the same result if you have two different accounts associated with these processes.

These elevated privileges can have effect on the overall management of the workflows and need to be properly discussed with the administrators managing the SharePoint servers. For more information on security planning for workflows please refer to MSDN at: `http://technet.microsoft.com/en-us/library/ee428324.aspx`.

Sandboxed activities

One thing that is to be noted here is that we cannot create a sandboxed workflow using Visual Studio. Visual Studio workflows are also called code-only workflows and are not allowed due to the fact that the deployment of the assemblies happens to the GAC. Deploying to GAC or accessing root folders and so on are not allowed in the sandboxed environment. If your company only allows sandboxed solutions or hosting SharePoint in a cloud environment like Office 365 / SharePoint online where sandboxed solutions are the only option, developing custom workflows can be done only via SharePoint designer. The workflows that are developed using SharePoint designer are called **declarative workflows**.

Visual Studio can still come in handy in the case of the sandboxed environment for workflows. You can create custom activities that can be used in declarative workflows. However, the custom activity that we developed here cannot be deployed in a sandboxed environment as you would have to make changes to `web.config` which is not allowed. Apart from that the custom activity uses **User Profile Manager** to get the manager information of a user. This is not allowed in the sandboxed environment either. If you want to mimic this kind of functionality in a sandboxed mode, create a custom list that stores the manager information of a user and retrieve it from there. The other approach is to create an external list with user and manager information. **External lists** are those that provide a way to view and manipulate external data. External data could be from databases or web services and so on. They rely on external content types. We will learn more about external content types in *Chapter 4, List Definitions and Content Types*. For more information on what you can do in a sandboxed environment, refer to MSDN at: `http://msdn.microsoft.com/en-us/library/gg615464.aspx`.

See also

▶ *Chapter 3, Creating a custom activity for a sandboxed solution* recipe

▶ *Chapter 3, Creating a state machine workflow* recipe

Creating a custom activity for a sandboxed solution

Even with the limited capabilities of sandboxed solutions, you can still develop custom activities that can be used in SharePoint designer without making changes to `web.config` or adding the `.ACTIONS` file to the root folder.

In this recipe, we will create a custom activity that can be deployed in a sandboxed environment. This activity will create an event in the calendar for a given date.

Getting ready

The concepts of custom activities need to be understood before following this recipe. Hence you should have completed the previous recipe successfully.

How to do it...

1. Create an empty SharePoint project called **SandboxedActivity** and make sure to select deploy as a sandboxed solution.

2. Add a class file and name it **SandboxActivity**. Also make sure to change the access modifier to public.

3. Add the following code `using` statements to the class:
   ```
   using System.Collections;
   using Microsoft.SharePoint;
   using Microsoft.SharePoint.UserCode;
   using Microsoft.SharePoint.Workflow;
   ```

4. Within the class, add a public method called `AddCalendarEvent` that accepts an argument of type `SPUserCodeWorkflowContext` and returns a value of type `Hashtable`. The argument that accepts the type `SPUserCodeWorkflowContext` should be the first argument. This method defines the workflow action. Also add arguments that accept `calendarName`, `eventTitle`, `startDate`, `endDate`, and `location`. The method signature is as follows:
   ```
   public Hashtable AddCalendarEvent(SPUserCodeWorkflowContext
     context, string calendarName, string eventTitle, DateTime
     startDate, DateTime endDate, string location)
   ```

5. Add code to the `AddCalendarEvent` method to create the new event in the calendar. In this method you can return values by using key/value pairs via the `Hashtable` object. Your code should be as follows:

```
public Hashtable AddCalendarEvent(SPUserCodeWorkflowContext
  context, string calendarName, string eventTitle, DateTime
startTime, DateTime endTime, string location)
        {
            Hashtable results = new Hashtable();
            using (SPSite site = new SPSite
            (context.CurrentWebUrl))
                {
                    using (SPWeb web = site.OpenWeb())
                    {
                        SPList calendarList = web.
Lists[calendarName];
                        if (calendarList != null)
                        {
                            try
                            {
            SPListItem newEvent = calendarList.Items.Add();
                        newEvent["Location"] = location;
                        newEvent["Start Time"] = startTime;
                        newEvent["End Time"] = endTime;
                        newEvent["Description"] = description;
                        newEvent["Title"] = title;
                        newEvent.SystemUpdate();
                                results["success"] = true;
                                results["exception"] = string.Empty;
                            }
                            catch (Exception e)
                            {
                                results["success"] = false;
                                results["exception"] = e.Message;
                            }
                        }
                    }
                }
            return results;

        }
```

6. To create a workflow action definition, add an empty element to the project and name it **SandboxedAction**. Visual Studio will create a folder named **SandBoxedAction** and in it an `Elements.xml` file. This will add a feature as well to the project to deploy the element file added. Make sure to set the scope of this feature to `Site` as it needs to be deployed to the Site Collection.

7. Add a `WorkflowActions` element in this `Elements.xml`.file This is used to create the `ACTIONS` metadata for SharePoint to display the custom activity in the menu. Your actions XML should be as follows:

```xml
<Elements xmlns="http://schemas.microsoft.com/sharepoint/">
  <WorkflowActions>
    <Action Name="Sandboxed Activity"
      ClassName="SandboxedActivity.SandboxedActivity"
      Assembly="$SharePoint.Project.AssemblyFullName$"
      Category="Chapter2 Actions"
      SandboxedFunction="true"
      AppliesTo="all"
      FunctionName="AddCalendarEvent"
      UsesCurrentItem="true">
      <RuleDesigner Sentence="Add an event to %1 with event %2 and
        with %3 and %4 at %5 (Exception output to %6)">
        <FieldBind Field="calendarName" Text="Calendar Name"
          Id="1" DesignerType="TextBox" />
        <FieldBind Field="eventTitle" Text="Title" Id="2"
          DesignerType="TextBox" />
        <FieldBind Field="startTime" Text="Start Date" Id="3"
          DesignerType="Date" />
       <FieldBind Field="endTime" Text="End Date" Id="4"
          DesignerType="Date" />
        <FieldBind Field="location" Text="Location" Id="5"
        DesignerType="TextBox" />
        <FieldBind Field="exception" Text="Exception" Id="6"
        DesignerType="ParameterNames" />
      </RuleDesigner>
      <Parameters>
        <Parameter Name="__Context"
            Type="Microsoft.SharePoint.WorkflowActions.Workflow
            Context,Microsoft.SharePoint.WorkflowActions"
            Direction="In" DesignerType="Hide" />
        <Parameter Name="exception" Type="System.String, mscorlib"
Direction="Out" DesignerType="ParameterNames" />
        <Parameter Name="calendarName" Type="System.String,
mscorlib" Direction="In" />
        <Parameter Name="eventTitle" Type="System.String,
mscorlib" Direction="In" />
        <Parameter Name="startTime" Type="System.DateTime,
```

```
mscorlib" Direction="In" />
        <Parameter Name="endTime" Type="System.DateTime, mscorlib"
Direction="In" />
        <Parameter Name="location" Type="System.String, mscorlib"
Direction="In" />
      </Parameters>
    </Action>
  </WorkflowActions>
</Elements>
```

8. Build and package this activity. Visual Studio will create a `.WSP` solution file that can be uploaded to the solution store. Navigate from your site's **SiteActions | Site Settings | Galleries | Solutions** and upload the `WSP` file. You can activate this solution file for the site collection right here as shown in the following screenshot:

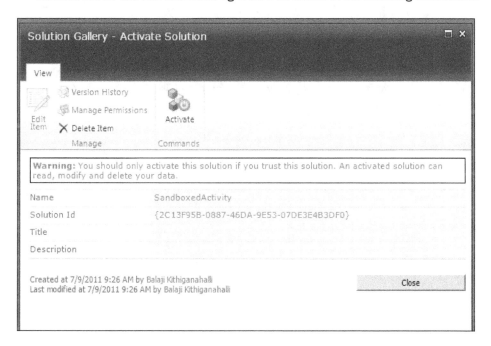

9. Open SharePoint designer, connect to the website and create a new workflow. You should see your custom action listed in the **Actions** menu as shown in the following screenshot:

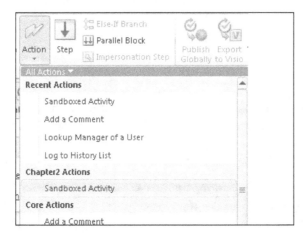

10. Add the activity and test out your newly created activity. The end result of the event added to the calendar is as shown in the following screenshot:

Thursday	Friday	Saturday
	1	2
	8	9 12:00 am - 12:00 am From Sandboxed Custom Action
	15	16

How it works...

Since we cannot deploy the actions file to the root folder, the actions file is now part of the solution file itself. To define this we created an empty `Elements.xml` file and added the required information for SharePoint designer to recognize our custom activity.

The actions file defined for the sandboxed solution is not that different compared to the one in `.ACTIONS` file. A couple of attributes like `SandboxedFunction` and `FunctionName` are the new items. The `SandboxedFunction` attribute indicates that this action is in the sandboxed environment. The `FunctionName` attribute provides the name of the method that needs to be invoked during the runtime. The rest of the other information is similar to that of the `.ACTIONS` file.

See also

- ▶ *Chapter 3, Creating a custom activity* recipe
- ▶ *Chapter 3, Creating a state machine workflow* recipe
- ▶ *Chapter 4, Creating an external content type* recipe

Creating a state machine workflow

So far we learnt how to create a sequential workflow as a list or as a site workflow. We also learnt how to add a custom initiation and task form to the workflow. In this recipe, we will create a state machine workflow that defines a project approval process.

Here are the steps that this workflow will follow through:

1. Workflow starts automatically on uploading the document to the document library.
2. A task is created to the manager for the approval.
3. The manager can either approve, reject, or request more information. In case of rejection, the workflow ends.
4. On approval from the manager, a task is created to the customer. The customer can either approve, reject or request more information from either the manager or the originator. On rejection or approval from the customer, the workflow ends.
5. On request for more information from originator will always flow through the manager, as the manager has to approve any changes.

This is a fairly complicated workflow that utilizes all the basics of task creation and applying InfoPath task forms that we learnt about in the previous recipes.

Getting ready

The workflow makes use of the Shared Documents Library that comes with the team site. You should have Forms services enabled and running on your SharePoint server as this workflow makes use of the InfoPath forms for creating the task forms.

How to do it...

1. Using InfoPath Designer, create a form named `ManagerTaskForm.xsn` with a drop-down list control for the status with values **Approved**, **Rejected**, and **More Info**. The end result of the InfoPath screen is as shown in the following screenshot:

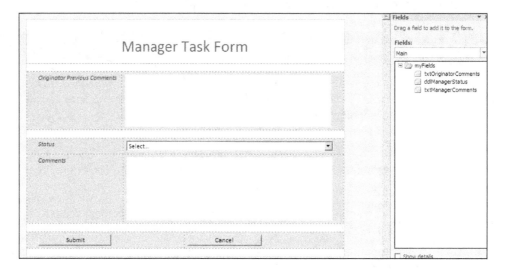

2. Similarly create a customer task form with the status values of **Approved, Rejected, More Info from Originator**, and **More Info from Manager**. The end result of the screen is as follows:

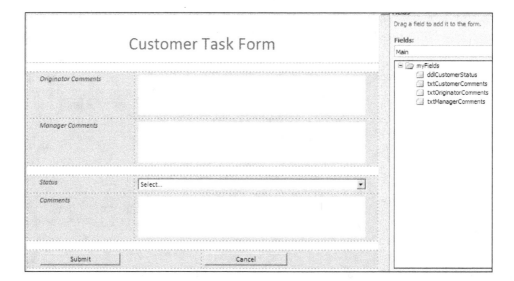

3. Create a task form for the originator as well with a status value of `Submitted`. The end result of the screen is as follows:

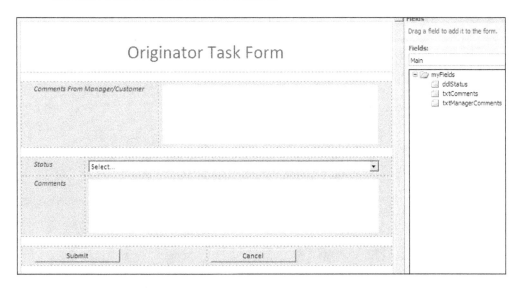

4. Create a new XML file called `ItemMetadata.xml`. Add the following content to this file:

```xml
<?xml version="1.0" encoding="utf-8"?>

<z:row xmlns:z="#RowsetSchema"
ows_OriginatorComments=""
ows_ManagerComments=""
/>
```

5. Add a receive data connection to the InfoPath forms with the previously created XML file.

6. Also create a submit data connection that submits the form to the rosting environment.

7. Follow the same procedure outlined in the recipe for creating the InfoPath initiation form to publish this form. Follow all the steps in that recipe from 3 to 9. For task forms there is no need to save the InfoPath source files and create the class file using `XSD.exe` as indicated in that recipe.

8. Launch your Visual Studio 2010 IDE as an administrator (right-click the shortcut and select **Run as administrator**).

9. Select **File | New | Project**. The new project wizard dialog box as shown will be displayed. (Make sure to select **.NET Framework 3.5** in the top drop-down box.)

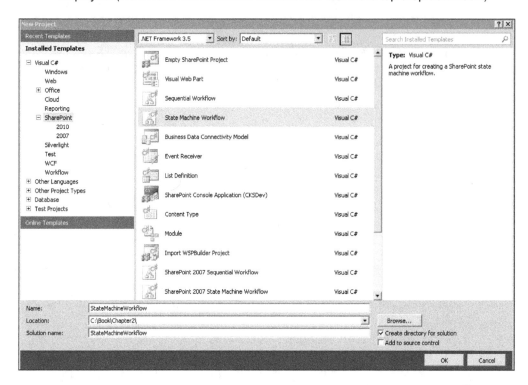

10. Select **State Machine Workflow** under the **Visual C# | SharePoint | 2010** node from **Installed Templates** section on the left-hand side.

11. Name the project **StateMachineWorkflow** and provide a directory location where you want to save the project and click **OK** to proceed to the next step in the wizard.

12. By default, Visual Studio selects the SharePoint site available on the machine. Select **Deploy as Farm Solution** and click on **Next** to proceed to the next step in the wizard.

13. Take the defaults in the next step of the wizard and finish the wizard to create the state machine workflow project. By default, Visual Studio adds a state with an event driven activity inside the state as shown in the following screenshot:

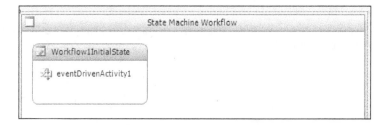

14. Name this default state as **initialState** from the **Properties** window. This may show a red exclamation mark icon on the workflow indicating that the starting state that the workflow associated with is not available. From the **Properties** window, change the name to **initialState** as shown in following screenshot:

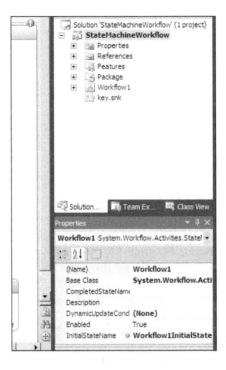

15. Also add four more states from the tool box to the workflow designer. Name them `ManagerState`, `OriginatorState`, `CustomerState`, and `endState`. From the workflow properties window set the `CompletedStateName` to `endState`.

16. Right-click on **ManagerState** and from the context menu select **Add StateInitialization** as shown in the following screenshot:

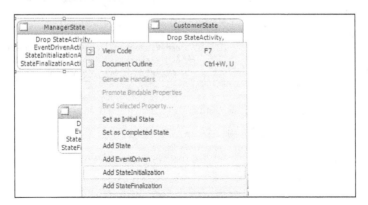

17. Visual Studio adds the **StateInitialization** activity to **ManagerState** and brings up the activity in the designer. To this activity add a **CreateTask** activity and name it **CreateManagerTask** and also add a **LogToHistoryListActivity** and set the **HistoryDescription** to **Manager Activity Created**. Your end result should be as shown in the following screenshot:

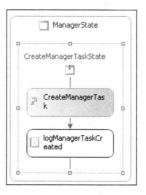

18. Set the **CorrelationToken** property of the **CreateManagerTask** to **managerToken** and the **OwnerActivityName** to **ManagerState**. Also bind a variable **managerTaskId** for the **TaskID** property and **managerTaskProps** for the **TaskProperties** property. Also generate an event handler method for this activity. The following screenshot shows the properties window of the **CreateManagerTask**:

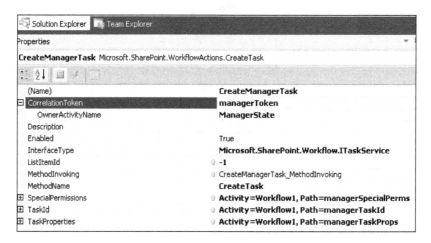

19. In the code file of the workflow, define the following Boolean variables:

```
public bool _managerNeedInfo = false;
public bool _managerApproved = false;
public bool _managerRejected = false;
```

20. Back in the workflow designer again, add an **EventDriven** activity to **ManagerState** by following the same process as indicated in step 9. Visual Studio will add an **EventDriven** activity to the **ManagerState** and bring this activity to the front on the designer surface. Name this **EventDriven** activity **managerEventDriven** and add an **onTaskChanged** activity inside it. Make sure to set the **CorelationToken** and **TaskId** to the same values that were created in step 11. Add an event handler method to this activity. Also add an **IfElse** activity beneath the **onTaskChanged** activity. By default, the **IfElse** activity starts with two branches and to this add an extra branch. Name these branches **ManagerApproved**, **ManagerRejected**, and **ManagerNeedsInfo**.

21. Under the **ManagerRejected** branch add a **LogToHistoryListActivity** and set the **HistoryDescription** to **Manager Rejected the project**. Under this activity add a **SetState** activity found in the **Windows Workflow V3.0** section of the **Toolbox** as shown in the following screenshot:

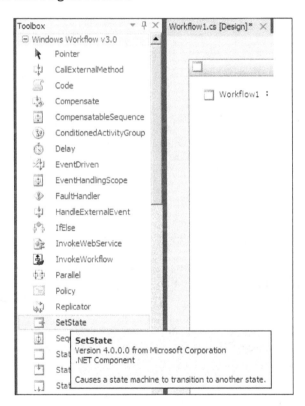

22. Set the state property of this activity to **endState**. Follow the same process and set the **ManagerApproval** branch **SetState** activity to **CustomerState** and **ManagerNeedsInfo** branch **SetState** to **OriginatorState** activity. Your end result of the process workflow should look as follows:

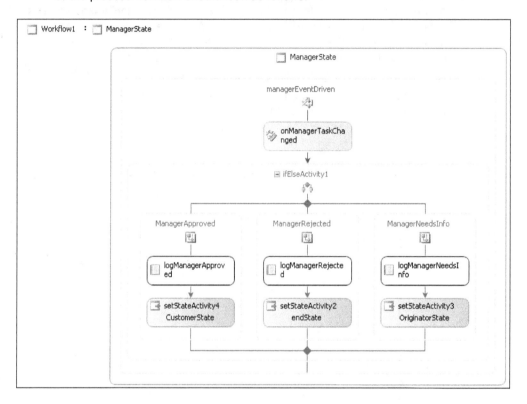

23. Define a declarative rule condition to the **ManagerApproved** branch. Set the name to **Manager Approved** and the condition expression to as follows:

```
this._managerApproved == True
```

24. Follow the same process and declare rule conditions to other branches as well. The expression for **ManagerRejected** and **ManagerNeedsInfo** is as follows respectively:

```
this._managerRejected == True
this._managerNeedInfo = True
```

25. Back on the **Workflow1** designer surface follow the process described in step 9 to add a **StateFinalization** activity to the **ManagerTask**. To this activity add a **CompleteTask** activity and set the **CorrelationToken** and bind the **TaskId** to the same variable that was created in step 11.

26. This completes the **ManagerState** settings. Follow the same process and set up the **CustomerState** and **OriginatorState**. The **originatorEventDriven** process flow should look as shown in the following screenshot:

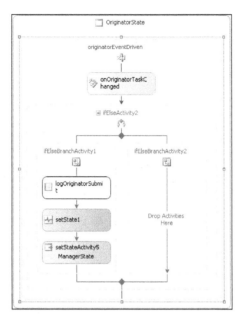

27. The **customerEventDriven** process flow should be as shown in the following screenshot:

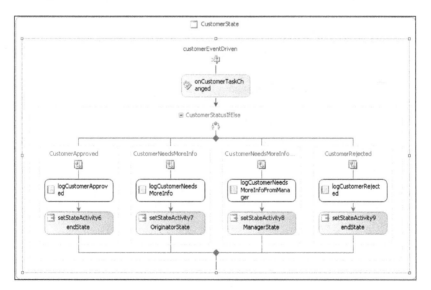

28. The finished process flow should look like the following screenshot:

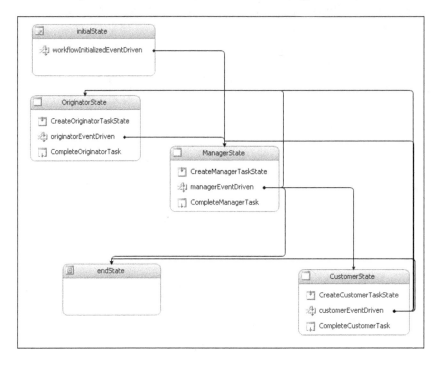

29. Follow the steps from 6 through 10 listed in the recipe *Creating a custom task form* from *Chapter 2* to add the InfoPath forms to the workflow project and set the proper properties of the workflow feature.

30. Follow the same process as described in the previous recipes to add code for creating the tasks for the manager, customer, and originator. The accompanying code for this book provides more information if needed.

31. Build and run the solution by pressing *F5*. When you upload a document, the workflow should start automatically. The following screenshot shows the manager task form during execution of the workflow:

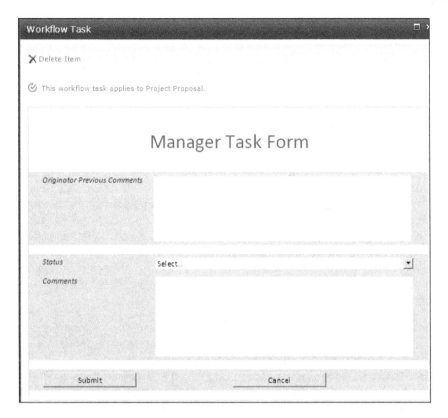

32. The following screenshot shows the history list with status during the state transition and also during the task status verification:

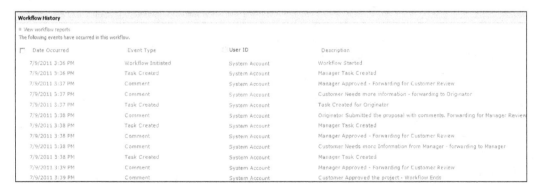

How it works...

The code is similar to what we went through in the previous recipes. Each state in the state machine workflow contains a series of activities that are executed in sequential order. It can be seen as a mini sequential workflow. Hence each state is also described as the stable condition of the workflow.

Usually, a stable condition is the idle state of the workflow. Most often workflows are in this state waiting for something or someone to take an action. When some action happens an event is triggered and a series of activities are executed and then the workflow goes back to idle again usually to a different state. In our example, when the document is uploaded, an event is triggered to start the workflow. The workflow then creates a task for the manager and goes to idle state until the manager comes back and makes changes to his/her task. Once again it becomes idle until the originator or the customer takes action on their task. This is the normal pattern of how workflows execute. In the state machine we model these idle conditions as **States**. Hence in our example we have a manager state, a customer state, and an originator state. When you want to model a state machine workflow for your needs, follow this rule of thumb.

State activity is inherited from sequence activity but with unique rules. Since it is a child of Sequence activity, it can hold multiple activities and execute those in a sequential order. State activities can only hold four other activities. Those are an `EventDriven` activity, `StateFinalization`, `StateInitialization`, and a `State` activity itself. When you embed a state activity inside a state activity, the embedded state activity is called a **Substate**. Using this method you can manage a state machine inside a state.

`StateInitialization` and `StateFinalization` are used for state initialization and the clean-up process respectively. They are not required activities and to replace with one can exist without the other. Hence in our example we used `StateInitialization` to create the task and `StateFinalization` to complete the task. You can set it to a different state in the `StateInitialization` activity thus bypassing the one that was getting initialized whereas you cannot transition to a different state in `StateFinalization` activity.

To transition from one state to another we use `SetStateActivity`. The `SetStateActivity` is normally used in the `EventDriven` activity to move from one state to another based on the conditions of the events.

 There are two activities named `SetState` in the toolbox. As indicated in the recipe, the `SetState` that we want to use for transition is located in Windows Workflow V3.0. The one located in SharePoint activities is used for setting properties (status) on the workflow. You cannot use this for state transition. Refer to Adding a custom workflow status recipe for how to make use of the SetState located in the SharePoint activities.

State activities can have more than one `EventDriven` activities. As the name indicates, `EventDriven` activities deal with events. In our example, we put in the `onTaskChanged` activity to tackle the task changed event. When you created the project, by default, Visual Studio added a state activity that contained an `EventDriven` activity that dealt with the `onWorkflowActivated` event.

There's more...

The workflow always provides a default status of its state on the item it is running. By default, it provides statuses such as **In Progress** or **Completed** or **Error Occurred**, and so on. The following screenshot shows the status for the workflow that we created in this recipe:

These statuses of the workflow are also called the state it is in. So when the workflow is running without any error, it is in a state of **In Progress**. If there is an error during its execution it goes into **Error Occurred** state and when the execution is completed it goes into **Completed** state. These workflow states are not the same as what the state machine workflow states. These two are unrelated. These states of workflows happen on both sequential and state machine workflows. These are just statuses of the workflow step or condition it is in. For the sake of clarity, I will only use the term workflow status.

There are occasions where you may want to change these workflow statuses from the default values to custom ones. Say in our example, when the workflow is in **Manager Review** state, you may want to indicate that in the workflow status as well. This can be done by adding your own custom statuses in the workflow `Elements.xml` file and adding a new activity called **SetState** activity found in the **SharePoint Workflow** section of the toolbar as shown in the following screenshot:

See also

▶ *Adding a custom workflow status* recipe

▶ *Creating a pluggable workflow service* recipe

Adding a custom workflow status

In this recipe, we will make modifications to the previous state machine workflow to show a custom workflow status during the state transition.

Getting ready

Since this recipe is a modification of the *Creating state machine workflow* recipe, you should have successfully completed that one to follow this recipe.

How to do it...

Open the **StateMachineWorkflow** solution if it is closed.

1. In the `MetaData` section of the workflow's `Elements.xml` file, add the `ExtendedStatusColumnValues` element and define your custom statuses in the `StatusColumnValue` element. The following code shows the custom status for our workflow created in this recipe. For the sake of brevity, I have only shown a part of the `Elements.xml` file:

```
<MetaData>
        <AssociationCategories>List</AssociationCategories>

        <StatusPageUrl>_layouts/WrkStat.aspx</StatusPageUrl>
        <ExtendedStatusColumnValues>
          <StatusColumnValue>Manager Review</StatusColumnValue>
          <StatusColumnValue>Originator Review</StatusColumnValue>
          <StatusColumnValue>Customer Review</StatusColumnValue>
          <StatusColumnValue>Rejected</StatusColumnValue>
          <StatusColumnValue>Completed</StatusColumnValue>
        </ExtendedStatusColumnValues>
```

2. Add the `SetState` activity found in the SharePoint workflow section to your workflow process flow where you find it appropriate to set the status (Usually during a state transition in a state machine workflow or during a change in the step in a sequential workflow.) The following screenshot shows the `SetState` activity during the state transition from `workflowActivation` to `ManagerState`:

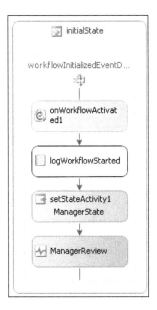

3. Set the `CorrelationToken` to `workflowToken` as it is not associated with any tasks. Also bind a variable to the `State` property. In our example the variable is called `workflowState`. The following screenshot shows the properties window of the `SetState` activity:

4. Generate an event handler for this activity and add the following code:

```
workflowState = (Int32)SPWorkflowStatus.Max;
```

5. Build and run the application. When the workflow is initiated, you should see your custom status shown instead of the default ones. The following screenshot shows the end result:

	Type	Name	Modified	Modified By	StateMachineWorkflow - Workflow1
☐	[W]	Project Proposal ☐NEW	7/9/2011 12:54 PM	Balaji Kithiganahalli	Manager Review

＋ Add document

How it works...

The `ExtendedStatusColumnValues` in the `Elements.xml` file is used to define the custom status messages. These status messages are accessed in the code by using the `SPWorkflowStatus.Max` property. The integer value of the `Max` is 15. From 0 through 14, the numbers are reserved for internal and built-in values such as **In Progress**, **Completed**, **Error occurred**, and so on. For the statuses we define in the `ExtendedStatusColumnValues` element we start with 15 for the first `StatusColumnValue` element and keep incrementing from there onwards. So to set the `OriginatorReview` status the value will be:

```
workflowState = (Int32)SPWorkflowStatus.Max + 1;
```

and for `CustomerReview` status the value will be

```
workflowState = (Int32)SPWorkflowStatus.Max + 2;
```

The activity `SetStatus` has the functionality to add the custom message to the `Status` column of the workflow hence the use of this activity. Like `LogToHistoryListActivity`, this activity also makes use of the `ISharePointService` interface and implements the `SetState` functionality. For more information on `SPWorkflowStatus` enumeration refer to MSDN at: `http://msdn.microsoft.com/en-us/library/microsoft.sharepoint.workflow.spworkflowstatus.aspx`.

There's more...

Versioning workflows are an important aspect in the real world development. When the workflow is idle, its state is stored in the database. This process of saving the state in database is called **hydration**. When it resumes, it is dehydrated out of the database and the workflow starts processing. During this time, if you modify the workflow assembly, and if it does not match the previous assembly construct, there is a chance for the workflow dehydration to break. For this purpose, it is better to treat the workflow modifications as a new workflow itself.

If your modification includes adding new activities or adding a new flow process and changing the existing flow process, consider this as a new workflow. Provide a new feature and increment the version number before deploying.

If your modifications only include bug fixes, you can overwrite the existing assembly and still be able to run the previous instances of the workflows without breaking them.

See also

▶ *Creating a state machine workflow* recipe

▶ *Creating a pluggable workflow service* recipe

Creating a pluggable workflow service

For our recipe here, we will rewrite the *Chapter 2, Creating a sequential workflow* recipe that enacts the credit approval system in such a way that we will remove all the `IfElse` activities that we used there to verify the credit check. In this recipe, we will have an external method to do that logic for us and raise an event when it is done with its decision. The event will also contain the response back from this external method.

Getting ready

Modify the Credit Approval list that we created in *Creating a sequential workflow* in *Chapter 2* and add a new field named `Credit Status` of `Single line of Text` type. The field is not a required field. This is the field where we will store the response from the external method.

How to do it...

1. Create a new sequential list workflow associated with the **Credit Approval List** named **PluggableWS**.

2. Add a new class file named `CreditCheck.cs`. Add the `Serializable()` attribute to the class and define the properties that correspond to the **Credit Approval List** columns. The class definition should be as follows:

```
[Serializable()]
    public class CreditCheck
    {
        public string Title { get; set; }
        public string CreditRequested { get; set; }
        public string EmploymentHistory { get; set; }
        public string CreditHistory { get; set; }
        public string CreditStatus { get; set; }
    }
```

3. Add one more class file named `CreditApprovalService.cs` and add the following `using` statements to this class file:

```
using Microsoft.SharePoint.Workflow;
using System.Workflow.Activities;
```

4. Define an interface in the previous class file, named `ICreditCheckService`. The interface will define a method called `GetCreditResponse` that will be invoked by the workflow to process the credit request and an event called `CreditCheckEvent` that will be raised by the method once it completes the credit request process. The code for `ICreditCheckService` is as follows:

```
[ExternalDataExchange]
public interface ICreditCheckService
      {
            event EventHandler<CreditCheckEventArgs> CreditCheckEvent;
            void GetCreditResponse(CreditCheck credit);
      }
```

5. Define the `CreditCheckEventArgs` type provided in the `EventHandler` delegate. This should contain a string variable called `CreditInfo` to hold event data. This class should be inherited from `ExternalDataEventArgs` and also make sure to decorate this class with a `Serializable()` attribute. The code should be as follows:

```
[Serializable()]
    public class CreditCheckEventArgs : ExternalDataEventArgs
      {
            public CreditCheckEventArgs(Guid id) : base(id) { }
            public string CreditInfo;
      }
```

6. Define a class named `WFContextState` to store the `SPWeb` object and workflow `instanceId`. The class definition should be as follows:

```
class WFContextState
      {
            public SPWeb web { get; set; }
            public Guid instanceId { get; set; }
            public WFContextState(Guid instanceId, SPWeb web)
            {
                this.instanceId = instanceId;
                this.web = web;
            }
      }
```

7. Define another class named `CreditApprovalService` that implements the abstract class `Microsoft.SharePoint.Workflow.SPWorkflowExternalDataExchangeService` and the interface `ICreditCheckService`. Your code for this class should be as follows:

```
    public class CreditApprovalService :
SPWorkflowExternalDataExchangeService, ICreditCheckService
      {
            public override void CallEventHandler(Type eventType,
```

```csharp
string eventName, object[] eventData, SPWorkflow workflow, string
identity, System.Workflow.Runtime.IPendingWork workHandler, object
workItem)
        {
            if (eventName.Trim().ToLower() == "creditcheckevent")
            {
                var args = new CreditCheckEventArgs
                (workflow.InstanceId);
                args.CreditInfo = eventData[0].ToString();
                this.CreditCheckEvent(null, args);
            }
        }

        public event EventHandler<CreditCheckEventArgs>
CreditCheckEvent;

        public void GetCreditResponse(CreditCheck credit)
        {
            ThreadPool.QueueUserWorkItem(delegate(object state)
            {
                WFContextState wfState = (WFContextState)state;
                if (wfState != null)
                {
                    Random rnd = new Random();
    //Simulating External System taking more time to respond
    by delay
                    Thread.Sleep(TimeSpan.FromMinutes(rnd.Next(1,
5))); //Thread sleep for 1 through 5 minutes
                    try
                    {
                        if (credit.EmploymentHistory.Trim().
ToLower() == "good")
                        {
                            if (credit.CreditHistory.Trim().
ToLower() == "good")
                                credit.CreditStatus = "Approved";
                            else
                                credit.CreditStatus = "Bad Credit
History";
                        }
                        else
                            credit.CreditStatus = "Bad Employment
History";
                    }
                    catch
```

```
                    {
                            credit.CreditStatus = "Cannot access the
      Credit Check System";
                    }

                        RaiseEvent(wfState.web, wfState.instanceId,
                            typeof(ICreditCheckService),
      "creditcheckevent", new object[] { credit.CreditStatus });
                    }
                }, new WFContextState( WorkflowEnvironment.
      WorkflowInstanceId,
                    this.CurrentWorkflow.ParentWeb)
                );
        }
```

8. Now build the workflow by adding **CallExternalMethodActivity** and **HandleExternalEvent** activity. Your workflow flowchart should look as follows:

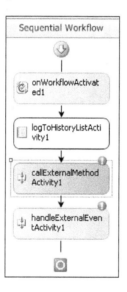

9. From the properties window of **CallExternalMethodActivity**, set the interface type to **ICreditCheckService** and **MethodName** to **GetCreditResponse**. As you associate the **MethodName** it also provides a **bindable** property for credit object (the parameter that needs to be passed to the **GetCreditResponse** method). Bind a variable to this property as well. The **Properties** window should be as shown in the following screenshot:

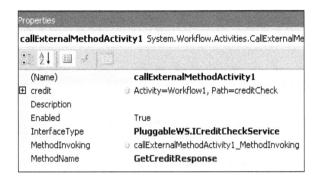

10. Similarly for **HandleExternalEventActivity** set the **InterfaceType** to **ICreditCheckService** and **EventName** to **CreditCheckEvent**. Also bind a variable to the **e** property as shown in the following screenshot:

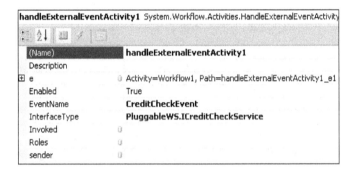

11. Generate event handlers to both of these activities and add code to `CallExternalMethodActivity` handler so that we set the values of the list item fields to the credit parameter that needs to be passed to the method. Your code should be as follows:

```
private void callExternalMethodActivity1_MethodInvoking(object
sender, EventArgs e)
        {
        creditCheck.CreditRequested = workflowProperties.
        Item["Credit Requested"].ToString();
        creditCheck.EmploymentHistory = workflowProperties.
        Item["Employment History"].ToString();
        creditCheck.CreditHistory = workflowProperties.
        Item["Credit History"].ToString();
        creditCheck.Title = workflowProperties.Item["Title"].
         ToString();
        }
```

12. Add code to `HandleExternalEventActivity` to update the list item with the status received from the `GetCreditResponse` method. Your code should be as follows:

```
private void handleExternalEventActivity1_Invoked(object sender,
ExternalDataEventArgs e)
        {
            SPListItem item = workflowProperties.Item;
            item["Credit Status"] = handleExternalEventActivity1_
            e1.CreditInfo;
            item.Update();

        }
```

13. Build and add an entry in the `web.config` file of your web application under the `WorkflowServices` element as shown in the following code (make sure to change the public key token to your assembly):

```
<WorkflowService Assembly="PluggableWS, Version=1.0.0.0,
Culture=neutral, PublicKeyToken=c236390f67db5b33"
Class="PluggableWS.CreditApprovalService"></WorkflowService>
```

14. Run the application and when you add a new item to your list, the workflow will start automatically and update the **Credit Status** column with the result. The following screenshot shows the end result:

		Title	Credit Requested	Employment History	Credit History	Credit Status	PluggableWS
		John Doe's Credit History	$1,000.00	Good	Good	Approved	Completed
		Bad Credit History	$100.00	Good	Bad	Bad Credit History	Completed
		Should give Bad Employment History	$56,565.00	Bad	Good	Bad Employment History	Completed

Add new item

How it works...

The workflow foundation provides external data exchange infrastructure to workflows through `CallExternalMethodActivity` and `HandleExternalEventActivity`. `CallExternalMethodActivity` as the name indicates is used to invoke a method in the workflow host synchronously and the `HandleExternalEventActivity` will handle the event raised by the workflow host. Behind the scenes, it is the workflow host that is responsible for correctly calling the external method, waiting for the event from the external source, and route it to the right workflow instance.

When developing a custom SharePoint workflow local service, the first thing to do is to implement a custom class that inherits from `SPWorkflowExternalDataExchangeService`. This class (in our example scenario, it is named `CreditApprovalService`) should also implement the custom communication interface that we define. This communication interface provides a way of invoking and receiver parties know what type of data to pass to each other. For external data exchanges, we need to decorate this custom interface with the `ExternalDataExchange` attribute. This attribute indicates to the workflow engine that it can be used in the external data exchange scenarios. It can also define the event that is raised from the method. Similarly the `EventArgs` of the event handler delegate (in our case `CreditCheckEventArgs` of event `CreditCheckEvent`) should always be inherited from `ExternalDataEventArgs`. This should also be decorated with a `Serializable()` attribute so in case of workflow persistence, this object can be persisted using the runtime serialization. The GUID parameter in the constructor is the workflow instance ID. This way the workflow host engine knows where to route the event when it is raised.

The class `CreditApprovalService` as explained previously should implement methods from `SPWorkflowExternalDataExchangeService`. The main method is the `CallEventHandler` which is invoked every time an event is requested in the service. This is requested when the `RaiseEvent` method is called. The `RaiseEvent` method is called from the `GetCreditResponse` method in our example, when it is done processing the credit request. This passes the event name it is requesting. Based on this event name, the `CallEventHandler` method constructs the event arguments. Since all services are uniquely identified by their interface type, only one instance of service is allowed for each of the service interfaces. This means when there is multiple workflow instances calling the same method of service at the same time, the only way to identify the workflow instance that invoked the method is through the workflow instance ID. Hence this is passed as a parameter to the `RaiseEvent` method which in turn raises an event in the workflow host passing this ID which in turn again routes the event to the right instance identified by this instance ID.

Since the method invocation from the workflow host is synchronous, in our method we created a background thread and delegated our credit check process to this thread. Our background thread needs the `SPWeb` object and the workflow instance ID to raise the event. To accommodate that we created a custom context state class to store this information. By creating the background thread, we can complete the synchronous method call from the `CallExternalMethodActivity` and let the workflow go idle to conserve resources. Our background thread now waits for the external system to provide the response and raises the event. As we are not accessing any external systems in our example, we put in a delay for simulation purposes and completed our credit check process before raising the event. This event is now routed to the right instance identified by the instance ID.

SharePoint workflow runtime when initialized creates an instance of all the local services identified in the `web.config`. To make sure this happens we need to add an entry in the `web.config` of the web application where the workflow is deployed.

You can register as many number of local services as you want as long as each implements a different interface.

There's more...

We manually made changes to the `web.config` file in the preceding example. This may not be an acceptable practice in the production environment. These changes can be made by adding a feature receiver to your workflow and writing code to make these entries. This same technique can be used to add database configuration strings as well. Refer to MSDN on how to make changes to `web.config` programmatically at: `http://msdn.microsoft.com/en-us/library/bb861909.aspx`.

See also

▶ *Chapter 1, Creating a Feature Receiver* recipe

4
List Definitions and Content Types

In this chapter, we will cover:

- ▸ Creating a site column
- ▸ Extending an existing content type
- ▸ Creating a custom content type using an object model
- ▸ Associating a document template to a content type
- ▸ Associating a workflow to a content type
- ▸ Creating an external content type
- ▸ Creating a list definition

Introduction

Content type is defined as a reusable collection of metadata, a workflow, and other settings for a category of items which encapsulate data requirements and enable standardization.

In SharePoint, content is stored in some type of list in the site. Content can be pictures, documents, contacts, tasks, or custom items that you store in a list. You can specify in the SharePoint list what kind of content that it can store. Out of the box, SharePoint provides templates that you can use to create lists or libraries that store specific contents like documents or pictures or contacts. This is achieved through content types. For example, a document library is intended for storing documents like word, PDF or excel documents where as a contacts list stores contacts. SharePoint makes this distinction by having different content types associated with these lists.

Apart from defining the type of content a list can store, content types can also have metadata properties and processes associated with the content. For example, a project proposal can have a word document that describes the project in a specific format and has certain metadata properties like the department that it belongs to, the cost associated with the the project, project start and end date, and any workflows that the document has to follow through in order to get an approval. Taken together the document, the metadata properties, and the workflows will become a content type.

The content types can be reused. This is when you define a content type at a site collection level or site level and you can use it in different sites or lists in the same site using the content type. For example, if you create the project proposal content type at the site level, you can create multiple document libraries that use the content type. This way you can create different project proposal lists (or document libraries) for each of the departments in your company and have a consistent format across the company. Apart from this, you can customize it at the list level for each of the departments in the previous example without affecting the parent content type.

Out of the box, SharePoint provides several content types. The following image shows the categories of the content types that come with SharePoint server:

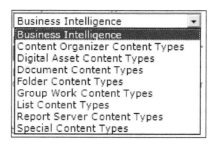

The list definition is a schema for defining lists in the SharePoint site. The list definition provides list structure with content type that is used in it. A list can have multiple content types which means it can have our example project proposal content type and also a resume content type. But each item in the list can only be associated with one content type. That is, the document in our example can only be a project proposal or resume but not both. The list is just a place holder for the content types.

> The other term that is used with Lists is list templates. They are very similar to list definitions. They mainly differ in how they are created. List templates are created by the end users using SharePoint UI by using an existing list as a starting point for the pattern. SharePoint designer also uses the term list templates. In Visual Studio terminology, it is always called **List Definitions**.

All content types in SharePoint are inherited from a parent content type. Whenever we create a new content type, we have to specify the parent content. All the attributes and settings of the parent content type are inherited in the child content type. When we make changes to the parent content type, the children are also updated with those changes. But when you make changes on the child content type, it does not affect the parent content type.

At the root of this inheritance is the `System` content type. This does not have any columns. Next in the inheritance is `Item` content type. We can derive content types from an `Item` content type but not directly from the `System`.

As indicated earlier, content types include metadata information as well. These metadata are stored as columns in the list or document library. These columns can be site columns or list columns. Site columns as the name suggests are created at the site level and can be reused in different lists.

A site column in SharePoint has the following four important parts:

- Column name
- Column type
- Column group
- Additional settings

Column name is a required attribute for a column. Column type provides information about its data type, that is, the type of information that the column can store like a number or text. The following screenshot shows the data types that SharePoint supports on the site columns:

The type of information in this column is:

- ⦿ Single line of text
- ○ Multiple lines of text
- ○ Choice (menu to choose from)
- ○ Number (1, 1.0, 100)
- ○ Currency ($, ¥, €)
- ○ Date and Time
- ○ Lookup (information already on this site)
- ○ Yes/No (check box)
- ○ Person or Group
- ○ Hyperlink or Picture
- ○ Calculated (calculation based on other columns)
- ○ Full HTML content with formatting and constraints for publishing
- ○ Image with formatting and constraints for publishing
- ○ Hyperlink with formatting and constraints for publishing
- ○ Summary Links data
- ○ Rich media data for publishing
- ○ Managed Metadata

A column group is not a required attribute but provides a way to organize your custom site columns. In additional settings, we can define whether a column is required or not, the maximum number of characters, currency format, and so on.

Visual Studio 2010 provides templates to create content types and list definitions. These templates allow you to create content types using declarative XML. You can always use an empty SharePoint project to create content types via a SharePoint object model. In this chapter, we will create content types using both code and declarative XML.

Creating a site column

A site column is the building block for creating a content type. In this recipe, we will create a site column using the SharePoint object model.

Getting ready

You should have a fully-functional development machine with SharePoint 2010 installed and configured. You also need Visual Studio 2010 IDE installed on the same development machine. For more information on this, refer to *Chapter 1, List and Event Receivers*.

How to do it...

1. Launch your Visual Studio 2010 IDE as an administrator (right-click on the shortcut and select **Run as administrator.**)

2. Select **File | New | Project**. The new project wizard dialog box as shown in the following screenshot will be displayed (make sure to select **.NET Framework 3.5** in the top drop-down box):

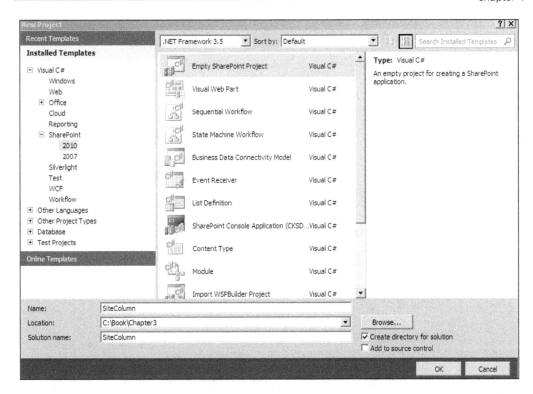

3. Select **Empty SharePoint Project** under **Visual C# | SharePoint | 2010** node from the **Installed Templates** section on the left-hand side.

4. Name the project **SiteColumn** and provide a directory location where you want to save the project and click on **OK** to proceed to the next step in the wizard.

5. By default, Visual Studio selects the SharePoint site available on the machine. Select **Deploy as Farm Solution** and click on **Next** to proceed to the next step in the wizard.

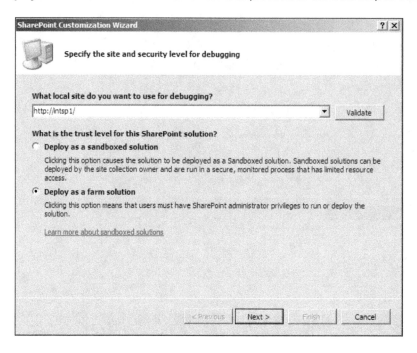

6. This should create an empty SharePoint project. To this project add a feature by right-clicking on the **Feature** folder as shown in the following screenshot:

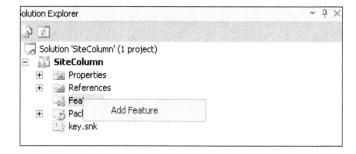

7. Add an event receiver to the new feature added by right-clicking on the feature and selecting **Add Event Receiver** as shown in the following screenshot:

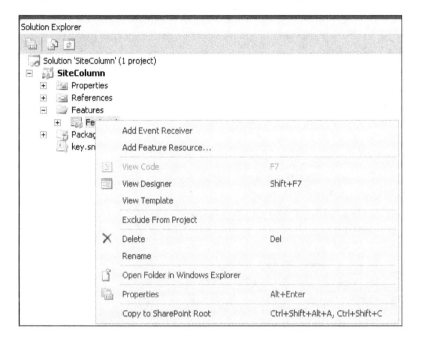

8. This should add a code file named `Feature1.EventReceiver.cs`. Uncomment `FeatureActivated` and `FeatureDeactivating` methods.

9. Add the following code to create a `TestColumn` in the `FeatureActivated` method:

```
public override void FeatureActivated(SPFeatureReceiverProperties
properties)
        {
            SPWeb web = null;
            if (properties.Feature.Parent is SPSite)
            {
                SPSite sites = (SPSite)properties.Feature.Parent;
                web = sites.RootWeb;
            }
            else
            {
                web = (SPWeb)properties.Feature.Parent;
            }
            if (web == null)
                return;

            string columnGroup = "Chapter3 Columns";
```

```
                // TEst Site Column
                string sTestSiteColumnFieldName = web.Fields.
     Add("TestColumn", SPFieldType.Text, true);
                SPFieldText fldTestCol = (SPFieldText)web.Fields.GetFi
     eldByInternalName(sTestSiteColumnFieldName);
                fldTestCol.Group = columnGroup;
                fldTestCol.MaxLength = 100;
                fldTestCol.Required = true;
                fldTestCol.Update();


        }
```

10. Add the code to delete the column in the `FeatureDeactivating` method. Your code should look like following:

```
public override void FeatureDeactivating(SPFeatureReceiverProperti
es properties)
        {
                SPWeb web = null;
                if (properties.Feature.Parent is SPSite)
                {
                    SPSite sites = (SPSite)properties.Feature.Parent;
                    web = sites.RootWeb;
                }
                else
                {
                    web = (SPWeb)properties.Feature.Parent;
                }
                if (web == null)
                    return;

                web.Fields["TestColumn"].Delete();


        }


        }
    }
```

11. When you build and run this solution, as indicated in the previous chapters, you should be directed to the site that you provided in the solution creation wizard.

12. Navigate to **Site Actions | Site Settings | Galleries | Site Columns**. You should see the new site column **Test Column** created under a new group **Chapter3 Columns** as shown here:

Site Column	Type	Source
Base Columns		
Append-Only Comments	Multiple lines of text	Book Portal
Categories	Single line of text	Book Portal
End Date	Date and Time	Book Portal
Language	Choice	Book Portal
Start Date	Date and Time	Book Portal
URL	Hyperlink or Picture	Book Portal
Workflow Name	Single line of text	Book Portal
Chapter3 Columns		
TestColumn	Single line of text	Book Portal

13. You can verify all the attributes like **Maximum number of characters** and **Require that is column contains information** properties by clicking on the **TestColumn** column. The following screenshot shows the attributes of our example column:

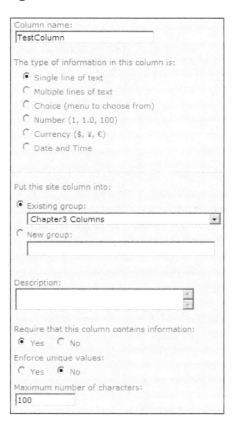

How it works...

Creating a feature receiver is explained in *Chapter 1*. This is a real-world example where feature receivers can come in handy.

The code is pretty simple in the sense; we add a field (the term field and column are used to refer to the same object) to the site's field collection. The add method on the field collection object is overloaded to take different parameters. We are using a method that takes in the display name of the column, the column type, and whether the column is required or not as the parameters. The method returns us the internal name of the field. This internal name is unique to a field. This way, you can use the same field in multiple lists and change the display name to suite your needs. By using this internal name, we retrieved the field object and set other additional attributes like the max length of the characters that it can hold and whether it is required or not. We also set the group name to which the field should belong. If the group does not exist, the SharePoint object model will create one and add the field to that group. When there are no fields in the group, the group is automatically deleted. So there is no exclusive code to create or delete the group.

There's more...

You can also use the site's field collection's `AddFieldAsXml` method to create a new site column. In this method, you will pass in the XML schema of the field you want to create. For our example, the following code shows the XML schema:

```
web.Fields.AddFieldAsXml("<Field DisplayName=\"TestColumn\" Type=\
"Text\" Required=\"TRUE\" Name=\"TestColumn\" Group=\"Chapter3
Columns\" MaxLength=\"100\" />");
```

Deleting the site columns on deactivation of the feature

In our recipe, we deleted the site column in the deactivating method of the feature. This is a normal way of cleaning up the site columns if they are not needed. Before deleting though make sure that it does not create any adverse effect on the content types that are already deployed and used in the site columns.

See also

- ▸ Extending an existing content type
- ▸ Creating a custom content type

Extending an existing content type

In the previous recipe, we learnt how to create a site column using the SharePoint object model. In this recipe, we will create a site column using a declarative XML and add it to the contacts content type.

Contacts content type provides a way to store the contacts in SharePoint. It provides various columns to store contact's name, phone number, fax, web page, and so on. Out of the box, it does not provide a way to categorize these contacts. We will extend this content type so we can categorize our contacts as sales lead, customer, or vendor

Getting ready

You should have completed the previous recipe successfully.

How to do it...

1. Launch your Visual Studio 2010 IDE as an administrator (right-click the shortcut and select **Run as administrator**).

2. Select **File | New | Project**. The new project wizard dialog box will be displayed (make sure to select **.NET Framework 3.5** in the top drop-down box).

3. Select **Content Type** project under **Visual C# | SharePoint | 2010** node from the **Installed Templates** section on the left-hand side.

4. Name the project **ContactsContentType** and provide a directory location where you want to save the project and click on **OK** to proceed to the next step in the wizard.

5. By default, Visual Studio selects the SharePoint site available on the machine. Select **Deploy as sandboxed Solution** and click on **Next** to proceed to the next step in the wizard.

6. In this step, make sure to select the **Contact** content type as the base content type as shown in the following screenshot and click on **Finish** to generate the project:

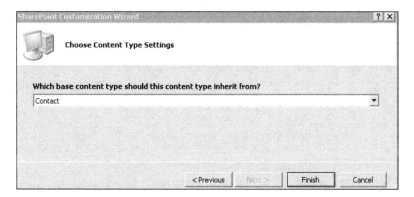

7. To this project, add a new empty element and call it **SiteColumns**. Your project structure should look like the following:

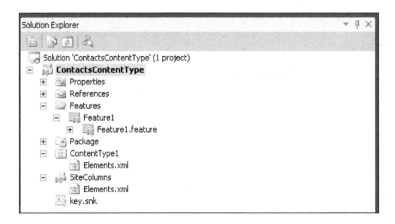

8. In the **Elements.xml** file underneath the **SiteColumns** element, add the xml to create a new site column. Your `Elements.xml` file should look similar to the following code:

```xml
<?xml version="1.0" encoding="utf-8"?>
<Elements xmlns="http://schemas.microsoft.com/sharepoint/">
  <Field ID="{CD822345-3D9D-45BC-8C7A-54198F77395C}"
Name="ContactType" Type="Choice" Required="FALSE" Group="Chapter3
Columns" DisplayName="Contact Type">
    <CHOICES>
      <CHOICE>Sales Lead</CHOICE>
      <CHOICE>Customer</CHOICE>
      <CHOICE>Vendor</CHOICE>
    </CHOICES>
  </Field>
</Elements>
```

9. We will reference this field in the content type. To do that, in the `Elements.xml` file underneath **ContentType1**, add the field reference to the created field in the previous step. Your `Elements.xml` file should look as follows:

```xml
<?xml version="1.0" encoding="utf-8"?>
<Elements xmlns="http://schemas.microsoft.com/sharepoint/">
  <!-- Parent ContentType: Contact (0x0106) -->
  <ContentType ID="0x01060016ac0527de4d4b989b1b9bcf8c9d2b38"
              Name="ContactsContentType - ContentType1"
              Group="Custom Content Types"
              Description="My Content Type"
              Inherits="TRUE"
              Version="0">
    <FieldRefs>
```

```
        <FieldRef ID="{CD822345-3D9D-45BC-8C7A-54198F77395C}"
Required="TRUE"/>
        </FieldRefs>
    </ContentType>
</Elements>
```

10. Run the project by pressing *F5*. This will create the content type and site column as shown in the following screenshot:

Site Content Type Information

Name:	ContactsContentType - ContentType1
Description:	My Content Type
Parent:	Contact
Group:	Custom Content Types

Settings

- Name, description, and group
- Advanced settings
- Workflow settings
- Delete this site content type
- Information management policy settings

Columns

Name	Type	Status	Source
Last Name	Single line of text	Optional	Item
Last Name Phonetic	Single line of text	Optional	Contact
First Name	Single line of text	Optional	Contact
First Name Phonetic	Single line of text	Optional	Contact
Full Name	Single line of text	Optional	Contact
E-Mail	Single line of text	Optional	Contact
Company	Single line of text	Optional	Contact
Company Phonetic	Single line of text	Optional	Contact
Job Title	Single line of text	Optional	Contact
Business Phone	Single line of text	Optional	Contact
Home Phone	Single line of text	Optional	Contact
Mobile Number	Single line of text	Optional	Contact
Fax Number	Single line of text	Optional	Contact
Address	Multiple lines of text	Optional	Contact
City	Single line of text	Optional	Contact
State/Province	Single line of text	Optional	Contact
ZIP/Postal Code	Single line of text	Optional	Contact
Country/Region	Single line of text	Optional	Contact
Web Page	Hyperlink or Picture	Optional	Contact
Comments	Multiple lines of text	Optional	Contact
Contact Type	Choice	Required	

11. Navigate to **Site Actions | Site Settings | Galleries | Site Columns**. You should see the new site column **Contact Type** created under a new group **Chapter3 Columns**.

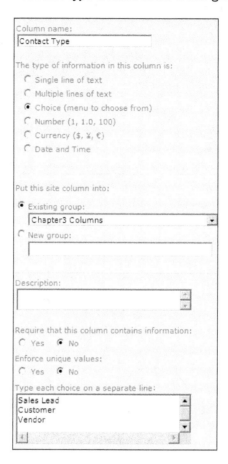

How it works...

In the strictest sense, whenever we develop a custom content type, we have to extend it from one of the available content types. In here, we extended the contacts content type. As indicated in the introduction of this chapter, the item (0x01) is the deepest we can go for inheriting the content type. We cannot inherit from the system content type (0x).

In the `Elements.xml` file underneath the **ContentType1** folder it describes the schema for the content type. It has attributes that define the name, group, description, and version. The ID attribute is GUID without any format. The ID of the content type is always prefixed with the parent content type ID and two zeros. Since we based our content type on a contact, the prefix is "0x010600". The ID attribute provides unique identification for the content type.

The `Inherits` attribute in the content type xml schema, specifies to SharePoint that all the fields from the parent content type are used in the derived child content type. So in our case, we still have all the fields defined in the contact content type, but we also added our own choice column for selecting the contact type.

When the feature is deployed, SharePoint reads the xml schema and creates the field based on the schema supplied. In our case, we created a new site column of type **Choice** and provided the choices that can be selected as well. All of this information was provided in the XML schema. Since Visual Studio does not have a specific template for creating site columns, we added a new empty element and provided the schema for creating the column in this element file. We do not have to do this. You can specify the field definitions in the content type `Elements.xml` file itself. It is a good practice though to have separate `Elements.xml` file when deploying fields and content types. In the later recipe, we will show how to include the field definitions in the content type `Elements.xml` file.

In the schema for the site column, you can see GUID for ID attribute. This is generated using the tool that Visual Studio provides. You can access this tool from the menu **Tools | Create GUID**. This will bring up a similar dialog box as the one follows:

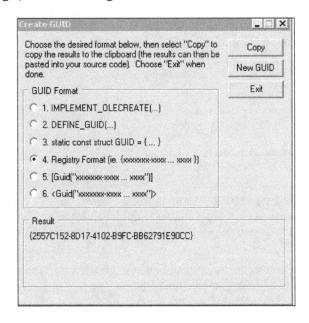

Select the registry format and copy to the ID attribute. This ID attribute is also used when referencing the field in the content type. The rest of the attributes in the field schema defines the column.

There's more...

To use the content type we created in this recipe, refer to the following steps:

1. From the SharePoint user interface, create a contacts list.

2. From the list settings page, click on the **Advanced Settings** and select **Yes** for the management of the content types. This will enable the content types section for the list.

3. Click on **Add** in the existing site content types link underneath the content types section in the list settings. Add **ContactContentType – ContentType1** as shown in the following screenshot:

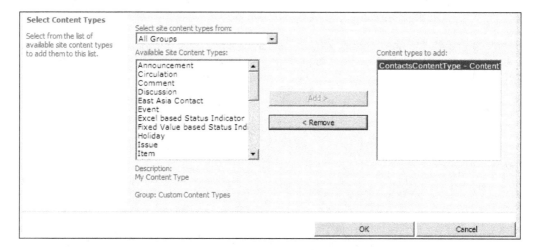

4. This will add our content type to the list. Now the list has Since list already has a default content type associated with it, by adding our content type, the list now has two content types associated with it. content types associated with it. Since we want to use our custom content type, remove the default content type associated with the list.

5. Add a new contact to the list, you should see the **Contact Type** field listed as required as shown in the following screenshot:

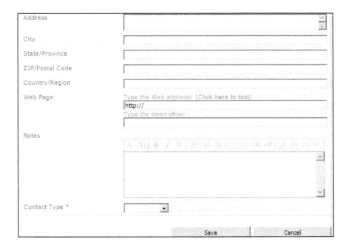

Deployment of previous solution

The previous example shows that the site column has to be deployed first in order for it to be referenced in the content type. To make sure that happens, we need to add a second feature to the project. To this feature, add the content type element and remove the same from the first feature. Also create a feature dependency such that feature 2 is dependent on the deployment of feature 1. This ensures that the site column is deployed before the content type gets deployed.

Here are steps to add feature dependency:

1. Double-click on **Feature 2** to open up the feature designer and click on the **+** next to the **Feature Activation Dependencies**.

2. Click on **Add** button to add the feature dependency as shown in the next screenshot:

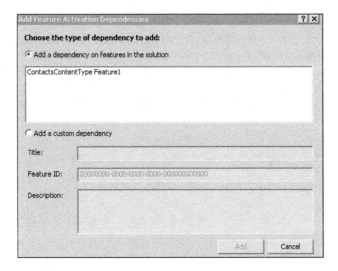

3. This will list the features that are in the project. In our case, we only have two features and hence **Feature 1** is shown in the list. Select **Feature 1** and click on **Add** to create the feature dependency.

Inherits attribute in content type

In the recipe, we learnt that the `Inherits` attribute specifies to SharePoint that all the fields from the parent content type is used in the child. If for some reason, you need to delete a column in the child that is available in the parent, make sure to set the `Inherits` attribute to false and use the `RemoveFieldRef` element as shown:

```
<RemoveFieldRef ID="ea8f7ca9-2a0e-4a89-b8bf-c51a6af62c73"/>
<RemoveFieldRef ID="fdc8216d-dabf-441d-8ac0-f6c626fbdc24"/>
```

By adding this preceding XML to content type `Elements.xml`, we will be removing the **First Name Phonetic** and the **Last Name Phonetic** columns from the content type.

See also

▸ *Creating a site column* recipe
▸ *Creating a custom content type using an object model* recipe

Creating custom content type using an object model

In the previous recipe, we extended a content type using an XML schema. This can get pretty difficult as Visual Studio does not provide ways to debug the XML schemas. Instead of using the xml schema method, you can always use object model APIs to create the content type. In this recipe we will do just that.

For this recipe, we will create a new content type called **Project Proposal** that has four custom columns **Amount**, **Department**, **Project Start Date**, and **Project End Date**. The `Department` field is a choice type where you can select the department to which the project belongs. The `Amount` field is of currency type and the `Project Start Date` and the `Project End Date` are of `DateTime` type. The content type will be inherited from the document content type.

Getting ready

You should have completed the previous recipes successfully.

How to do it...

1. Launch your Visual Studio 2010 IDE as an administrator (right-click the shortcut and select **Run as administrator**).

2. Select **File | New | Project**. The new project wizard dialog box will be displayed (make sure to select **.NET Framework 3.5** in the top drop-down box).

3. Select **Empty SharePoint Project** under **Visual C# | SharePoint | 2010** node from the **Installed Templates** section on the left-hand side.

4. Name the project **ProjectProposal** and provide a directory location where you want to save the project and click **OK** to proceed to the next step in the wizard.

5. By default, Visual Studio selects the SharePoint site available on the machine. Select **Deploy as Farm Solution** and click on **Next** to proceed to the next step in the wizard.

6. This should create an empty SharePoint project. To this project, add a feature by right-clicking on the **Feature** folder.

7. Add an event receiver to the new feature added by right-clicking on the feature and selecting **Add Event Receiver**.

8. This should add a code file named `Feature1.EventReceiver.cs`. Uncomment `FeatureActivated` and `FeatureDeactivating` methods.

9. Add the code to create a `Project Proposal` content type in the `FeatureActivated` method. The code is as follows:

```
public override void FeatureActivated
(SPFeatureReceiverProperties properties)
{
    SPWeb web = null;
    if (properties.Feature.Parent is SPSite)
    {
        SPSite sites = (SPSite)properties.Feature.Parent;
        web = sites.RootWeb;
    }
    else
    {
        web = (SPWeb)properties.Feature.Parent;
    }
    if (web == null)
        return;


    string columnGroup = "Chapter3 Project Proposal Site
     Column Group";

    // Project Amount
```

```
            string sAmountFieldName = web.Fields.Add("Chapter3
            Project Amount", SPFieldType.Currency, false);
            SPFieldCurrency fldAmount = (SPFieldCurrency)
            web.Fields.GetFieldByInternalName(sAmountFieldName);
            fldAmount.Group = columnGroup;
            fldAmount.DisplayFormat = SPNumberFormatTypes.
            TwoDecimals;
            fldAmount.MinimumValue = 0;
            fldAmount.Update();
            Guid fldGuid = fldAmount.Id;


            // Project Start Date
            string sProjectDateFieldName = web.Fields.
    Add("Chapter3 Project Start Date", SPFieldType.DateTime, false);
            SPFieldDateTime fldProjectStartDate =
    (SPFieldDateTime)web.Fields.GetFieldByInternalName(sProjectDateFie
    ldName);
            fldProjectStartDate.Group = columnGroup;
            fldProjectStartDate.DisplayFormat =
            SPDateTimeFieldFormatType.DateOnly;
            fldProjectStartDate.DefaultValue = "[today]";
            fldProjectStartDate.Update();

            // Project End Date
            string sProjectEndDateFieldName = web.Fields.
    Add("Chapter3 Project End Date", SPFieldType.DateTime, false);
            SPFieldDateTime fldProjectEndDate =
    (SPFieldDateTime)web.Fields.GetFieldByInternalName(sProjectEndDate
    FieldName);
            fldProjectEndDate.Group = columnGroup;
            fldProjectEndDate.DisplayFormat =
    SPDateTimeFieldFormatType.DateOnly;
            fldProjectEndDate.DefaultValue = "[today]";
            fldProjectEndDate.Update();

            // Department
            string sDepartmentFieldName = web.Fields.Add("Chapter3
            Department", SPFieldType.Choice, false);
            SPFieldChoice fldDepartment = (SPFieldChoice)web.
            Fields.GetFieldByInternalName(sDepartmentFieldName);
            fldDepartment.Choices.Add("Human Resources");
            fldDepartment.Choices.Add("Information Technology");
            fldDepartment.Choices.Add("Finance");
            fldDepartment.Choices.Add("Research and Development");
            fldDepartment.Choices.Add("Sales");
            fldDepartment.Choices.Add("Marketing");
            fldDepartment.Group = columnGroup;
```

```
fldDepartment.Update();


string contentTypeGroup = "Chapter3 Project Proposal
Content Type Group";

// We will use Document Content type as the parent
SPContentType documentCType = web.AvailableContentType
 s[SPBuiltInContentTypeId.Document];

// Create the Budget Proposal Content type.
SPContentType ctProjectProposal = new SPContentType
(documentCType, web.ContentTypes, "Chapter3 Project
Proposal");


ctProjectProposal = web.ContentTypes.
 Add(ctProjectProposal);
ctProjectProposal.Group = contentTypeGroup;

// Add columns created earlier
SPFieldLink projectStartDateFieldRef = new SPFieldLink
(fldProjectStartDate);
projectStartDateFieldRef.Required = true;
ctProjectProposal.FieldLinks.Add(projectStartDateField
Ref);

// Add columns created earlier
SPFieldLink projectEndDateFieldRef = new SPFieldLink
(fldProjectEndDate);
projectEndDateFieldRef.Required = true;
ctProjectProposal.FieldLinks.Add
(projectEndDateFieldRef);

SPFieldLink frAmount = new SPFieldLink(fldAmount);
ctProjectProposal.FieldLinks.Add(frAmount);

SPFieldLink frDepartment = new SPFieldLink
(fldDepartment);
ctProjectProposal.FieldLinks.Add(frDepartment);
// Commit changes.
ctProjectProposal.Update();


}
```

10. Add the code to delete the content type and columns in the `FeatureDeactivating` method. The code should be as follows:

```
public override void FeatureDeactivating(SPFeatureReceiver
Properties properties)
{
    SPWeb web = null;
    if (properties.Feature.Parent is SPSite)
    {
        SPSite sites = (SPSite)properties.Feature.Parent;
        web = sites.RootWeb;
    }
    else
    {
        web = (SPWeb)properties.Feature.Parent;
    }
    if (web == null)
        return;

    web.AllowUnsafeUpdates = true;

    web.ContentTypes["Chapter3 Project Proposal"].
    Delete();
    web.Fields.GetFieldByInternalName("Chapter3_x0020_
    Project_x0020_Amount").Delete();
    web.Fields.GetFieldByInternalName("Chapter3_x0020_
    Department").Delete();
    web.Fields.GetFieldByInternalName("Chapter3_x0020_
    Project_x0020_End_x0020_Date").Delete();
    web.Fields.GetFieldByInternalName("Chapter3_x0020_
    Project_x0020_Start_x0020_Date").Delete();
    web.Update();
    web.AllowUnsafeUpdates = false;

}
```

11. Build and run the project by pressing *F5*. Visual studio will launch the browser with the site you provided during the project creation. Navigate to **Site Actions | Site Settings | Galleries | Site Columns**. You should see the new site columns created under a new group **Chapter3 Project Proposal Site Column Group**. Similarly, navigate to **Site Actions | Site Settings | Galleries | Site Content Types** to see the **Project Proposal** content type as shown in the following screenshot:

Site Content Type	Parent	Source
Business Intelligence		
Excel based Status Indicator	Common Indicator Columns	Book Portal
Fixed Value based Status Indicator	Common Indicator Columns	Book Portal
Report	Document	Book Portal
SharePoint List based Status Indicator	Common Indicator Columns	Book Portal
SQL Server Analysis Services based Status Indicator	Common Indicator Columns	Book Portal
Web Part Page with Status List	Document	Book Portal
Chapter3 Project Proposal Content Type Group		
Chapter3 Project Proposal	Document	Book Portal
Content Organizer Content Types		
Rule	Item	Book Portal

How it works...

Instead of the schema, we made use of the object model APIs to create the site columns. This was explained in our first recipe. The addition to this recipe is to create the content type and reference the site columns that were created previously.

For this, we used the `SPContentType` constructor and passed in the parent content type and the name of the content type. We added this to our web content type collection.

To add a reference to the fields, we created an instance of `SPFieldLink` and added to the content type. The content type was updated with the reference to the fields when we called the update method on the content type.

See also

▸ *Associating a document template with the content type* recipe

Associating a document template with the content type

In the introduction to content types, we specified that a content type can include document templates and/or workflows. In this recipe, we will include a document template for our `Project Proposal` content type.

Getting ready

You should have completed the previous recipes successfully. Create a word template and name it `ProjectProposal.dotx`.

How to do it...

1. If you have closed Visual Studio IDE, launch it as an administrator.

2. Open the previously created **ProjectProposal** solution.

3. Right-click on the project and select **Add | SharePoint "Layouts" Mapped Folder** as follows:

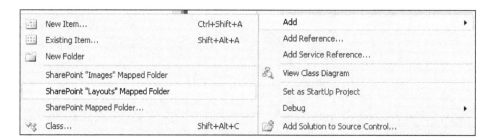

4. This will create a mapped folder to the **Layouts** folder and add a subfolder with the same name as the project underneath it. In our case it is called **ProjectProposal**.

5. Add your `ProjectProposal.dotx` file to this folder. Your project structure should be as follows:

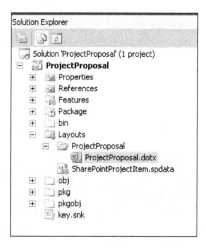

6. Open `Feature1.EventReceiver.cs` file and add code to associate the document template before the content type update method in feature activating method. Your code should look like the following:

```
SPFieldLink frDepartment = new SPFieldLink(fldDepartment);
        ctProjectProposal.FieldLinks.Add(frDepartment);

        //Associate the document template created.
```

```
ctProjectProposal.DocumentTemplate = "/_layouts/
ProjectProposal/ProjectProposal.dotx";

// Commit changes.
ctProjectProposal.Update();
```

7. Build and run the project. Navigate to **Site Actions | Site Settings | Gallery | Site content types** and select **Chapter3 Project Proposal**. Click on the **Advanced settings** link and you should see the URL for the document template attached as shown here:

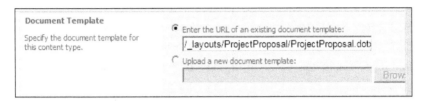

How it works...

From the previous chapters we understand the concept of the *Mapped folders*. As explained in the previous chapters, Visual Studio always creates a subfolder underneath the mapped folder when we add a reference to the mapped folders. We added our template file to this location. The layouts mapped folder can be referenced as _layouts and hence we provided the URL for the document template from this location.

You can associate this content type to a library as explained in the previous recipes. When you create a new document from this library, the template will be opened from the _layouts folder as shown in the next screenshot:

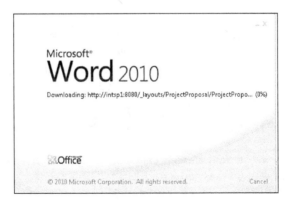

There's more...

In this recipe, we used the `_layouts` folder to deploy the document template. This will not work with sandboxed solutions. For sandboxed solutions, since you do not have access to the SharePoint root on the file system, you have to deploy the document templates to the content databases. For my example here, I have created an excel template called `BudgetProposal.xltx`. The content type is called **DocumentTemplateContentType**. Here is the step-by-step instructions on deploying the document template in a sandboxed solution:

1. Create a new content type project and make sure you select the **Sandboxed** solution in the wizard. Inherit the content type from a document content type.

2. Visual Studio creates the **ContentType1** folder and the `Elements.xml` file underneath it along with the feature to deploy the content type.

3. Add a new module item to the **ContentType1** folder and call it **Template**.

4. Delete the default `Sample.txt` and the `Elements.xml` file that Visual Studio adds. Your project structure should look like the following:

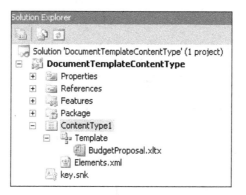

5. Edit the `Elements.xml` file of the content type and add the module information. The attribute's `Url` provides the path for clients to look for the template associated with the content type. The `Type` attribute specifies that the template is loaded into the content database. Your content type `Elements.xml` file should be as follows:

```xml
<?xml version="1.0" encoding="utf-8"?>
<Elements xmlns="http://schemas.microsoft.com/sharepoint/">

  <Module Url="_cts/DocumentTemplateContentType" Name="Template">
    <File Url="BudgetProposal.xltx" Name="BudgetProposal.xltx"
Type="Ghostable" Path="Template\BudgetProposal.xltx"/>
  </Module>

  <!-- Parent ContentType: Document (0x0101) -->
  <ContentType ID="0x010100a3c7c0095daf42ac924b1258ab88563c"
```

```
                    Name="DocumentTemplateContentType"
                    Group="Custom Content Types"
                    Description="My Content Type"
                    Inherits="TRUE"
                    Version="0">
        <FieldRefs>
        </FieldRefs>
        <DocumentTemplate TargetName="BudgetProposal.xltx"/>
      </ContentType>
    </Elements>
```

 For the list of built-in content types and their IDs refer to MSDN at: `http://msdn.microsoft.com/en-us/library/ms452896.aspx`.

See also

▸ *Associating a workflow to a content type* recipe

Associating a workflow to a content type

We added metadata columns to our content type, we added a document template that provides the common format for uploading project proposals to the library, and in this recipe we will add "Approval workflow" to our content type.

Approval Workflow is out-of-the-box workflow available in the SharePoint server. The same steps will work in case you want to associate custom workflows that we developed in *Chapter 2, Workflows*.

Getting ready

You should have completed the previous recipes successfully.

How to do it...

1. If you have closed Visual Studio IDE, launch it as an administrator.

2. Open the previously created `ProjectProposal` solution.

3. Open `Feature1.EventReceiver.cs` file and add code to associate the workflow before the content type update method in the feature's activating method. Your code should look like the following:

    ```
    //Associate the document template created.
            ctProjectProposal.DocumentTemplate = "/_layouts/
    ```

```
ProjectProposal/ProjectProposal.dotx";

SPWorkflowTemplate approvalTemplate = null;

for (int i = 0; i < web.WorkflowTemplates.Count; ++i)
{
    if (web.WorkflowTemplates[i].Name == "Approval -
    SharePoint 2010")
        approvalTemplate = web.WorkflowTemplates[i];
}

SPList wrkHistoryList = null;
// Try to get workflow history list
try
{
    wrkHistoryList = web.Lists["Workflow History"];
}
catch (Exception)
{
    // Create workflow history list
    Guid listGuid = web.Lists.Add("Workflow History",
    "", SPListTemplateType.WorkflowHistory);
    wrkHistoryList = web.Lists[listGuid];
    wrkHistoryList.Hidden = true;
    wrkHistoryList.Update();
}


SPList wrkTasksList = null;
// Try to get workflow tasks list
try
{
    wrkTasksList = web.Lists["Tasks"];
}
catch (Exception)
{
    // Create workflow tasks list
    Guid listGuid = web.Lists.Add("Tasks", "",
    SPListTemplateType.Tasks);
    wrkTasksList = web.Lists[listGuid];
    wrkTasksList.Hidden = true;
    wrkTasksList.Update();
}
```

```
            Microsoft.SharePoint.Workflow.SPWorkflowAssociation
    wrkAssoc = SPWorkflowAssociation.CreateListContentTypeAssocia
    tion(approvalTemplate, "Chapter3 Project Proposal Approval",
    wrkTasksList, wrkHistoryList);

            wrkAssoc.AutoStartCreate = false;
            ctProjectProposal.WorkflowAssociations.Add(wrkAssoc);

            // Commit changes.
            ctProjectProposal.Update();
```

4. Build and run the project. Navigate to **Site Actions** | **Site Settings** | **Gallery** | **Site Content Types** and select **Chapter3 Project Proposal**. Click on the **Workflow Settings** and you should be able to see our "Approval workflow" associated with the content type as shown in the following screenshot:

How it works...

The first step to associate a workflow to a content type is to get the workflow template that we need to associate. We loop through the web object to get our template. In our example, we got the template for "Approval – SharePoint 2010". This is the name of the workflow. When you know the name of the workflow, you can iterate through the web object for all the workflows that are available on that site. After this, we created the necessary supporting lists like the tasks and the workflow history list for the workflow. Based on the template, we created an association object for the content type and associated this object to our content type.

A workflow associated object represents the binding of the template to a particular content type or list. It has a static method to create the binding association. In our case, we used the `CreateListContentTypeAssociation` method to create the binding association. For more information on workflow association please refer to MSDN at: `http://msdn.microsoft.com/en-us/library/microsoft.sharepoint.workflow.spworkflowassociation.aspx`.

There's more...

You can also pass the association data to the workflow template. Association data is of the XML format and is different for each of the workflows. The following is the code to pass association data to the approval workflow that we have used. Make sure to substitute proper user IDs for your environment.

```
string sAssocData = "<dfs:myFields xmlns:xsd=\"http://www.w3.org/2001/
XMLSchema\" xmlns:dms=\"http://schemas.microsoft.com/office/2009/
documentManagement/types\" xmlns:dfs=\"http://schemas.microsoft.com/
office/infopath/2003/dataFormSolution\" xmlns:q=\"http://schemas.
microsoft.com/office/infopath/2009/WSSList/queryFields\" xmlns:
d=\"http://schemas.microsoft.com/office/infopath/2009/WSSList/
dataFields\" xmlns:ma=\"http://schemas.microsoft.com/office/2009/
metadata/properties/metaAttributes\" xmlns:pc=\"http://schemas.
microsoft.com/office/infopath/2007/PartnerControls\" xmlns:xsi=\
"http://www.w3.org/2001/XMLSchema-instance\"><dfs:queryFields></
dfs:queryFields><dfs:dataFields><d:SharePointListItem_RW><d:
Approvers><d:Assignment><d:Assignee><pc:Person><pc:DisplayName>Balaji
Kithiganahalli</pc:DisplayName><pc:AccountId>INTEGRATELLCDEV\\
balaji</pc:AccountId><pc:AccountType>User</pc:AccountType></pc:
Person><pc:Person><pc:DisplayName>SP Test1</pc:DisplayName><pc:Acco
untId>INTEGRATELLCDEV\\sptest1</pc:AccountId><pc:AccountType>User</
pc:AccountType></pc:Person></d:Assignee><d:Stage xsi:nil=\"true\"
/><d:AssignmentType>Serial</d:AssignmentType></d:Assignment><d:
Assignment><d:Assignee><pc:Person><pc:DisplayName>SP Test2</pc:
DisplayName><pc:AccountId>INTEGRATELLCDEV\\sptest2</pc:AccountId><pc:
AccountType>User</pc:AccountType></pc:Person></d:Assignee><d:Stage
xsi:nil=\"true\" xmlns:xsi=\"http://www.w3.org/2001/XMLSchema-
instance\" /><d:AssignmentType>Serial</d:AssignmentType></d:
Assignment></d:Approvers><d:ExpandGroups>true</d:ExpandGroups><d:
NotificationMessage /><d:DueDateforAllTasks xsi:nil=\"true\" /><d:
DurationforSerialTasks xsi:nil=\"true\" /><d:DurationUnits>Day</
d:DurationUnits><d:CC /><d:CancelonRejection>false</d:
CancelonRejection><d:CancelonChange>false</d:CancelonChange><d:EnableC
ontentApproval>false</d:EnableContentApproval></d:SharePointListItem_
RW></dfs:dataFields></dfs:myFields>";

approvalTemplate.AssociationData = sAssocData;
```

See also

▶ *Creating an external content type* recipe

Creating an external content type

External content types are defined as reusable objects with metadata descriptions of connectivity information to external systems and data definitions. They could also contain the behaviors you want to apply to the external data. They are similar to the content types that we have dealt so far. The difference is that we will be managing the external data in external content types. The external data can be from relational databases like SQL server or Oracle or data coming from some web service.

For our recipe, we will use a SQL server table and create a content type based on the table data. We will use the `HumanResources.Department` table in the `AdventureWorks` database. We will create a `GetDepartments` method that will retrieve the list of all departments and a `GetDepartment` method that retrieves the single department object.

We will use LINQ to SQL to access relational data as objects. You do not have to use LINQ to SQL for data access in external content types. In this example, we are using it for the sake of simplicity of the code. If you want to learn more about LINQ to SQL, refer to MSDN at: `http://msdn.microsoft.com/en-us/library/bb425822.aspx`.

Getting ready

For this recipe, you need to have access to the `AdventureWorks` database. You can download it from: `http://msftdbprodsamples.codeplex.com/`.

How to do it...

1. Create an empty SharePoint project with the farm level deployment option.

2. Add a new item to this project and select **Business Data Connectivity Model** and name the item as **DepartmentsModel** as shown here:

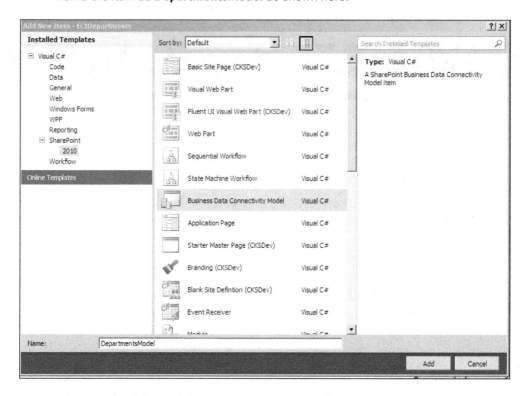

3. Visual Studio adds the necessary files and brings up the BDC designer with a default entity called **Entity1**. Delete this default entity. Also delete the files `Entity1.cs` and `Entity1Service.cs` associated with this entity.

4. From the ToolBox, add a new entity to the designer surface and rename this as **Department** in the properties window of the entity. Add a new identifier to this entity and call it **DepartmentID** and change the **Type Name** to `System.Int16`. Visual Studio will add a new service file called `DepartmentService.cs` in your solution explorer.

5. To the project, now add a new item and select **Data | LINQ to SQL Classes** and name it **Department** as shown in the following screenshot:

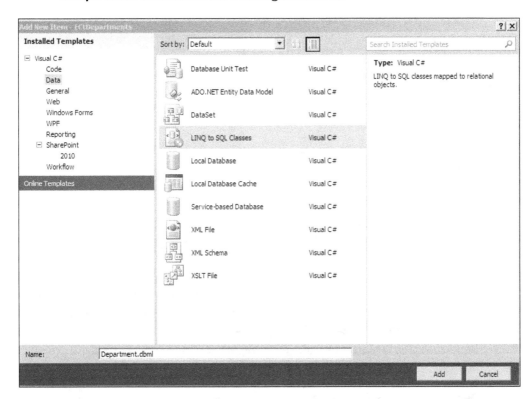

6. From the server explorer, add a new data connection to your **AdventureWorks** database. Now from your LINQ to SQL designer window, navigate through the Server Explorer to the tables node from the data connection you just added. Expand the tables node and drag the `Departments` table and it to the designer. Visual Studio will generate the necessary LINQ `DataContext` classes for the external table. You can refer to this `DataContext` class in the `Department.designer.cs` file. Close this designer surface. We will not be making any changes to this class file.

7. Now back in the **DepartmentsModel**, select the **Department Entity** created previously, and **Create a Finder Method** from the **BDC Method Details** window and name it GetDepartmentList. Also Create a Finder Specific method and name it GetDepartment. The final screenshot should look like the following:

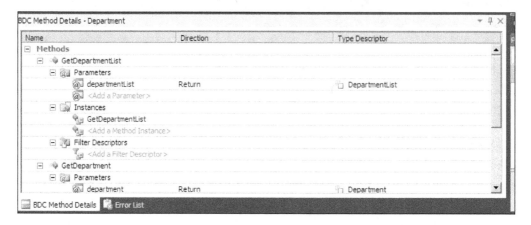

8. Select the **DepartmentList Type Descriptor** in the **BDC Method Details** window and from the drop-down select **Edit** menu option to bring up the BDC explorer window. In here, change the Type Name property to **Current Project | Department**. Make sure that the **Is Enumerable** checkbox is selected.

9. Underneath the **DepartmentList**, select **Department** and change the Type Name property to **Current Project | Department**. In this case, the **Is Enumerable** checkbox is not selected. Underneath this department, add a Type Descriptor and name it **DepartmentID**. The type name should be System.Int16. In the same manner, add three more **Type Descriptors** named **Name**, **GroupName**, and **ModifiedDate**. The **Type Name** for the **Name** and the **GroupName** is System.String and for **ModifiedDate** it is System.DateTime. The final screen should be as shown in the following screenshot:

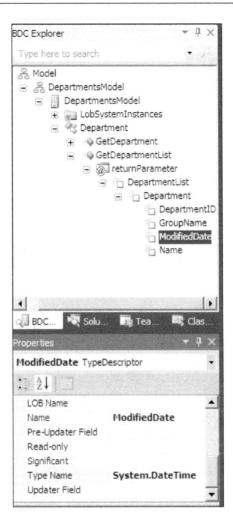

10. Open the `DepartmentService.cs` file and add code to retrieve the departments from the database to the `GetDepartmentList` method and add code to retrieve the single object to the `GetDepartment` method. Your code should be as follows. Make sure to change the database connection string to your environment:

```
public static IEnumerable<Department> GetDepartmentList()
    {
        DepartmentDataContext dx = new DepartmentData
         Context("Data Source=intsql;Initial Catalog=Adventure
         Works;Integrated Security=True");
        return dx.Departments;
    }


    public static Department GetDepartment(short id)
```

```
        {
            DepartmentDataContext dx = new DepartmentData
Context("Data Source=intsql;Initial Catalog=AdventureWorks;
Integrated Security=True");
            return dx.Departments.Single(d => d.DepartmentID ==
            id);
        }
```

11. Press *F5* to build and run the project. This should bring up the site that was provided during the project creation wizard. In here, from the site actions menu, create an external list called **Departments** and add the content type we just created as shown here:

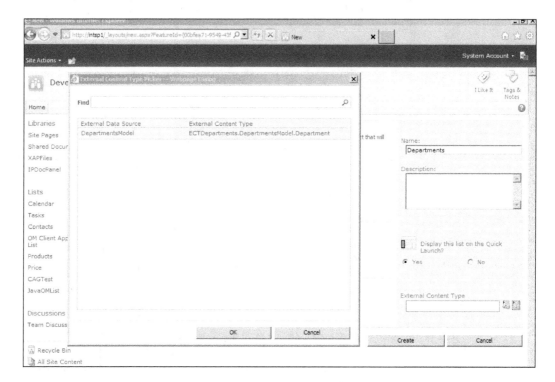

12. This should list all the departments from the `Departments` table in the `AdventureWorks` database as shown in the next screenshot:

	DepartmentID	Name	GroupName	ModifiedDate
	1	Engineering	Research and Development	6/3/2011 8:00 PM
☐	2	Tool Design	Research and Development	5/31/1998 8:00 PM
	3	Sales	Sales and Marketing	5/31/1998 8:00 PM
	4	Marketing	Sales and Marketing	5/31/1998 8:00 PM
	5	Purchasing	Inventory Management	5/31/1998 8:00 PM
	6	Research and Development	Research and Development	5/31/1998 8:00 PM
	7	Production	Manufacturing	5/31/1998 8:00 PM
	8	Production Control	Manufacturing	5/31/1998 8:00 PM
	9	Human Resources	Executive General and Administration	5/31/1998 8:00 PM
	10	Finance	Executive General and Administration	5/31/1998 8:00 PM
	11	Information Services	Executive General and Administration	5/31/1998 8:00 PM
	12	Document Control	Quality Assurance	5/31/1998 8:00 PM
	13	Quality Assurance	Quality Assurance	5/31/1998 8:00 PM
	14	Facilities and Maintenance	Executive General and Administration	5/31/1998 8:00 PM
	15	Shipping and Receiving	Inventory Management	5/31/1998 8:00 PM
	16	Executive	Executive General and Administration	5/31/1998 8:00 PM

How it works...

Visual Studio refers to external content types as an entity because BDC schema refers to this as entities. BDC Designer is built on top of ADO.Net Entity Designer and hence that reference. If you are familiar with ADO.Net Entity Designer, this will work the same way. In here, we can create entities and associate them with some relationship.

For our external content type to work, we need to create at least two methods of type `Finder` and `SpecificFinder` method. In our example, we created `GetDepartmentList` and `GetDepartment` that corresponds to these types. This is important because SharePoint calls these methods to render the list and display the selected item when the item is selected. There are other types of methods that can be used in external content types. Refer to MSDN at: `http://msdn.microsoft.com/en-us/library/ee557363(office.14).aspx` for more information on different method types that can be developed in the external content types.

The finder method, `GetDepartmentList` does not take any input parameters, but has one return parameter. This is defined in the **Method Details** window. In here, we provided information about the type of our parameter and direction of the parameter. The direction can be "In", "Out", "InOut", and "Return". The "In" direction is used on the parameters that are used to pass in the values to the methods. The "Out" direction, as the name refers to, is the output parameter and "InOut" is similar to "ref" parameter in C#. We also provided the type of our parameter. For this, we used the `Department` object that was created through LINQ to SQL. We set the type of the parameter through type descriptors. Type descriptors are metadata information that is used during the runtime to determine the type of the parameter passed or returned. There are other properties in type descriptors that tell SharePoint how to use this parameter. For example, the `Creator Field` property in a type descriptor tells that it is used in the form for user input. the collection property tells that the parameter is a collection. Not all of the type descriptors make sense for each of the parameters that pass in the method. It comes in handy, depending upon the type we want to retrieve or pass.

Each of the methods that we defined also has a method instance. This is because, in BCS, when we define a method, it is defined as an abstract piece of code. An instance is created during run time and executed.

There's more...

If you receive **Access denied by Business Data Connectivity** error as shown here, follow these steps:

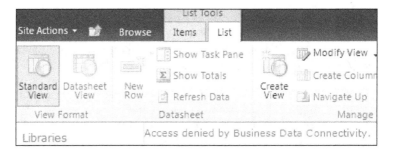

1. Open **Central Administration | Application Management | Manage Service applications** and select **Business Data Connectivity Service**. You should see the list of all external content types deployed.

2. From the drop-down menu select your content type and select **Set Permissions** as shown in the following screenshot:

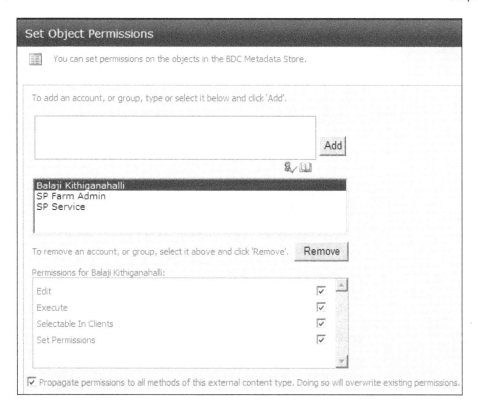

3. Add users and set appropriate permissions for the user executing the ECT.

Create, update, and delete methods

For our preceding example, to add other CRUD methods like create, update, and delete methods, follow these steps:

1. From the **BDC Method Details Window**, create **Creator Method** for creating the department. Name this method `CreateDepartment`. For updating, the method type should be `Updater Method` and for delete `Deleter Method`. Also name the updater method as `UpdateDepartment` and the deleter method as `DeleteDepartment`.

2. Visual Studio automatically wires up the necessary parameters and its type descriptors and adds method signatures in the `DepartmentService.cs`. Add the code in the `DepartmentService.cs` for create, update, and delete. Your code should look as follows:

```
        public static Department CreateDepartment(Department
newDepartment)
        {
```

```
            DepartmentDataContext dx = new DepartmentDataContext
    ("Data Source=intsql;Initial Catalog=AdventureWorks;Integrated
    Security=True");
                newDepartment.ModifiedDate = DateTime.Today;
                dx.Departments.InsertOnSubmit(newDepartment);
                dx.SubmitChanges();
                return dx.Departments.Single(d => d.DepartmentID ==
    newDepartment.DepartmentID);
            }


        public static void UpdateDepartment(Department department)
        {
            DepartmentDataContext dx = new DepartmentDataContext
    ("Data Source=intsql;Initial Catalog=AdventureWorks;Integrated
    Security=True");
                Department dept = dx.Departments.Single(d =>
    d.DepartmentID == department.DepartmentID);
                dept.GroupName = department.GroupName;
                dept.Name = department.Name;
                dept.ModifiedDate = DateTime.Today;
                dx.SubmitChanges();
        }


        public static void DeleteDepartment(short departmentID)
        {
            DepartmentDataContext dx = new DepartmentDataContext
    ("Data Source=intsql;Initial Catalog=AdventureWorks;Integrated
    Security=True");
                dx.Departments.DeleteOnSubmit(dx.Departments.Single(d
    => d.DepartmentID == departmentID));
                dx.SubmitChanges();
        }
```

Connection strings

In our example, we have hard coded the connection string. There are several ways you can access the connection string data without hard coding it like getting the connection string from `web.config` or from a custom SharePoint list that is used to store the configuration information. The other approach is to use the BCS `LobSystemInstance` object. For our example:

1. Navigate from BCS Explorer window **Model** | **DepartmentsModel** | **DepartmentsModel** | **LobSystemInstances** | **DepartmentsModel**.

2. From the properties windows, add a custom property in the custom property collection and add your connection string as shown:

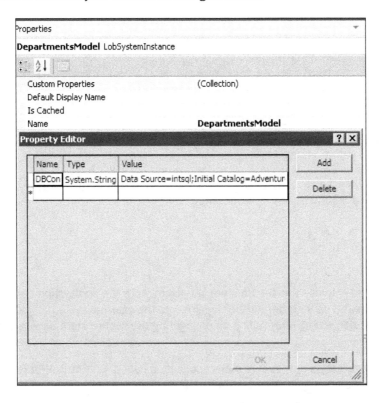

3. Add a reference to `Microsoft.BusinessData.dll` found in `\Program Files\Common Files\Microsoft Shared\Web Server Extensions\14\ISAPI`.

4. This connection string now can be accessed from the code by making `DepartmentService` implement the `IContextProperty` interface. The following is the code for getting the DB connection string.

```
public  string GetDBCon()
      {
           Microsoft.BusinessData.MetadataModel.Collections.
INamedPropertyDictionary dic = this.LobSystemInstance.
GetProperties();
           if (dic.ContainsKey("DBCon"))
               return dic["DBCon"].ToString();
           else
               return "";
      }


      public  Microsoft.BusinessData.Runtime.IExecutionContext
```

```
ExecutionContext
        {
            get;
            set;
        }

        public   Microsoft.BusinessData.MetadataModel.
ILobSystemInstance LobSystemInstance
        {
            get;
            set;
        }

        public   Microsoft.BusinessData.MetadataModel.
IMethodInstance MethodInstance
        {
            get;
            set;
        }
```

The other method is to use the secure store service to store the connection string. Although it is used to store the user credentials for logging into the external system, it can be used to store the connection string. Information on configuring the secure store service can be found on MSDN at `http://technet.microsoft.com/en-us/library/ee806866.aspx`.

For our example, create a new secure store application called **AdventureWorks** with one field of type **Generic**. Call that field **Connection String** as shown here:

Follow the next steps to get credentials from the secure store programmatically.

1. Add a new class to the project and call it `SecureStoreUtilities.cs`.

2. Add a reference to `Microsoft.BusinessData.dll` from the ISAPI folder.

3. Add a reference to `Microsoft.Office.SecureStoreService.dll` from `\Windows\assembly\GAC_MSIL\Microsoft.Office.SecureStoreService\14.0.0.0__71e9bce111e9429c\`.

4. Add the following code to `SecureStoreUtilities.cs` to retrieve and decrypt the string:

```
public static Dictionary<string, string> GetSSCreds(string
applicationID)
        {
            var credKVP = new Dictionary<string, string>(); //Key
Value pair
            using (SPSite site = new SPSite("http://intsp1/"))
            {
               //  Console.WriteLine(site.RootWeb.CurrentUser.
Name);
                SPServiceContext serviceContext =
SPServiceContext.GetContext(site);

                var secureStoreProvider = new SecureStoreProvider
{ Context = serviceContext };

                using (var creds = secureStoreProvider.
                GetCredentials(applicationID))
                {
                    var taFields = secureStoreProvider.GetTarget
                     ApplicationFields(applicationID);
                    for (var i = 0; i < taFields.Count; i++)
                    {
                        var field = taFields[i];
                        var credential = creds[i];
                        var decryptedCredential = DecryptCredential
(credential.Credential);

                        credKVP.Add(field.Name,
decryptedCredential);
                    }
                }
            }

            return credKVP;
        }

        public static string DecryptCredential(this SecureString
        encryptedString)
        {
            var ssBSTR = Marshal.SecureStringToBSTR
            (encryptedString);

            try
```

```
        {
                return Marshal.PtrToStringBSTR(ssBSTR);
        }
        finally
        {
                Marshal.FreeBSTR(ssBSTR);
        }
    }
```

5. Create a following utility method in your `DepartmentService.cs` called `GetDBConnectionString` and pass the return value from this method to the `DepartmentDataContext` constructor:

```
public static string GetDBConnectionString()
    {
        string sDbCon = "";
        Dictionary<string, string> ssList =
SecureStoreUtilities.GetSSCreds("AdventureWorks");
        foreach (KeyValuePair<string, string> kvp in ssList)
        {
            if (kvp.Key == "Connection String")
            {
                sDbCon = kvp.Value;
                break;
            }
        }

        return sDbCon;
    }
```

You can use this approach to dynamically construct a LOB connection string by storing the credentials in the secure store.

See also

▸   *Creating a list definition* recipe

Creating a list definition

In all the previous recipes, when we deployed the content type, we had to manually create a list based on the content type using the SharePoint UI. We can create list instances based on the content type using Visual Studio without going through the SharePoint UI.

In this recipe, we will create a custom content type called an `Expense` content type and based on that content type, we will create a list `Definition` and list `Instance`.

Our Expense content type will be based on an Item content type and will have three fields named Title, Amount, and Expense category which is a choice field.

Getting ready

You should have completed the previous recipes successfully.

How to do it...

1. Launch your Visual Studio 2010 IDE as an administrator (right-click the shortcut and select **Run as administrator**).

2. Select **File | New | Project**. The new project wizard dialog box will be displayed. (Make sure to select **.NET Framework 3.5** in the top drop-down box).

3. Select **List Definition** project under **Visual C# | SharePoint | 2010** node from **Installed Templates** section on the left-hand side.

4. Name the project **Chapter3ListDefinition** and provide the location to save the project.

5. Select **Deploy** as a farm solution and move to the next step in the wizard.

6. In the **Choose List Definition Settings** dialog box, provide the name for your list definition and select **Custom List** for **What is the type of the list definition?** and make sure to check **Add a list instance for this list definition** as shown here:

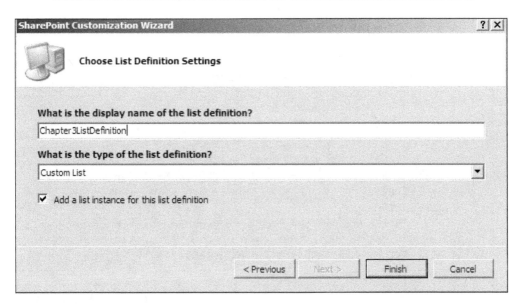

7. This creates a folder names **ListDefinition1** with two XML files named `Elements.xml` and `Schema.xml`. This folder also contains a subfolder named **ListInstance1**. This folder too has an XML file named `Elements.xml`. By default, Visual Studio opens the `Elements.xml` file from the folder `ListDefinition1`.

8. To this add the XML definition that creates the required fields, content type, and the list definition. Your `Elements.xml` file inside the **ListDefinition1** folder should be as follows:

```xml
<?xml version="1.0" encoding="utf-8"?>
<Elements xmlns="http://schemas.microsoft.com/sharepoint/">

  <Field ID="{ACFCD9F9-56D4-42B0-91E7-702511A41E0D}"
Name="Chap3Amt" Description="Chap3 Expense Amount" Type="Currency"
DisplayName="Chap3 Expense Amount" Required="TRUE" LCID="1033"></
Field>
  <Field ID="{1C9A5A95-12EA-4FED-8D2B-419C0E883DAF}"
Name="Chap3Cat" Description="Chap3 Expense Category" Type="Choice"
DisplayName="Chap3 Expense Category" Required="TRUE">
    <CHOICES>
      <CHOICE>Books</CHOICE>
      <CHOICE>Food</CHOICE>
      <CHOICE>Rent</CHOICE>
      <CHOICE>Entertainment</CHOICE>
      <CHOICE>ISP</CHOICE>
      <CHOICE>Cable</CHOICE>
    </CHOICES>
  </Field>

  <ContentType ID="0x0100794FFBC7EB4A4441AFC07DA551BB610E"
               Name="Chap3ExpenseCT"
               Group="Custom Content Types"
               Description="Expense Content Type -
               Chapter 3 example"
               Version="0">
    <FieldRefs>

      <FieldRef ID="{ACFCD9F9-56D4-42B0-91E7-702511A41E0D}"/>
      <FieldRef ID="{1C9A5A95-12EA-4FED-8D2B-419C0E883DAF}"/>
    </FieldRefs>
  </ContentType>
    <!-- Do not change the value of the Name attribute below. If
it does not match the folder name of the List Definition project
item, an error will occur when the project is run. -->
    <ListTemplate
        Name="Chapter3ListDef"
```

```
            Type="10999"
            BaseType="0"
            OnQuickLaunch="TRUE"
            DisallowContentTypes="FALSE"
            SecurityBits="11"
            Sequence="410"
            DisplayName="Chapter3ListDefinition"
            Description="My List Definition"
            Image="/_layouts/images/itgen.png"/>
    </Elements>
```

9. In the `Elements.xml` file inside the `ListInstance1` folder, change the `TemplateType` attribute to the same number as the one provided in the `ListDefinition Elements.xml` file for the attribute type. Also add a default row to the list instance that gets populated when the list instance gets created. Your `Elements.xml` in the `ListInstance1` folder should look as follows:

```xml
<?xml version="1.0" encoding="utf-8"?>
<Elements xmlns="http://schemas.microsoft.com/sharepoint/">
    <ListInstance Title="Chapter3ListDefinition - Chapter3ListInst"
                OnQuickLaunch="TRUE"
                TemplateType="10999"
                Url="Lists/Chapter3ListInst"
                Description="My List Instance">
        <Data>
          <Rows>
            <Row>
              <Field Name="Title">Movie</Field>
              <Field Name="Chap3Amt">10.00</Field>
              <Field Name="Chap3Cat">Entertainment</Field>
            </Row>
          </Rows>
        </Data>
    </ListInstance>
</Elements>
```

10. In the `Schema.xml` file underneath the `ListDefinition1` folder, add a new attribute `EnableContentTypes="True"` to the list node. Part of the list node is provided as follows:

```xml
<List xmlns:ows="Microsoft SharePoint" Title="Chapter3ListDefiniti
on" EnableContentTypes="TRUE"
```

11. Add the field definitions that we added to the `Elements.xml` file under the `ListDefinition1` folder to the `<Fields>` section in `Schema.xml`. The following is the `Fields` section in `Schema.xml`:

```xml
<Fields>
        <Field ID="{ACFCD9F9-56D4-42B0-91E7-702511A41E0D}"
Name="Chap3Amt" Description="Chap3 Expense Amount" Type="Currency"
```

```
DisplayName="Chap3 Expense Amount" Required="TRUE" LCID="1033"></
Field>
        <Field ID="{1C9A5A95-12EA-4FED-8D2B-419C0E883DAF}"
Name="Chap3Cat" Description="Chap3 Expense Category" Type="Choice"
DisplayName="Chap3 Expense Category" Required="TRUE">
            <CHOICES>
                <CHOICE>Books</CHOICE>
                <CHOICE>Food</CHOICE>
                <CHOICE>Rent</CHOICE>
                <CHOICE>Entertainment</CHOICE>
                <CHOICE>ISP</CHOICE>
                <CHOICE>Cable</CHOICE>
            </CHOICES>
        </Field>
    </Fields>
```

12. Add a `ContentTypeRef` node to the `<ContentTypes>` section in `Schema.xml`. The ID attribute for this element should be the same as the one defined in the `Elements.xml` underneath the `ListDefinition1` folder. The `ContentRef` node is as follows:

```
<ContentTypeRef ID="0x0100794FFBC7EB4A4441AFC07DA551BB610E"></
ContentTypeRef>
```

13. Add the `FieldRef` elements to the default view in the section `<ViewFields>`. The following code shows the listing of `ViewFields` section:

```
<ViewFields>
        <FieldRef Name="Attachments"></FieldRef>
        <FieldRef Name="LinkTitle"></FieldRef>
        <FieldRef Name="Chap3Amt"></FieldRef>
        <FieldRef Name="Chap3Cat"></FieldRef>
    </ViewFields>
```

14. Press *F5* to build and run the application. This will bring up the site that was provided during the project creation wizard. Your list is created with a row already populated as follows:

How it works...

In the previous recipes, we have explained how the XML schema is used by the SharePoint to create the necessary fields and content types. In this recipe, the added item is a list definition. A list definition, also referred to as a list template provides the information on what the list contains. It is like an architectural diagram for a building. You can use it to build many buildings of the same type. Similarly, a list definition provides information on whether we allow management of content types, if so, what content type the list uses, whether we need to allow it on the quick launch toolbar and so on. The main attributes of a list template are as follows:

Attribute Name	Description
AllowDeletion	A Boolean flag to indicate whether the list can be deleted or not. When set to false, you do not get the menu item delete in this list in the settings page.
Name	Provides the unique name for the list template.
Type	Not to conflict with the default list types provided, always use number above 10000.
DisallowContentTypes	When set to false, it allows the management of the content types.
SecurityBits	Item level security on the list.

More information on the attributes that can be passed in the `ListTemplate` can be found on MSDN at: `http://msdn.microsoft.com/en-us/library/ms439434.aspx`.

Using this list definition, we created a list instance and provided a default row. A list instance can override some of the properties like `VersioningEnabled`, `OnQuickLaunch`, and `Hidden` that are set on list definition. The properties on the list instance will always prevail over the properties set on list definition. More information on all the attributes that can be set on list instance can found on MSDN at: `http://msdn.microsoft.com/en-us/library/ms476062.aspx`.

See also

▶ *Working with Web Parts* recipe

5
Web Parts

In this chapter, we will cover:

- ▶ Creating a visual web part
- ▶ Creating a code-only web part (sandboxed solution)
- ▶ Creating AJAX enabled web parts
- ▶ Adding configuration properties to web parts
- ▶ Creating connectable web parts
- ▶ Creating a Silverlight web part

Introduction

Today's web pages are very dynamic showing different information. Usually this is done by dividing up the web page into multiple regions. For example, a portal can show news in one region and weather information in another. These regions occupy some portion of the web page and provide unique functionality to end users. End users also have opportunities to customize these regions like adding them to a different location in the web page or entirely removing them from the page. Different technologies call these regions by different names like portlets or widgets. These regions are called **Web Parts** in SharePoint. From an end user perspective a web part is a region on the web page that can be customized using browser interface. Whereas from a developer perspective, it is a class that renders content on a particular location on the web page. SharePoint introduced web parts way back in SharePoint Team Services. Since then, the technology is evolved and is available to ASP.Net developers also. Now the SharePoint web parts are derived from their ASP.Net counterparts. Since web parts run under the context of the page that it is hosted on and also on the security context of the user accessing the page, the same web part can be made to show different data based on the user's security context. For example, if we have a web part that lists information about a department's budget, the VP of finance is able to see all the different department's budget information whereas a department director can only see his/her department's budget information.

Web parts are ASP.Net custom controls that are inherited from the `WebPart` class in the `System.Web.UI.WebControls.WebParts` namespace. Web parts cannot just be added to any page. The pages that can host web parts are called **Web Part Pages**. The web pages that can host a web part should have `WebPartManager` objects and `WebPartZone` controls.

Web part zones are container controls that can host one or more web parts. The web part manager object keeps track of all the web parts on the page and their customizations. In SharePoint, web part manager and web part zones are inherited from `SPWebPartManager` and `SPWebPartZone` class respectively. The web pages that can host web parts are inherited from `WebPartPage` in the `Microsoft.SharePoint.WebPartPages` namespace. For more information on the web part pages refer to MSDN at the following URL: `http://msdn.microsoft.com/en-us/library/microsoft.sharepoint.webpartpages.webpart.aspx`.

In SharePoint, web parts can also be inherited from `Microsoft.SharePoint.WebPartPages.WebPart`. This is only provided for legacy compatibility purposes. It is not recommended to inherit your custom web parts from this class. But there are situations like cross page connections, communication of web parts between zones, and web part caching where you may want to use this class instead. If you have a need to develop a web part that falls in the above said situations, refer to SharePoint Services 2003 SDK.

In the previous versions of Visual Studio, developing web parts were not intuitive as we did not have a visual graphics designer to place the controls and provide a proper layout. Some SharePoint developers developed ASP.Net web user controls and used that as a web part in the previous versions of SharePoint, as user control development provided designer support. If you did use the web user control approach to develop the web part, you had to build a wrapper to use it in the SharePoint environment or use open source generic wrappers such as SmartPart. This is not the case with Visual Studio 2010. It provides templates to create the visual web parts. The reason it is called visual web part is because we get visual graphics designer support to place the controls and provide a proper layout. We do not have to resort to writing wrappers or using open source generic wrappers. There is support for code-only web parts too. In this chapter, we will use both the templates and develop web parts for different deployment targets.

Creating a visual web part

In this recipe, we will learn how to create a visual web part. The web part will show data from an external database in a grid format. For our recipe, we will make use of the `AdventureWorks` database.

Getting ready

For this recipe, you need to have access to the `AdventureWorks` database. You can download it from: `http://msftdbprodsamples.codeplex.com/`.

How to do it...

1. Launch your Visual Studio 2010 IDE as an administrator (right-click on the shortcut and select **Run as administrator**).

2. Select **File | New | Project**. The new project wizard dialog box will be displayed (make sure to select **.NET Framework 3.5** in the top drop-down box).

3. Select **Empty SharePoint Project** under **Visual C# | SharePoint | 2010** node from **Installed Templates** section on left-hand side.

4. Name the project **EmployeeList** and provide a directory location where you want to save the project and click on **OK** to proceed to the next step in the wizard.

5. By default, Visual Studio selects the SharePoint site available on the machine. Select **Deploy as Farm Solution** and click on **Next** to proceed to the next step in the wizard.

6. This should create an empty SharePoint project. To this project add a new item and select **Visual Web Part** as shown and provide **EmployeeList** as the name.

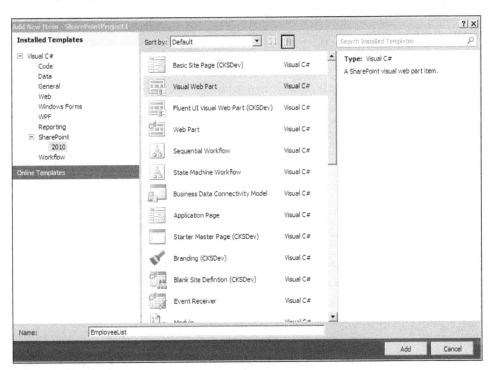

7. Visual Studio creates a folder named EmployeeList and adds some files. The designer also opens up the EmployeeListUserControl.ascx. control.

8. To this user control, add an ASP.Net GridView control as shown in the following image and set its width property to 100%.

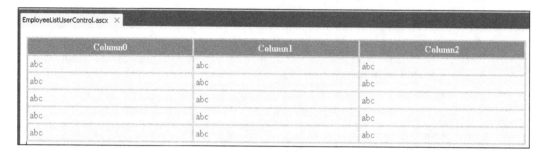

9. Open the code file EmployeeListUserControl.ascx.cs and add the code to display data from the employee table in the AdventureWorks database. Your code file should look as follows (Make sure to change the necessary database connection strings to your environment):

```csharp
using System;
using System.Web.UI;
using System.Web.UI.WebControls;
using System.Web.UI.WebControls.WebParts;
using System.Data.SqlClient;
using System.Data;

namespace EmployeeList.EmployeeList
{
    public partial class EmployeeListUserControl : UserControl
    {
        protected void Page_Load(object sender, EventArgs e)
        {
            bindGridView();
        }

        private void bindGridView()    {

            string connStr = "Server=intsql;Database=AdventureWork
s;Integrated Security=true";
```

```
SqlConnection mySQLconnection = new SqlConnection
(connStr);

if (mySQLconnection.State == ConnectionState.Closed)
{
    mySQLconnection.Open();
}
    SqlCommand mySqlCommand = new SqlCommand("SELECT top 10
Person.Contact.LastName,Person.Contact.FirstName,Person.Contact.
EmailAddress, HumanResources.Employee.HireDate, HumanResources.
Employee.BirthDate, HumanResources.Employee.Title FROM  Person.
Contact INNER JOIN HumanResources.Employee ON Person.Contact.
ContactID = HumanResources.Employee.ContactID", mySQLconnection);
    SqlDataAdapter mySqlAdapter = new SqlDataAdapter
    (mySqlCommand);
    DataSet myDataSet = new DataSet();
    mySqlAdapter.Fill(myDataSet);
    DataView myDataView = new DataView();
    myDataView = myDataSet.Tables[0].DefaultView;

    GridView1.DataSource = myDataView;
    GridView1.DataBind();

    if (mySQLconnection.State == ConnectionState.Open)
    {
        mySQLconnection.Close();
    }
    }
}
}
```

10. Open the `EmployeeList.webpart` file and change the description to **Employee List Demo Web Part**.

11. Build and run this solution. Edit the page and navigate to **Insert | Web Parts** and from the web parts list, select **Custom** category to insert our newly created **EmployeeList** web part as follows:

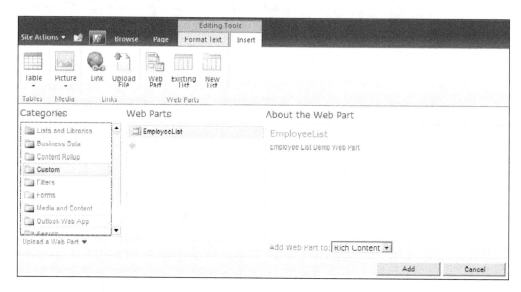

12. The web part will retrieve the data from the database as it is added to the page. The final result will be similar to the following screenshot:

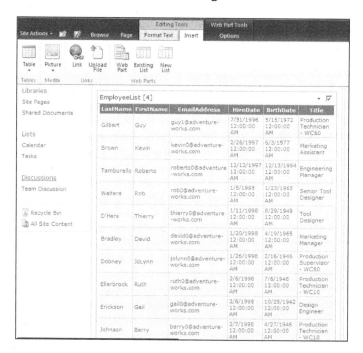

How it works...

When you create a visual web part in Visual Studio 2010, it creates a series of files. The file that we worked on is an ASP.Net web user control. This control has a designer interface, and VS 2010 also generates the code behind a file. Visual Studio also generates a wrapper class `EmployeeList` in the file `EmployeeList.cs`. This is the class that is inherited from the `WebPart` class. This class also overrides the `CreateChildControls` method where it loads the user control that we created.

By default, Visual Studio deploys the user control to the SharePoint root. It deploys the user control to the `ControlTemplates` folder underneath the `Templates` folder. In here, it creates a folder with the same name as the project name and underneath it creates a subfolder in the name of the visual web part and deploys the user control here. In our case, both are named `EmployeeList` and hence you will see two folders.

If you open the `EmployeeList.cs`, you will see there are only two lines of code in the `CreateChildControls` method. It loads the control from the `ControlTemplates` location and adds it to the web parts' controls collection. If you were not using a visual web part method of development, this is where you would have written code to create controls and add them to the web part.

Visual Studio also creates a `.webpart` file. This file provides information to the SharePoint environment to show the web part in the web part gallery of the site collection. This can be thought of as the metadata file for our web part. In here you will provide information such as title, description, chrome state, any icon that you want to associate to the web part, and other properties. It also contains information on the code assembly of the web part. Refer to MSDN at: `http://msdn.microsoft.com/en-us/library/ms227561(VS.80).aspx` for all the properties that you can set for the web part.

Even though the `.webpart` file can provide definitions for more than one web part in the solution, Visual Studio 2010 always generates a separate `.webpart` file for each of the web parts in the solution.

The `Elements.xml` file as described in the previous chapters provides the configuration information to the feature definition about the web part. This is where you can set the category under which your web part will be listed. By default, it is listed under `Custom` category. Another important piece of information you notice in this `Elements.xml` file is the `List=113` attribute in the `Module` element. This tells the SharePoint where to deploy the web part. `113` is the template ID for the document library `_catalogs/wp`.

There's more...

Even though there is a visual web part template in the Visual Studio, you might be wondering why we started with an empty SharePoint project? The reason is when we use the visual web part template, it does not provide an opportunity for us to name the web part item. You can always change it in the IDE and sometimes you may have to rename some instances manually. If you are not careful and miss one or two of these renaming instances, it can cause annoying errors while deploying. Hence, to make life easier, you can always start with empty SharePoint project, add an item, provide the name you want to use for the web part and VS 2010 will take care of generating the files with the name you provided for the item.

Visual web parts and sandboxed solution

When you create a visual web part solution in Visual Studio, it does not provide an opportunity to select the sandboxed mode for deployment. This is because, the web user control generated is stored in the root folder. In sandboxed mode, you cannot acces the root folder and hence cannot develop the Visual web parts. The option for developing web parts in the sandboxed mode is a code-only web part. Apart from that, you cannot access the database or web services in sandboxed mode via a web part.

Web Parts Gallery

Navigate to **Site Actions | Site Settings | Gallery | Web Parts** on your site. This is where you can see all the web parts deployed for your site collection. You can see the `.webpart` files deployed to this location. Whenever you add the web part to your page, this is where SharePoint goes to get the metadata information for your web part. You may also come across some `.dwp` files which are also the web part files, the previous version of SharePoint (version 2, that is, SharePoint 2003) used.

See also

▶ *Creating a code-only web part (sandboxed solution)* recipe

Creating a code-only web part (sandboxed solution)

In this recipe, we will develop a code-only web part that can be deployed as a sandboxed solution. For this recipe, we will create a data entry screen to add an item to a SharePoint list.

In this example, we will provide a user interface for bug reporting. Testers can come into the site and enter information about the bug they found during testing. The web part then inserts this data to a SharePoint list. Based on the category selected, we would associate the bug to a developer. In case we had a workflow associated with this list, we could have created a task for the developer and sent an alert about the entered bug.

Getting ready

Create a custom list named **Bugs** with columns **Title**, **Description**, **Category**, and **Developer**. The **Description** column is of **multiple lines of text** type, whereas others are **single lines of text** type. All the columns are required.

How to do it...

1. Launch your Visual Studio 2010 IDE as an administrator (right-click on the shortcut and select **Run as administrator**).

2. Select **File | New | Project**. The new project wizard dialog box will be displayed (make sure to select **.NET Framework 3.5** in the top drop-down box).

3. Select **Empty SharePoint Project** under **Visual C# | SharePoint | 2010** node from **Installed Templates** section on the left-hand side.

4. Name the project **SandboxWebPart** and provide a directory location where you want to save the project and click on **OK** to proceed to the next step in the wizard.

5. By default, Visual Studio selects the SharePoint site available on the machine. Select **Deploy as Sandboxed Solution** and click on **Finish** to create the project.

6. Add a new item to this project and select **Web Part** from the list and name it **BugList**. This will create a folder named **BugList** with `BugList.cs`, `BugList.webpart`, and `Elements.xml` files in it.

7. Visual Studio will have automatically opened the `BugList.cs` and if you look through the code, it has already added a method `CreateChildControls` in it. This is where you create the user interface for our data entry screen. The code in `CreateChildControls` method is as follows:

```
protected override void CreateChildControls()
    {
        bugTitle = new TextBox();
        bugDescription = new TextBox();
        ddlCategory = new DropDownList();
        btnAdd = new Button();

        bugTitle.MaxLength = 100;
        bugTitle.Columns = 50;
        bugTitle.ID = "bugTitle";

        bugDescription.MaxLength = 255;
        bugDescription.TextMode = TextBoxMode.MultiLine;
        bugDescription.Columns = 50;
        bugDescription.Height = new Unit(172, System.Web.
UI.WebControls.UnitType.Pixel);
        bugDescription.Width = new Unit(100, System.Web.
```

```
I.WebControls.UnitType.Percentage);
            bugDescription.ID = "bugDescription";

        ddlCategory.Items.Add(new ListItem("SharePoint",
        "SharePoint"));
        ddlCategory.Items.Add(new ListItem("ASP.Net", "ASP.
         Net"));
        ddlCategory.Items.Add(new ListItem("Database",
        "Database"));
        ddlCategory.ID = "ddlCategory";

        btnAdd.Click += new EventHandler(btnAdd_Click);
        btnAdd.Height = new Unit(27, System.Web.
        UI.WebControls.UnitType.Pixel);
        btnAdd.Text = "Add Bug to List";
        btnAdd.Width = new Unit(130, System.Web.
        UI.WebControls.UnitType.Pixel);
        btnAdd.ID = "btnAdd";


        Controls.Add(new LiteralControl("<table>"));

        Controls.Add(new LiteralControl("<tr><td><b>Bug
        Title:</b></td><td>"));
        Controls.Add(bugTitle);
        Controls.Add(new LiteralControl("</td></tr>"));

        Controls.Add(new LiteralControl("<tr><td><b>Bug
        Description:</b></td><td>"));
        Controls.Add(bugDescription);
        Controls.Add(new LiteralControl("</td></tr>"));

        Controls.Add(new LiteralControl("<tr><td><b>Bug
        Category:</b></td><td>"));
        Controls.Add(ddlCategory);
        Controls.Add(new LiteralControl("</td></tr>"));

        Controls.Add(new LiteralControl("<tr><td
        colspan=\"2\">"));
        Controls.Add(btnAdd);
        Controls.Add(new LiteralControl("</td></tr>"));

        Controls.Add(new LiteralControl("</table>"));
    }
```

8. Add the code for the button click event handler to create the list item when a user clicks the button. The code to create the list item should be as follows:

```
void btnAdd_Click(object sender, EventArgs args)
{
    AddListItem();
}

private void AddListItem()
{
    SPWeb web = SPContext.Current.Web;
    SPList bugs = web.Lists["Bugs"];

    if (bugs != null)
    {
        SPListItemCollection itemCol = bugs.Items;
        SPListItem bug = itemCol.Add();

        bug["Title"] = bugTitle.Text;
        bug["Description"] = bugDescription.Text;
        string sCat = ddlCategory.SelectedValue;
        string sDeveloper = "";

        switch (sCat)
        {
            case "SharePoint":
                sDeveloper = "Balaji";
                break;
            case "Database":
                sDeveloper = "DB Developer";
                break;
            case "ASP.Net":
                sDeveloper = "Web Developer";
                break;

        }

        bug["Category"] = sCat;
        bug["Developer"] = sDeveloper;

        bug.Update();
    }
}
```

9. Open the `BugList.webpart` file and change the description to **Bug List Demo Web Part**.

10. Build and run the project. Add the web part to the page. When you click the **Add Bug to List** button, the item will be added to the **Bugs** list with the developer selected based on the category as shown in the following screenshot:

How it works...

The code is self-explanatory. We take the values from the controls and create a list item based on the server object model.

Compared to the previous recipe, in this, we do not have ASP.Net web user control. Hence there is no ASCX file and there is no deployment to the `ControlTemplates` location either. Not having a ASCX file means, no designer support and hence we had to manually create the controls and add it to the controls collection. This is exactly what we did in the `CreateChildControls` method. We had to manually provide a user interface format and event handler for the button click.

The rest of the elements are similar to the previous recipe. We have the `.webparts` file where we provide the metadata information for the web part. The `Elements.xml` will provide the configuration information for the feature definition.

There's more...

As we saw in this recipe, creating a good UI based web part is a very tedious process without designer support. Microsoft has released the Visual Studio 2010 SharePoint power tools. These tools provide support to the visual web part in sandboxed mode. You can download these power tools from the Visual Studio Gallery at the following URL: `http://visualstudiogallery.msdn.microsoft.com/8e602a8c-6714-4549-9e95-f3700344b0d9/`.

As indicated previously, in sandboxed mode there is no access to the root folder. So, in the visual web part support for `sandboxed` mode, there is no web user control deployed to the root folder. Instead as we add the controls to the designer and make modifications to properties of the control, behind the scenes, Visual Studio adds the code to the `CreateChildControls` method automatically. So in principle, it works the same as our recipe here.

Deployment of web parts

In SharePoint 2010, you can deploy web parts in three locations:

1. **Solution gallery**: This applies to sandboxed web parts like the one we created in this recipe. This same concept can also be used to deploy the web parts if you are using a hosting or cloud solution, such as Office 365 or SharePoint online where you do not have access to the SharePoint root. This is the new method and applies to this version of SharePoint only. In here, you will just upload the solution file to the solution gallery and your solution will be available for use in the site collection.

2. **Bin directory**: You can deploy to the `bin` directory of the web application. This method helps in releasing your web part to a specific web application and you can have local permission set for that web application. By default, Visual Studio always deploys to **Global Assembly Cache (GAC)**. If you want to deploy to the web application bin directory, then change the **Assembly Deployment Target** property of your project to **WebApplication** as shown in the following screenshot:

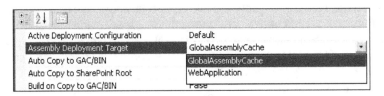

3. **Global Assembly Cache (GAC)**: You can deploy to the global assembly cache. Here, code libraries and web parts are shared across all the web applications in the server farm. In order to deploy assemblies to GAC, one should be an administrator (local or domain).

When you deploy a web part at the farm level, you need to mark the web part as `SafeControl` in the `web.config`. You can set the `SafeControl` settings in the Visual Studio 2010 by navigating to the **Safe Control Entries** collection of the web part as shown in the following screenshot:

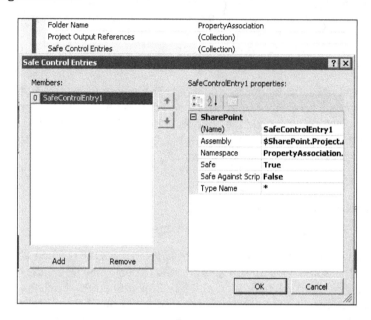

Here is an example of one of the web parts listed in the `web.config SafeControls` section:

```
<SafeControl Assembly="PropertyAssociation, Version=1.0.0.0,
Culture=neutral, PublicKeyToken=b0efe28e77dc8482" Namespace="PropertyA
ssociation.PropertyAssociation" TypeName="*" Safe="True" SafeAgainstSc
ript="False" />
```

In SharePoint 2010, users who are in designer roles and higher are the only ones that can configure the web part properties. Before contributor role, users also had access to the configuration properties. The changes are due to the fact that SharePoint 2010 provides a Client Object Model that can be used in web parts and can manipulate data on sites. More information on Client Object Model can be found in *Chapter 7, Working with Client Object Model*. If you want to change this default behavior, change the `SafeAgaintScript` attribute to **True** in the `SafeControl` element.

Regardless of the method used to deploy, the `.webpart` file is the main component that provides metadata information about the web part for SharePoint. This file is included in the solution file and you can use `STSADM` or `PowerShell` commands to deploy the solution to either bin location or GAC.

Versioning of web parts

Versioning of web parts are a little trickier than deployment. If your web part was just a bug fix without any changes to the public interface or assembly versions, then you could just install over the existing web part and it should be reflected on the sites where the web part is used.

If you have changed the assembly versions, deploy the new assembly to GAC or bin based on your deployment process and add a redirect directive in the `web.config` of the site where the web part is loaded. The reason is that the web parts that are already deployed on the pages refer to the older version of the assembly and now are not able to reference the assemblies as the versions have changed. Hence you need to add the redirection directive in the `web.config`. This redirects the references that are used by older versions to the newer ones. Here is an example of the redirect directive in the `web.config`:

```
<runtime>
    <assemblyBinding xmlns="urn:schemas-microsoft-com:asm.v1">
      <dependentAssembly>
        <assemblyIdentity name="MyWebPart.MyWebPart" publicKeyToken="7
1e9bce111e9429c" culture="neutral" />
        <bindingRedirect oldVersion="1.0.0.0" newVersion="2.0.0.0" />
      </dependentAssembly>
</assmeblyBinding>
</runtime>
```

If you have changed the public properties of the web part, your code has to manage those changes. You have two options to do this conversion.

1. If you are migrating from old SharePoint version web parts to newer ones, override the `AfterDeserialize` method. This method is invoked the first time the page loads and you can map the properties from the old ones to the newer ones.

2. The second method is by implementing the `IVersioningPersonalizable` interface.

The `IVersioningPersonalizable` interface has one method called `Load` that needs to be implemented. The following is the signature of the `Load` method:

```
public interface IVersioningPersonalizable
    {

    void Load(IDictionary unknownProperties);

    }
```

The `unknownProperties` contains both **User** and **Shared** scope properties. When the page is running in **User** mode, only the **User** scoped unknown properties are supplied. The `unknownProperties` are key/value pairs of the missing properties where the key is the name of the property that is missing.

The `Load` method provides a list of all the unknown properties and you loop through it and map it to the newer ones. The following is the code that can be used to loop through and associate the old property to the new one.

```
// Find the property we want to update...
            foreach (System.Collections.DictionaryEntry kvPair in
this.missingProperties)
                {
                this.Controls.Add(new LiteralControl(kvPair.Key + ": "
+ kvPair.Value + "<br/>"));
                // Let's save OldProperty value into NewProperty
                if (kvPair.Key.ToString() == "OldProperty")
                {
                    this.NewProperty = "Updated: " + kvPair.Value;
                    this.SetPersonalizationDirty();
                }
            }
```

The accompanying code for this book contains an example that shows how the entire code works. It is recommended that you come back to this example after you have completed the *Adding Configuration Properties to web part* recipe. Here are the steps you need to take in order to deploy the `PropertyAssociation` web part.

1. Uncomment the old property in `PropertyAssociation.cs`. Compile and deploy the web part. Add it to the page. You should see two properties, `OldProperty` and `NewProperty` in the web part properties pane.

2. Set **Hello World** as the value for the `OldProperty` and save the page.

3. Comment the `OldProperty` in the code and redeploy the web part. When you refresh the page, you should see the **OldProperty:Hello World** message as shown here:

PropertyAssociation

OldProperty: Hello World

See also

▶ *Creating AJAX enabled web parts* recipe

Creating AJAX enabled web parts

In this recipe, we will rewrite the first recipe to utilize the AJAX. For this recipe, we will create a visual web part that shows the data from the `AdventureWorks` database. We will add pagination to the `GridView` that we used in the first recipe.

Getting ready

You should complete the previous recipes successfully to follow this one.

How to do it...

1. Launch your Visual Studio 2010 IDE as an administrator (right-click on the shortcut and select **Run as administrator**).

2. Select **File | New | Project**. The new project wizard dialog box will be displayed (Make sure to select **.NET Framework 3.5** in the top drop-down box.)

3. Select **Empty SharePoint Project** under **Visual C# | SharePoint | 2010** node from the **Installed Templates** section on the left-hand side.

4. Name the project **AJAXEnabled** and provide a directory location where you want to save the project and click on **OK** to proceed to the next step in the wizard.

5. By default, Visual Studio selects the SharePoint site available on the machine. Select **Deploy as Farm Solution** and click on **Finish** to proceed to the next step in the wizard.

6. This should create an empty SharePoint project. To this project add a new item and select **Visual Web Part** and provide **AJAXEmployeeList** as the name.

7. Visual Studio creates a folder named **AJAXEmployeeList** and adds a series of files. The designer also opens up the `AJAXEmployeeListUserControl.ascx`.

8. To this user control add an `UpdatePanel` found in the **AJAX Extensions** section in the **Toolbox** tab. Add `ASP.Net GridView` control to this `UpdatePanel` and also set its width property to **100%**.

9. From the properties window of **GridView**, set **AllowPaging** to **true** and add an event handler to the **GridView** instance's `PageIndexChanging`.

10. Open the code file AJAXEmployeeListUserControl.ascx.cs and add the code to display the data from the employee Table in the AdventureWorks database. Also add code to the GridView PageIndexChanging event handler to handle the pagination events. Your code should be as follows:

```
using System;
using System.Web.UI;
using System.Web.UI.WebControls;
using System.Web.UI.WebControls.WebParts;
using System.Data.SqlClient;
using System.Data;

namespace AJAXEnabled.AJAXEmployeeList
{
    public partial class AJAXEmployeeListUserControl : UserControl
    {
        protected void Page_Load(object sender, EventArgs e)
        {
            bindGridView();
        }

        private void bindGridView()
        {

            string connStr = "Server=intsql;Database=AdventureWork
s;Integrated Security=true";

            SqlConnection mySQLconnection = new
SqlConnection(connStr);

            if (mySQLconnection.State == ConnectionState.Closed)
            {
                mySQLconnection.Open();
            }
            SqlCommand mySqlCommand = new SqlCommand("SELECT
Person.Contact.LastName,Person.Contact.FirstName,Person.Contact.
EmailAddress, HumanResources.Employee.HireDate, HumanResources.
Employee.BirthDate, HumanResources.Employee.Title FROM  Person.
Contact INNER JOIN HumanResources.Employee ON Person.Contact.
ContactID = HumanResources.Employee.ContactID", mySQLconnection);
            SqlDataAdapter mySqlAdapter = new SqlDataAdapter(mySql
Command);
            DataSet myDataSet = new DataSet();
            mySqlAdapter.Fill(myDataSet);
            DataView myDataView = new DataView();
            myDataView = myDataSet.Tables[0].DefaultView;
```

```
            GridView1.DataSource = myDataView;
            GridView1.DataBind();

            if (mySQLconnection.State == ConnectionState.Open)
            {
                mySQLconnection.Close();
            }
        }

        protected void GridView1_PageIndexChanging(object sender,
    GridViewPageEventArgs e)
        {
            GridView1.PageIndex = e.NewPageIndex;
            bindGridView();
        }
    }
}
```

11. Open `AJAXEmployeeList.cs` and override the `OnInit` method and add code to verify if the `ScriptManager` exists in the page or not. If not, add an instance of a `ScriptManager`. Your code should look like the following:

```
protected override void OnInit(EventArgs e)
        {
            if (Page != null && ScriptManager.GetCurrent(Page) ==
            null)
            {
                Page.Form.Controls.AddAt(0, new ScriptManager());
            }
            base.OnInit(e);
        }
```

12. Open the `AJAXEmployeeList.webpart` file and change the description to **AJAX Employee List Demo Web Part** and the title to **AJAX Employee List**.

13. Build and run this solution. Edit the page and navigate to **Insert | Web Parts** and from the web parts list select the **Custom** category to insert our newly created **Ajax Employee List** web part as shown in the following screenshot. Try out pagination; you can see there is no flicker of the entire page due to `PostBack`.

AJAX Employee List

LastName	FirstName	EmailAddress	HireDate	BirthDate	Title
Poland	Carole	carole0@adventure-works.com	1/20/1999 12:00:00 AM	11/19/1973 12:00:00 AM	Production Technician - WC30
Li	George	george0@adventure-works.com	1/22/1999 12:00:00 AM	5/18/1967 12:00:00 AM	Production Technician - WC30
Yukish	Gary	gary0@adventure-works.com	1/23/1999 12:00:00 AM	6/17/1978 12:00:00 AM	Production Technician - WC40
Petculescu	Cristian	cristian0@adventure-works.com	1/23/1999 12:00:00 AM	5/13/1974 12:00:00 AM	Production Supervisor - WC10
Sam	Raymond	raymond0@adventure-works.com	1/24/1999 12:00:00 AM	4/2/1957 12:00:00 AM	Production Technician - WC20
Bueno	Janaina	janaina0@adventure-works.com	1/24/1999 12:00:00 AM	3/3/1975 12:00:00 AM	Application Specialist
Hohman	Bob	bob0@adventure-works.com	1/25/1999 12:00:00 AM	9/16/1969 12:00:00 AM	Production Technician - WC50
Mohamed	Shammi	shammi0@adventure-works.com	1/25/1999 12:00:00 AM	11/5/1970 12:00:00 AM	Production Technician - WC40
Moschell	Linda	linda0@adventure-works.com	1/26/1999 12:00:00 AM	8/17/1977 12:00:00 AM	Production Technician - WC50
Martin	Mindy	mindy0@adventure-works.com	1/26/1999 12:00:00 AM	12/22/1974 12:00:00 AM	Benefits Specialist

1 2 3 4 5 6 7 8 9 10 ...

How it works...

Asynchronous JavaScript and XML (AJAX) is a way to utilize XML to respond to control events and user inputs by making HTTP asynchronous requests in the background. In ASP.Net, the `ScriptManager` object is the key to making AJAX run on ASP.Net applications. This non-visual control helps to load the JavaScript necessary to do AJAX calls. SharePoint 2010 provides native support for AJAX. That means we can use ASP.Net AJAX controls without modifying the `web.config`.

The `ScriptManager` should be the first control on the page before any of the other controls are added. This is because, the scripts has to be loaded first for the AJAX controls to render properly. We verified this by overriding the `OnInit` method. Some of the master pages already have the `ScriptManager` object loaded. That is the reason, we verified: to find out if it already existed or not. Some custom master pages may have omitted the `ScriptManager`, and this code will make certain that the `ScriptManager` is added to the page.

In this recipe, we made use of the `UpdatePanel`. This control provides an opportunity for us to manage which controls need to be asynchronously updated and at what events. We used this `UpdatePanel` on the `GridView` and by default, it responds to all the events on the `GridView`.

The rest of deployment and other properties are exactly similar to the previous recipe.

There's more...

The `UpdatePanel` is a simple control to use but is not very efficient or scalable. Whenever you invoke the page that contains the `UpdatePanel` asynchronously, on the server side, the entire page is recreated. When the response is received by the client, the AJAX JavaScipt, only updates the area that the `UpdatePanel` belongs to. This makes the server load more even for a small portion of update. Hence in real world programming, coders code to respond to the AJAX low-level events and make the update process more effective. There are different alternatives and you can use some of these methods in SharePoint as well. Refer to MSDN for more information on ASP.Net AJAX at the following URL: `http://msdn.microsoft.com/en-us/magazine/cc163480.aspx`.

See also

- ▶ *Creating a visual web part* recipe
- ▶ *Adding configuration properties to web parts* recipe

Adding configuration properties to web parts

The web parts are configured by authorized users. You can use that as an opportunity and provide properties that can be set during the configuration time rather than hard coding in the code. In this recipe, we will learn how to add those configuration properties to the web parts.

In our first recipe, we had hard coded the database connection string. In this recipe, we will modify the web part to get the database connection string from the configuration property.

Getting ready

Since this recipe is a modification of the first recipe, you should complete that recipe successfully in order to follow this one.

How to do it...

1. If you have closed your Visual Studio IDE, launch it now as an administrator and open the solution file that we created in the first recipe.

2. Open the `EmployeeList.cs` and add a property called `DBConnectionString` with attributes as follows:

   ```
   Personalizable(PersonalizationScope.Shared),
   WebBrowsable, Category("DB Connection"),
   WebDisplayName("DB Connection String"),
   WebDescription("DB Connection string.")]
   public string DBConnectionString { get; set; }
   ```

3. Open the `EmployeeListUserControl.ascx.cs` file and add a property called `EmpList` as follows:

   ```
   public EmployeeList EmpList { get; set; }
   ```

4. In the `bindGridView` method, comment the connection string and add the following lines of code:

   ```
   string connStr = EmpList.DBConnectionString;

       if (string.IsNullOrEmpty(connStr)) return;
   ```

5. Make changes to the `CreateChildControls` method in `EmployeeList.cs` so that the `EmpList` property is set to the user control that is created. Your code in the `CreateChildControls` method should look like the following:

   ```
   //Control control = Page.LoadControl(_ascxPath);
      EmployeeListUserControl control = Page.LoadControl(_ascxPath) as
   EmployeeListUserControl;

                if (control != null)
                    control.EmpList = this;

             Controls.Add(control);
   ```

6. Build and run the project and follow the same steps as the previous recipes to add the web part to the page. This time the web part will not list the data from the table as it has no default connection string. Edit the web part to open the properties dialog and you should see our newly defined property listed as shown in the following screenshot:

7. Enter connection string to your environment and click on the **OK** button and you should see the web part listing the data in the Employee table from the AdventureWorks database.

How it works...

The web part properties area or editor area as it is called, is implemented by a set of SharePoint specific classes called **Tool parts**. By default, SharePoint provides a WebPartToolPart class that is used to display the standard properties like appearance, layout, and other category properties. The CustomPropertyToolPart class is used to render the custom properties deployed to the web parts. When we deployed our property, the web part utilized this and displayed our property. The property type is used to determine the type of control that needs to display on the property sheet. The following table provides the different controls displayed based on the property type.

Custom Property Type	Control displayed
Boolean	Check box
String	Text box
Integer	Text box
DateTime	Text box
Enum	Drop-down list

The web part base class exposes many attributes that can be used to decorate a standard property that will be displayed in the web part properties page. In this recipe, we created a property called DBConnectionString and decorated it with attributes such as Personalizable, WebBrowsable, Category, WebDisplayName, and WebDescription. These properties tell the framework that it is a custom configuration property and hence needs to be displayed in the property page.

The `Personalizable` property defines that the property can be personalized and the scope is set to `Shared`. The other scope setting would be user-level personalization. When you define a property you need to be aware of the difference between `Shared-` and `user level` scope. A user-level scope makes this setting be changed and sets this as per user basis. A `Shared` scope is shared across all the users of the web part. Since we set our property as `Shared`, to verify it, navigate the page by adding a query string parameter called `PageView=Personal` to the URL of the page. This will not show the `DBConnection` property of the web part. You can toggle back to `Shared`, by changing the `PageView` value to `Shared`.

The `WebBrowsable` property instructs the SharePoint environment that this property should be made available in the property pages of the web part. The `Category` helps you to organize your custom properties under its own category in the property page. If you do not provide the `Category` attribute, by default SharePoint puts your custom property in the `Miscellaneous` category. You cannot add your custom properties to reserved categories like appearance, advanced, and layout. Through `WebDisplayname` and `WebDescription`, you will provide the property name and description respectively.

There's more...

By default, your custom category always comes at the bottom of the property page. Sometimes this may not be a suitable idea as inexperienced users can easily miss the property category. And also, if your web part requires complex property settings, you can always create your own `EditorPart` to add custom panes to the property pages of the web part. For more information on `EditorPart` refer to MSDN at: `http://msdn. microsoft.com/en-us/library/system.web.ui.webcontrols.webparts. editorpart(v=VS.90).aspx`.

See also

- ▶ *Creating a visual web part* recipe
- ▶ *Creating connectable web parts* recipe below

Creating connectable web parts

The connectable web parts or master-detail web parts are two different web parts that are connected to each other in a provider/consumer fashion. In this recipe, we will create two web parts where one is a provider and the other a consumer.

For this recipe, we will create a `DepartmentList` web part that acts as a provider and a `DepartmentEmployees` web part that acts as a consumer. Based on the row selected in the `DepartmentList` web part, we will list all the employees of the department in the `DepartmentEmployees` web part.

Getting ready

You should complete the previous recipes successfully so you understand the concept of web parts and its deployment to follow this one.

How to do it...

1. Launch your Visual Studio 2010 IDE as an administrator (right-click on the shortcut and select **Run as administrator**).

2. Select **File | New | Project**. The new project wizard dialog box will be displayed (make sure to select **.NET Framework 3.5** in the top drop-down box).

3. Select **Empty SharePoint Project** under **Visual C# | SharePoint | 2010** node from the **Installed Templates** section on the left-hand side.

4. Name the project **ConnectableWP** and provide a directory location where you want to save the project and click on **OK** to proceed to the next step in the wizard.

5. By default, Visual Studio selects the SharePoint site available on the machine. Select **Deploy as Farm Solution** and click on **Next** to proceed to the next step in the wizard.

6. This should create an empty SharePoint project. To this project add a new item and select **Visual Web Part** and provide **DepartmentList** as the name.

7. Visual Studio creates a folder named `DepartmentList` and adds some files. The designer also opens up the `DepartmentListUserControl.ascx`.

8. To this user control add an `ASP.Net GridView` control and set its width property to 100% and set its ID to `gvDepartments` and set the `AutoGenerateSelectButton` property to **true**.

9. To the project add an interface named `IDepartmentProvider` and define a `DepartmentId` property as follows:

```
using System;
using System.Collections.Generic;
using System.Linq;
using System.Text;

namespace ConnectableWP
{
    public interface IDepartmentProvider
    {
        string DepartmentId { get; }
    }
}
```

10. Open `DepartmentList.cs` and implement the `IDepartmentProvider` interface. Also add a method named `GetDepartmentProvider` that returns `IDepartmentProvider`. Decorate this method with the attribute `ConnectionProvider` and pass in a string parameter `DepartmentProvider`. Make changes to `CreateChildControls` such that the control is casted to the `DepartmentListUserControl`. Your code in `DepartmentList.cs` should be as follows:

```csharp
using System;
using System.ComponentModel;
using System.Web;
using System.Web.UI;
using System.Web.UI.WebControls;
using System.Web.UI.WebControls.WebParts;
using Microsoft.SharePoint;
using Microsoft.SharePoint.WebControls;

namespace ConnectableWP.DepartmentList
{
    [ToolboxItemAttribute(false)]
    public class DepartmentList : WebPart, IDepartmentProvider
    {
        // Visual Studio might automatically update this path when
        you change the Visual Web Part project item.
        private const string _ascxPath = @"~/_CONTROLTEMPLATES/
ConnectableWP/DepartmentList/DepartmentListUserControl.ascx";

        protected DepartmentListUserControl control;
        protected override void CreateChildControls()
        {
            // Control control = Page.LoadControl(_ascxPath);
            control = Page.LoadControl(_ascxPath) as
DepartmentListUserControl;

            if (control != null)
                Controls.Add(control);
        }

        [ConnectionProvider("DepartmentProvider")]
        public IDepartmentProvider GetDepartmentProvider()
        {
            return (this);
        }
```

```csharp
        string IDepartmentProvider.DepartmentId
        {
            get { return control.DepartmentId; }
        }
    }
}
```

11. Open the `DepartmentListUserControl.cs` and add a public property named
    `DepartmentId` of type string and also add code to get the department data from the
    `Adventureworks` database and bind it to the `GridView` control. Your code should
    be as follows. Make sure to change the connection strings to your environment.

```csharp
using System;
using System.Web.UI;
using System.Web.UI.WebControls;
using System.Web.UI.WebControls.WebParts;
using System.Data.SqlClient;
using System.Data;

namespace ConnectableWP.DepartmentList
{
    public partial class DepartmentListUserControl : UserControl
    {
        protected void Page_Load(object sender, EventArgs e)
        {
            bindGridView();
        }

        public string DepartmentId
        {
            get
            {
                if (this.gvDepartments.SelectedIndex >= 0)
                {
                    string sTemp = this.gvDepartments.
SelectedDataKey.Value.ToString(); ;
                    return (sTemp);
                }
                else
                {
                    return (String.Empty);
                }
            }
        }
```

```
        private void bindGridView()
        {

                string connStr = "Server=intsql;Database=AdventureWor
    ks;Integrated Security=true";


                if (string.IsNullOrEmpty(connStr)) return;

                SqlConnection mySQLconnection = new
    SqlConnection(connStr);

                if (mySQLconnection.State == ConnectionState.Closed)
                {
                    mySQLconnection.Open();
                }
                SqlCommand mySqlCommand = new SqlCommand("SELECT
    DepartmentId, Name, GroupName from AdventureWorks.HumanResources.
    Department", mySQLconnection);
                SqlDataAdapter mySqlAdapter = new SqlDataAdapter(mySql
    Command);
                DataSet myDataSet = new DataSet();
                mySqlAdapter.Fill(myDataSet);
                DataView myDataView = new DataView();
                myDataView = myDataSet.Tables[0].DefaultView;

                gvDepartments.DataSource = myDataView;
                gvDepartments.DataBind();

                if (mySQLconnection.State == ConnectionState.Open)
                {
                    mySQLconnection.Close();
                }
            }
        }
    }
```

12. To the project add another visual web part and name it DepartmentEmployees. As before, Visual Studio will create a folder named DepartmentEmployess with files and open up the DepartmentEmployeesUserControl.ascx in the designer tab.

13. To this user control add an ASP.Net GridView control and set its width property to 100% and set its ID to gvDepartmentsEmployees.

14. Open `DepartmentEmployees.cs` and add the `SetDepartmentProvider` method that takes one parameter of type `IDepartmentProvider`. Decorate this method with an attribute `ConsumerProvider` and pass in the string parameter `Department Consumer`. Your code should be as follows:

```
[ConnectionConsumer("Department Consumer")]
        public void SetDepartmentProvider(IDepartmentProvider
deptProvider)
        {
            this._deptProvider = deptProvider;
        }
```

15. Modify the `CreateChildControls` method such that the control is casted to `DepartmentEmployeesUserControl`. Your code should be as follows:

```
    protected override void CreateChildControls()
        {
            control = Page.LoadControl(_ascxPath) as
DepartmentEmployeesUserControl;
        }
```

16. Also override the `OnPreRender` method and add code to pass the `DepartmentId` to the `DepartmentEmployeeUserControl` as follows:

```
    protected override void OnPreRender(EventArgs e)
        {
            if (this._deptProvider != null)
            {
                this.departmentId = this._deptProvider.
                DepartmentId;

                if (!String.IsNullOrEmpty(this.departmentId))
                {
                    this.EnsureChildControls();
                    control.DepartmentId = departmentId;
                    Controls.Add(control);
                }
                else
                {
                    this.Controls.Add(new LiteralControl
                    ("Please select a Department"));
                }
            }
            else
            {
                this.Controls.Add(new LiteralControl("Please
connect this Web Part to Department Web Part"));
            }
```

```
                    base.OnPreRender(e);
            }
```

17. Add code to the `DepartmentEmployeeListUserControl.cs` to get the data based on the `DepartmentId`. Your code should look as follows:

```csharp
using System;
using System.Web.UI;
using System.Web.UI.WebControls;
using System.Web.UI.WebControls.WebParts;
using System.Data.SqlClient;
using System.Data;


namespace ConnectableWP.DepartmentEmployees
{
    public partial class DepartmentEmployeesUserControl :
UserControl
    {
        public string DepartmentId { get; set; }

        protected void Page_Load(object sender, EventArgs e)
        {
            bindGridView();
        }

        private void bindGridView()
        {

            string connStr = "Server=intsql;Database=AdventureWor
ks;Integrated Security=true";

            if (string.IsNullOrEmpty(connStr)) return;

            SqlConnection mySQLconnection = new
SqlConnection(connStr);

            if (mySQLconnection.State == ConnectionState.Closed)
            {
                mySQLconnection.Open();
            }
            SqlCommand mySqlCommand = new SqlCommand("SELECT
Person.Contact.FirstName, Person.Contact.LastName,
HumanResources.Employee.HireDate, HumanResources.
Department.Name, HumanResources.EmployeeDepartmentHistory.
```

```
StartDate, HumanResources.EmployeeDepartmentHistory.EndDate
FROM HumanResources.Employee INNER JOIN HumanResources.
EmployeeDepartmentHistory ON HumanResources.Employee.
EmployeeID = HumanResources.EmployeeDepartmentHistory.
EmployeeID INNER JOIN Person.Contact ON HumanResources.Employee.
ContactID = Person.Contact.ContactID INNER JOIN HumanResources.
Department ON HumanResources.EmployeeDepartmentHistory.
DepartmentID = HumanResources.Department.DepartmentID AND
HumanResources.EmployeeDepartmentHistory.DepartmentID =
HumanResources.Department.DepartmentID Where HumanResources.
EmployeeDepartmentHistory.DepartmentID = " + DepartmentId,
mySQLconnection);

            SqlDataAdapter mySqlAdapter = new SqlDataAdapter
            (mySqlCommand);
            DataSet myDataSet = new DataSet();
            mySqlAdapter.Fill(myDataSet);
            DataView myDataView = new DataView();
            myDataView = myDataSet.Tables[0].DefaultView;

            gvDepartmentEmployees.DataSource = myDataView;
            gvDepartmentEmployees.DataBind();

            if (mySQLconnection.State == ConnectionState.Open)
            {
                mySQLconnection.Close();
            }
        }
    }
}
```

18. Build and run the project. Add the web parts to your page and use the
    `DepartmentList` web part's menu to make a connection between the
    two web parts as shown:

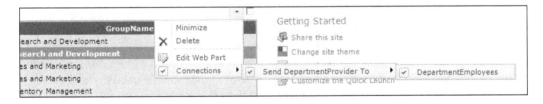

19. Select any of the departments and you should be able to see the data based on the department selected. The following screenshot shows the end result:

DepartmentList

	DepartmentId	Name	GroupName
Select	1	Engineering	Research and Development
Select	2	Tool Design	Research and Development
Select	3	Sales	Sales and Marketing
Select	4	Marketing	Sales and Marketing
Select	5	Purchasing	Inventory Management
Select	6	Research and Development	Research and Development
Select	7	Production	Manufacturing
Select	8	Production Control	Manufacturing
Select	9	Human Resources	Executive General and Administration
Select	10	Finance	Executive General and Administration
Select	11	Information Services	Executive General and Administration
Select	12	Document Control	Quality Assurance
Select	13	Quality Assurance	Quality Assurance
Select	14	Facilities and Maintenance	Executive General and Administration
Select	15	Shipping and Receiving	Inventory Management
Select	16	Executive	Executive General and Administration

DepartmentEmployees

FirstName	LastName	HireDate	Name	StartDate	EndDate
Rob	Walters	1/5/1998 12:00:00 AM	Tool Design	7/1/2000 12:00:00 AM	
Thierry	D'Hers	1/11/1998 12:00:00 AM	Tool Design	1/11/1998 12:00:00 AM	
Ovidiu	Cracium	1/5/2001 12:00:00 AM	Tool Design	1/5/2001 12:00:00 AM	
Janice	Galvin	1/23/2001 12:00:00 AM	Tool Design	1/23/2001 12:00:00 AM	

How it works...

Web part development is similar to what we saw in the previous recipes. The important aspect of connectable web parts is the communication between the two web parts. For that to happen, we defined a common interface that both of these web parts can implement. There are no restrictions on the property type or signatures of the methods that you implement in this interface. Web part infrastructure will deal with the connection using this interface. You can also define a complex property based on your class. The only requirement is that the class has to be serializable.

A typical interface only defines properties that need to be shared among the web parts. In our case, it is the department ID and hence our interface only had one property called DepartmentID. Each web part that is part of the connection implements the interface and decorates the method with an attribute to indicate whether the connection is a provider or a consumer connection. A provider would decorate the method with ConnectionProvider, and the consumer will decorate the method with the ConnectionConsumer attribute. Each of these attributes also take an input parameter of string type that is used to display the connection description. The following table provides the list of all properties that can be set on these attributes.

Property Name	Description
DisplayName	The name that is used in the browser UI to display the connection name. This is what we passed in our example.
AllowsMultipleConnections	A Boolean property to indicate whether a web part can either provide connections for multiple consumers or can receive from multiple providers. By default, provider web parts have this property set to true and consumer web parts set it to false.
ConnectionPointType	Represents whether a web part is consumer or provider. This is set automatically based on the attribute type. You can also create a custom class and set this attribute.
ID	A unique ID that represents the provider or consumer.

Based on these attribute, the web part infrastructure knows which is the provider and which is the consumer.

Since our provider also implements the interface, the method GetDepartmentProvider returns "this" (the instance of the current web part). The web part connection infrastructure now gets the object returned by the GetDepartmentProvider and looks for the corresponding consumer method. In our case, it is called SetDepartmentProvider which takes in the interface as the input parameter. This is how the consumer will get an instance of the provider web part. The consumer can now have access to the public properties of the web part. Hence, we implemented a property DepartmentID that returns the selected department ID from the GridVeiw control.

On the consumer web part, we will verify if the connection to the provider is made in the OnPreRender event handler and if so, we will retrieve the data based on the department ID provided by the provider web part.

Since SharePoint is based on ASP.Net infrastructure, it follows the same page life cycle pattern as the ASP.Net page. Hence the verification of the provider web part reference in the OnPreRender event handler rather than in CreateChildControls. On a quick note, web part life cycle starts with OnInit where configuration information like those from the web part properties pane is loaded. OnInit is followed by LoadViewState, CreateChildControls, and User events like button clicked and others. User events is followed by OnPreRender event. OnPreRender is followed by RenderControls which outputs the HTML and then goes on to SaveViewState and then disposes and unloads. For more information on the ASP.Net page life cycle, please refer to MSDN at: http://msdn.microsoft.com/en-us/library/ms178472.aspx.

SharePoint also provides some native interfaces that can be used instead of creating your own interfaces. This is becoming obsolete and you should refrain from using these interfaces. If you have web parts from previous versions, these interfaces can come in handy. The recipe we provided here is the approach that is recommended to create the connectable web parts. The following is the list of some of the interfaces that SharePoint provides by default:

Interface	Description
ICellProvider	Used to consume or provide a single value.
ICellConsumer	
IRowProvider	Used for rows of data.
IRowConsumer	
IListProvider	Used in the case of lists data.
IListConsumer	

There's more...

An interface transformer is provided by the web part infrastructure. It helps users to connect two different interfaces in a natural and transparent mode. This is only possible where one web part requires connecting to another web part that does not have the exact identical interface.

For example, a user might require connecting a phone list to a picture viewer. However, the phone list has the IRowProvider interface, and the picture viewer has the ICellConsumer interface. To resolve this discrepancy, an interface transformer is provided that permits these two interfaces to connect to each other.

See also

- ▸ *Creating a visual web part* recipe
- ▸ *Creating a code-only web part (sandboxed solution)* recipe
- ▸ *Creating a Silverlight web part* recipe

Creating a Silverlight web part

In this recipe we will create a Silverlight application that retrieves data from the contacts list that we used in *Chapter 1*.

Getting ready

The previous recipes should be completed successfully so that you understand the concept of a web part and its deployment. Apart from that, create a new document library on your site using SharePoint UI and name it XAPFiles.

How to do it...

1. If you have closed Visual Studio IDE, launch it as an administrator.

2. Create a new empty SharePoint project called **SilverlightOM**. Take defaults on the next steps of the wizard.

3. To this solution add a new Silverlight application project and name it **ContactsListSilverlight**.

4. Now to your empty SharePoint project, add a new module and name it **XAPFiles**.

5. Delete the Sample.txt file it adds to the module. The Elements.xml file will be automatically updated by VS 2010.

6. In the **Properties** window for this module, click on the ellipsis (**...**) for **Project Output References** as shown in the following screenshot:

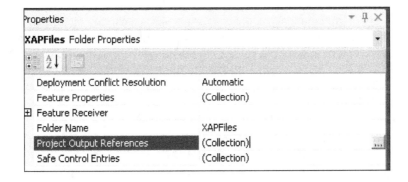

7. This should bring up the **Project Output References** collection window. Click on the **Add** button and add the **ContactsListSilverlight** project as a member project and set the deployment type to **ElementFile** as shown in the following screenshot:

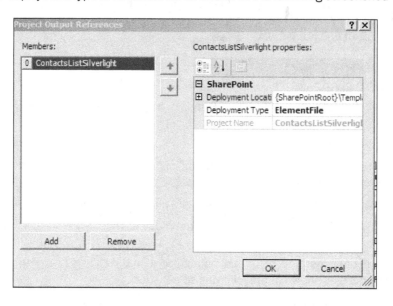

8. Visual Studio automatically updates your elements file in the module with the XAP files. Open the `Elements.xml` file from the module and add a `Url` attribute to the `Module` element and set the value to the document library name. In our case it is `XAPFiles`. Also add the `Type` attribute to the `File` element and set the value to `GhostableInLibrary`. Your `Elements.xml` file in the `XAPFiles` module should look as follows:

```
<?xml version="1.0" encoding="utf-8"?>
<Elements xmlns="http://schemas.microsoft.com/sharepoint/">
  <Module Name="XAPFiles" Url="XAPFiles">
   <File Path="XAPFiles\ContactsListSilverlight.xap" Url="XAPFiles/
ContactsListSilverlight.xap" Type="GhostableInLibrary" />
  </Module>
</Elements>
```

9. Add references to the Silverlight client object assemblies to your **ContactsListSilverlight** project. The client object assemblies can be found in the `Layouts\ClientBin` directory in your SharePoint root. The Silverlight assemblies are as follows: `Microsoft.SharePoint.Client.Silverlight.Runtime.dll` and `Microsoft.SharePoint.Client.Silverlight.dll`.

10. Add a datagrid and a button to your `MainPage.xaml` and your XAML file should look as follows:

```
<UserControl x:Class="ContactsListSilverlight.MainPage"
    xmlns="http://schemas.microsoft.com/winfx/2006/xaml/
presentation"
    xmlns:x="http://schemas.microsoft.com/winfx/2006/xaml"
    xmlns:d="http://schemas.microsoft.com/expression/blend/2008"
    xmlns:mc="http://schemas.openxmlformats.org/markup-
compatibility/2006"
    mc:Ignorable="d"
    d:DesignHeight="290" d:DesignWidth="508" xmlns:data="clr-
namespace:System.Windows.Controls;assembly=System.Windows.
Controls.Data">

    <Grid x:Name="LayoutRoot" Background="#B4ECFFE6" Height="264"
Width="466">
        <Button Content="Get Data" Height="23" HorizontalAlignment
="Left" Margin="268,12,0,0" Name="button1" VerticalAlignment="Top"
Width="105" Click="button1_Click" />
        <data:DataGrid AutoGenerateColumns="True" Height="200"
HorizontalAlignment="Left" Margin="12,52,0,0" Name="dataGrid1"
VerticalAlignment="Top" Width="420" />
    </Grid>
</UserControl>
```

Add a class named "MyContacts" and define the properties to store the contact information. Your code should be as follows:

```
public class MyContacts
{
    public string LastName { get; set; }
    public string FirstName { get; set; }
    public string BusinessPhone { get; set; }
    public string EmailAddress { get; set; }
}
```

11. Now add code to the button click event handler to retrieve contacts from the contacts list that we have used in the previous chapters and recipes. Your code in `MainPage.xaml.cs` should be as follows:

```
private void button1_Click(object sender,
RoutedEventArgs e)
{
    ClientContext context = new ClientContext
    (ApplicationContext.Current.Url);
    _web = context.Web;
    context.Load(_web);
```

```
        _list = _web.Lists.GetByTitle("Contacts");
        var query = new CamlQuery();
        var rowLimit = "<View><RowLimit>5</RowLimit></View>";
        query.ViewXml = rowLimit;
        _listItemCol = _list.GetItems(query);
        context.Load(_listItemCol);
        context.Load(_list);
        context.ExecuteQueryAsync(new ClientRequestSucceeded
        EventHandler(OnSuccessRequest), new ClientRequest
        FailedEventHandler(OnFailedRequest));
    }


    private void OnSuccessRequest(Object sender,
    ClientRequestSucceededEventArgs args)
    {
        Dispatcher.BeginInvoke(FillGrid);
    }


    private void OnFailedRequest(Object sender,
    ClientRequestFailedEventArgs args)
    {
        MessageBox.Show("Request Failed: " + args.Message + ",
Stack Trace:" + args.StackTrace);
    }


    private void FillGrid()
    {
      List<MyContacts> _myContacts = new List<MyContacts>();
      foreach(ListItem item in _listItemCol)
      {
          _myContacts.Add(new MyContacts
          {
              LastName = item["Title"].ToString(),
              FirstName = item["FirstName"].ToString(),
              BusinessPhone = item["WorkPhone"].ToString(),
              EmailAddress = item["Email"].ToString()
          });
      }
      dataGrid1.ItemsSource = _myContacts;
    }
```

12. Build and run the project by pressing *F5*. You should see the XAP file deployed to your documents folder XAPFiles created before the beginning of this recipe.

13. Add the Silverlight web part to your page and provide the URL of the XAP file as shown in the following screenshot:

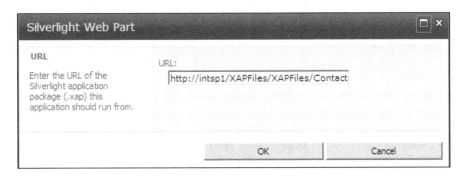

14. The output of the Silverlight web part is as shown in the following screenshot:

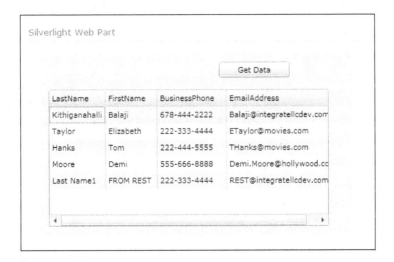

How it works...

Silverlight is a development platform to develop rich internet applications that are cross-browser and cross platform compatible. Silverlight applications are executed through a browser plug-in.

In this recipe, we are using a Silverlight managed object model to retrieve data from the **Contacts** list. In *Chapter 7*, we will explore more about the Client Object Model.

SharePoint supports Silverlight throughout its platform. Some of the features like creating lists, adding web parts to the web page are all implemented via Silverlight. If Silverlight is not installed on the machine that is browsing the SharePoint site, SharePoint falls back to the HTML view.

By default, SharePoint provides a generic Silverlight web part that is used to host the Silverlight applications. This is exactly what we did in this recipe. We created a Silverlight application and the resultant XAP file was uploaded to a document library and used the generic web part to host our Silverlight application.

A XAP (pronounced as *Zap*) file is a Silverlight application package file. This is nothing but a compressed ZIP file that can be renamed to `.zip` and opened up to see the contents of it. To deploy these application packages to the SharePoint environment, we need to store it at some location and hence we created a document library called `XAPFiles`. We uploaded our Silverlight application to this location via feature. To do that, we added a module called XAPFiles to our SharePoint project and then we provided a reference to the output of our Silverlight application. We also changed the `Elements.xml` file to reflect the `Url` location to our XAPFiles document library. Then we provided the path to this location to the generic Silverlight web part that comes by default in the SharePoint environment. Since the Silverlight application we created is not a web part, we had to create the document library to store this application. As noted in the previous recipes, web parts, when deployed, get stored in the `_catalogs/wp` document library.

There's more...

To enable Silverlight applications debugging in Visual Studio 2010 SharePoint projects, go to the project properties of your SharePoint project and navigate to the SharePoint tab and select the **Enable Silverlight debugging (instead of Script debugging)** checkbox as shown in the following screenshot:

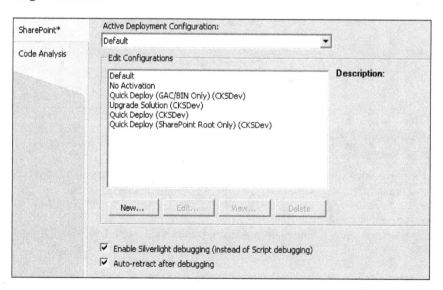

See also

- ▶ *Chapter 1, Validating data when an item is added to a list* recipe
- ▶ *Chapter 6, Web Services and REST* recipe

6
Web Services and REST

In this chapter, we will cover:

- ▶ Getting data through REST
- ▶ Filtering list data
- ▶ Fiddling with Fiddler
- ▶ Creating a REST consumer
- ▶ Inserting new contacts through REST
- ▶ Creating a custom SharePoint WCF service

Introduction

The web services expose common functionality of the SharePoint that can be utilized by the client applications to extract and input data to SharePoint sites. If these exposed web services, do not provide you with the necessary functionality, you can always create custom web services that use the SharePoint object model.

Web services can be developed, using the old ASP.NET style by creating the `.ASMX` files or the **Windows Communication Foundation (WCF)** services. Using WCF, you can create either the SOAP style or REST web services.

For more information on the differences between ASP.NET web services versus WCF services, refer to MSDN at: `http://msdn.microsoft.com/en-us/library/aa738737.aspx`.

Simple Object Access Protocol (**SOAP**) uses XML behind the scenes to do client and server transactions. With SOAP, you can only use the HTTP POST method to do client and server transactions. It does not make use of the GET method, and hence does not provide better caching mechanisms for read-only data. In ASP.NET, if you create a web service, it uses the POST method to create the web services.

Representational State Transfer (**REST**) is another way to do a client/server request/response transaction. It was first introduced and defined by Roy Fielding, who is also one of the principle authors of HTTP specifications 1.0 and 1.1.

REST is not a protocol, but an architectural style as defined by the author. It is used in situations, where web services are used without the additional overhead of the SOAP. Even though you can use some or all of the REST specifications with other protocols, it provides its best benefits when used with HTTP protocol. Services that follow these REST architectural styles are also called RESTful services.

In the .NET Framework 3.5, WCF provides a very good support for RESTful services. SharePoint 2010 based on this framework, provides a very robust support for operations that clients can make use of by using RESTful services.

REST, like SOAP web services are for remote clients who are not running on SharePoint servers locally. These clients can make server calls by using these REST APIs and get the information from SharePoint objects.

Creating a custom ASP.NET style web service involves:

1. Creating a web service in Visual Studio.
2. Creating WSDL and discovery files.
3. Creating a class file that contains the logic of your web service.
4. Deploying your web service to the _vti_bin (ISAPI) directory in the SharePoint root.
5. Making your web service discoverable from SPDisco.aspx.

In this case, the end point (the URL location that you use to access the web service) of the web service was defined well before and is static.

In this chapter, we will go through the process of creating a custom WCF web service for SharePoint and consuming it with a client application.

Using REST, you can perform read, create, update, and delete operations on SharePoint resources using flexible URL notation. Each of these actions corresponds to HTTP's GET, POST, PUT, and DELETE verbs. Actually they are directly mapped to these HTTP verbs. Even though the PUT method is used for update purposes, it updates the entire entity. So, WCF also uses a MERGE request when only updating certain fields that are changed.

The data that you retrieve using REST API need not always be XML. You can request data in **JavaScript Object Notation** (**JSON**) and AtomPub standards. For more information on AtomPub refer to: http://atompub.org/ and on JSON refer to: http://json.org/.

Getting data through REST

In this recipe, we will issue a GET request to SharePoint from the browser using REST service to get data.

Getting ready

Open Internet Explorer. In this recipe, we will be using the default installation of **Internet Explorer 9** (**IE9**). It should work the same with **Internet Explorer 8** (**IE8**).

How to do it...

In order to get data through REST, adhere to the following steps:

1. In Internet Explorer navigate to **Tools | Internet Options | Content Tab | Feeds and Web slice settings.** Make sure you have checked the **Turn on feed reading view** in the **Advanced** section.

2. Issue a Get request to your SharePoint site: http://YOURSERVERNAME/_vti_bin/ListData.svc. Make sure to substitute your server name in the URL.

3. This should display all the lists information from the site you are referring to in the URL. In our case, we are using a team site and the following screenshot shows the output:

4. The result is an XML response in Atom format.

How it works...

When you issue a GET request to SharePoint through the REST services as we did earlier, behind the scenes it uses the object model to query the lists on the site and gets the result set back. In the preceding case, it uses the context under which the GET request is issued and retrieves all the lists for that site.

As indicated in the previous chapters, all the sites are configured with some SharePoint Root folders as virtual folders, automatically for each of the web applications you create in SharePoint. This way you can access these farms wide functionalities from any web application, site collection, or site. ISAPI underneath the Root is one such folder which is a virtual directory under IIS and is mapped as virtual folder _vti_bin for every web application that you create in SharePoint. This is where all the out-of-the-box web services are located. The preceding URL uses this approach and issues a call to ListsData.SVC that is deployed in the ISAPI folder in the SharePoint root.

There's more...

When you navigate to the SharePoint Root from your Windows Explorer, in the ISAPI directory, you can see all the ASP.NET web services and WCF services that come out-of-the-box with SharePoint. These ASP.NET web services were also available in SharePoint 2007. The Lists.asmx can be used to issue SOAP calls to SharePoint lists to get list items, add new items, and so on. This is an example of ASP.NET web service. This is available in the current SharePoint version as well. Use the browser and navigate to this web service to see all the methods it supports.

Why is the ISAPI folder named _vti_bin?

This comes from the mid-nineties when Microsoft acquired a company called Vermeer Technologies Inc, which was the parent company for FrontPage product. The _vti_bin folder was used to store the FrontPage server-side extensions. In SharePoint as indicated earlier, is where all the web services are stored.

See also

▶ *Filtering list data* recipe

Filtering list data

Using the REST calls, we can issue complicated queries to the SharePoint and get data. In the previous recipe, we got names of all the lists that are present in the site. In this recipe, we will issue a query to our contacts list and filter data based on the LastName column.

Getting ready

You need to have the contacts list that we created in *Chapter 1*. Alternatively, create a list called "Contacts" using the Contacts template via the SharePoint user interface and fill in with some data

How to do it...

In order to filter list data, adhere to the following steps:

1. In Internet Explorer navigate to **Tools | Internet Options | Content Tab | Feeds and Web slice settings**. Make sure you have checked the **Turn off feed reading view** in the **Advanced** section. This time we will receive the data in XML format.

2. Issue a `Get` request to your SharePoint site: `http://YOURSERVERNAME/_vti_bin/listdata.svc/Contacts()?$filter=startswith(LastName,'Kithi')&$select=LastName,FirstName,BusinessPhone,EMailAddress`. Make sure to substitute your server name in the URL and fix the filter parameter to your contacts information. You should see the end result as shown in the following screenshot:

```xml
<?xml version="1.0" encoding="utf-8" standalone="yes" ?>
- <feed xml:base="http://intsp1/_vti_bin/listdata.svc/"
    xmlns:d="http://schemas.microsoft.com/ado/2007/08/dataservices"
    xmlns:m="http://schemas.microsoft.com/ado/2007/08/dataservices/metadata"
    xmlns="http://www.w3.org/2005/Atom">
    <title type="text">Contacts</title>
    <id>http://intsp1/_vti_bin/listdata.svc/Contacts</id>
    <updated>2011-04-23T16:08:15Z</updated>
    <link rel="self" title="Contacts" href="Contacts" />
  - <entry m:etag="W/"1"">
      <id>http://intsp1/_vti_bin/listdata.svc/Contacts(10)</id>
      <title type="text">Kithiganahalli</title>
      <updated>2011-04-23T11:04:53-04:00</updated>
    - <author>
        <name />
      </author>
      <link rel="edit" title="ContactsItem" href="Contacts(10)" />
      <category term="Microsoft.SharePoint.DataService.ContactsItem"
        scheme="http://schemas.microsoft.com/ado/2007/08/dataservices/scheme" />
    - <content type="application/xml">
      - <m:properties>
          <d:LastName>Kithiganahalli</d:LastName>
          <d:FirstName>Balaji</d:FirstName>
          <d:EMailAddress>Balaji@integratellcdev.com</d:EMailAddress>
          <d:BusinessPhone>678-444-2222</d:BusinessPhone>
        </m:properties>
      </content>
    </entry>
  </feed>
```

How it works...

In SharePoint 2010, out of the box all the lists are exposed as WCF RESTful service using OData protocol. We use the `ListData.svc` service to request data from the lists in SharePoint. The preceding URL sends the REST statement to SharePoint server. The REST service translates this to SharePoint CAML and executes the object model to get the data.

There's more...

You can use the same concept as earlier and filter or sort data on the list. Here are some of the example queries that can be used to sort and filter data.

- To get data ordered by last name in a descending order, use the following URL syntax: `http://YourserverName/_vti_bin/listdata.svc/Contacts?$orderby=LastName desc`.

- To get data of a list item whose ID is 3 use the following URL syntax: `http://YourserverName/_vti_bin/listdata.svc/Contacts(3)`.

- To get data ordered by multiple columns use the following URL syntax: `http://YourserverName/_vti_bin/listdata.svc/Contacts?$orderby=LastName desc, id asc`.

- The following query will skip the first three items and get the next two items and order them on the `LastName` column from the list specified. This approach can be used for paging purposes: `http://YourserverName/_vti_bin/listdata.svc/Contacts?$skip=3&$top=2&$orderby=LastName`.

See also

Chapter 1, Validating data when an item is added to a list recipe

Chapter 6, Fiddling with Fiddler recipe

Fiddling with Fiddler

Fiddler is a freeware developed by Eric Lawrence. This tool is used to debug HTTP traffic from any application including Internet Explorer, Firefox, and other browsers. From the Fiddler's website, the description of Fiddler is as follows:

Fiddler is a Web Debugging Proxy which logs all HTTP(S) traffic between your computer and the Internet. Fiddler allows you to inspect all HTTP(S) traffic, set breakpoints, and fiddle with incoming or outgoing data. Fiddler includes a powerful event-based scripting subsystem, and can be extended using any .NET language.

In this recipe, we will use Fiddler to get a result as a JSON response.

Getting ready

Fiddler needs to be installed and configured properly. If you do not have Fiddler, you can get this freeware from: `http://www.Fiddler2.com`. The installation of this tool is pretty easy, and all the needed documentation is available on the site.

How to do it...

Follow the given steps:

1. Open **Fiddler** and with your browser running, issue a REST call like in the previous recipe to your server.

2. Once **Fiddler** is running, it automatically monitors all the traffic and you should see a screen similar to the following screenshot:

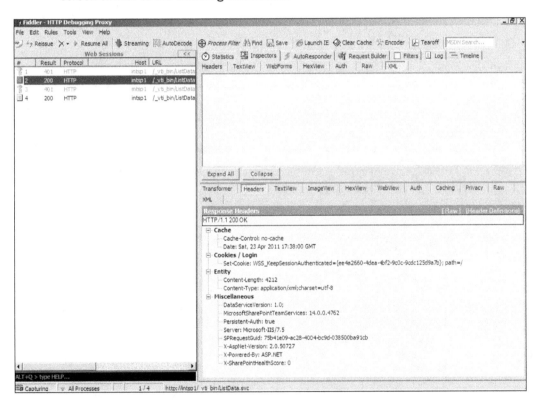

3. If you notice, under the **Inspectors** tab in the **Headers** section, you see the content type is **application/xml**. As indicated in the previous recipes, we are getting our responses in XML format. You can click on the **Raw** tab in the same section to see the output that you saw in the browser. Here is the screenshot of **Fiddler** showing the **Raw** XML format output:

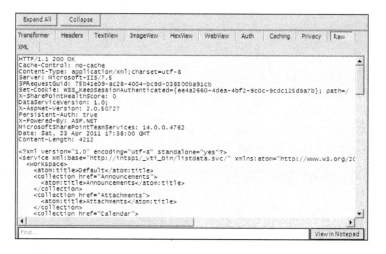

4. To change the output, we can fiddle with the request format. To do this, click on the **Customize Rules** menu item from the **Fiddler** menu **Rules**. This will open up the JavaScript in the notepad that is used by the **Fiddler**.

5. Find the `OnBeforeRequest` method, add the following line in the end of the method, and save the script.

```
oSession.oRequest["Accept"] = "application/json";
```

6. Reissue the request and this time you should see your request in JSON format as shown in the following screenshot:

How it works...

By using **Fiddler** we modified the header that was sent to the SharePoint server to indicate how the data needs to be received. Headers are a way to indicate to SharePoint, in which way we need to receive the data. In the previous recipes, we used **application/xml** as the header to indicate that we need data in XML format. That was neatly displayed in Internet Explorer. The JSON format may not be shown in the browser. Use the **Raw** tab in **Fiddler** to check the JSON response.

See also

▸   *Creating a REST consumer* recipe

Creating a REST consumer

In this recipe, we will use the SharePoint REST APIs to retrieve data from the SharePoint list to display in a Windows application.

Getting ready

You need to have completed the previous recipes and understood the REST calls that were made in the previous recipes.

How to do it...

In order to create a REST consumer, adhere to the following steps:

1.   Open Visual Studio 2010 and create a `Windows Forms` Application project.

2.   Name the project **RESTConsumer**.

3. Visual Studio will create the necessary files for the Windows project and should bring up the project with an empty form as follows:

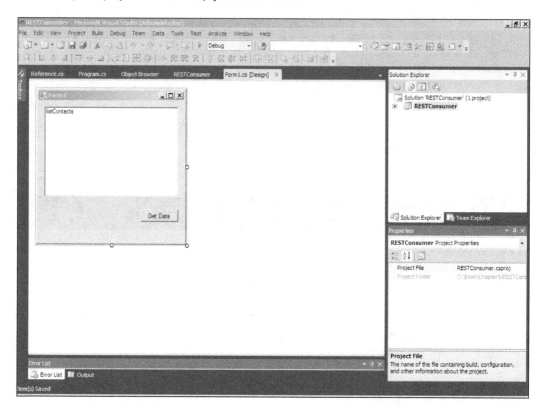

4. Add a list box and a button as shown in the previous screenshot and name the list box as **listContacts** and the button **btnGetData**. Change the label on the button to **Get Data.** The completed form is as shown in the previous screenshot.

5. Right-click on the references and click on **Add Service Reference**. This will bring up the **Service Reference** wizard as shown in the following screenshot:

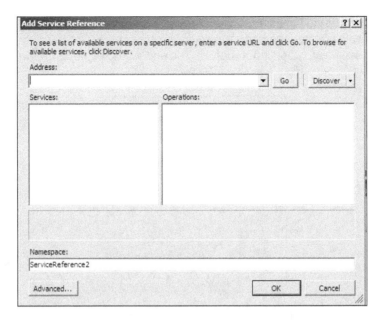

6. Alternatively, you can add the same through **Data | Add new data source** and then selecting **SharePoint**.

7. Add the `ListData.svc` URL to your server in the address bar and click on the **Go** button. Services will be listed in the **Services List** box. Use the default for **Namespace** and click **OK**. Visual Studio will add the necessary files to the project.

8. Double-click on the **btnGet** to add the event handler to the click event. This is where you will write your code to retrieve data from the SharePoint list. Add the following lines of code. Make sure to change the URL and context name to your environment.

```
string URL = "http://intsp1/_vti_bin/ListData.svc";
ServiceReference1.DevelopmentPortalDataContext context = new Devel
opmentPortalDataContext(new Uri(URL));
context.Credentials = System.Net.CredentialCache.
DefaultCredentials;
foreach(ServiceReference1.ContactsItem item in context.Contacts)
  {
    listContacts.Items.Add(item.LastName + ", " + item.FirstName);
  }
```

9. Build and run the project from menu **Debug | Start Debugging** or by pressing *F5*. This should bring up the form, and when you click on the **Get Data** button you should see the contacts from your list. The end result will be as shown in the following screenshot:

How it works...

When we added the reference to the ListData.svc in the Visual Studio, it created a folder named Service References and underneath it for your service reference, you should see a Reference.cs file. This file has all the necessary code for you to execute all the queries on your server and retrieve the data. If you cannot see all the files that it created, go to menu **Project | Show all files**. This should bring up all the hidden files as well.

Reference.cs is the proxy file that is generated by Visual Studio from the metadata information of the service. This file is the shell that hides all the complexity of sending, serializing or deserializing, and receiving the messages over the wire. Clients make use of this proxy to talk to the service.

In our code, we first created a context under which our code needs to run. The context uses the URL we specify. This way we know our code will run on the site or site collection we are specifying. Next we pass on the default credentials that are used while running the application. This means, it passes whatever the credentials that are used to run the application. If the user running this application does not have access to the site, to perform a lookup, or any transactions then it will throw an unauthorized exception. The next series of lines of code use the proxy class to retrieve all the contacts and uses the familiar foreach loop to add the contacts to the list box.

There's more...

You can execute all the queries we listed in the previous recipes. The easiest way to execute the filter query from the previous recipe is to use the code as follows:

```
ContactsItem item = context.Contacts.Where(i => i.LastName ==
"Kithiganahalli").FirstOrDefault();
```

The LINQ statements are first converted to URL based REST requests before they are submitted to the REST interface. You can use **Fiddler** to check the REST statements that are passed to the server. On the SharePoint server, these requests are then converted into CAML statements and executed using the object model. But whenever you write a LINQ query, it is always converted to CAML to get the data from the object model.

See also

- ▶ *Getting data through REST* recipe
- ▶ *Filtering list data* recipe
- ▶ *Fiddling with Fiddler* recipe
- ▶ *Inserting new contacts through REST* recipe

Inserting new contacts through REST

We now know we can use REST requests to get data from SharePoint lists, how about adding data to the list from the client applications? In this recipe, we will see how to do just that.

Getting ready

You need to have completed the previous recipes and understand the REST calls that are made in the previous recipes.

How to do it...

In order to insert a new contact through REST, adhere to the following steps:

1. Open Visual Studio 2010, and create a console application project.

2. Name the project **RESTUpdate**. Visual Studio will create the necessary files and bring you to `Program.cs`. This is where you will write your code to add the new contact.

3. Right-click on the references and click on **Add Service Reference**. This will bring up the **Service Reference** wizard.

4. Add the `ListData.svc` URL to your server in the address bar, and click on the **Go** button. Services will be listed in the **Services List** box. Use the default for **Namespace** and click on the **OK** button. Visual Studio will add necessary `proxy` files to the project.

5. In the `Program.cs`, in the `Main` method add the following lines of code. Make sure to change the URL and context name to your environment.

```
string URL = "http://intsp1/_vti_bin/ListData.svc";
ServiceReference1.DevelopmentPortalDataContext context = new Devel
opmentPortalDataContext(new Uri(URL));
context.Credentials = System.Net.CredentialCache.
DefaultCredentials;
ServiceReference1.ContactsItem newItem = new ContactsItem();
newItem.LastName = "Last Name";
newItem.FirstName = "FROM REST";
newItem.EMailAddress = "REST@integratellcdev.com";
newItem.BusinessPhone = "222-333-4444";
context.AddToContacts(newItem);
context.SaveChanges();
```

6. Build and run the project from menu **Debug | Start Debugging**, or by pressing *F5*. This should run the console application and insert the list item to our contacts list. The end result will be as shown in the following screenshot:

Last Name↑	First Name	Business Phone	E-mail Address	Created	Created By	
Hanks ☐ NEW	Tom	222-444-5555	THanks@movies.com	4/23/2011 11:06 AM	Balaji Kithiganahalli	4
Kithiganahalli ☐ NEW	Balaji	678-444-2222	Balaji@integratellcdev.com	4/23/2011 11:04 AM	Balaji Kithiganahalli	4
Last Name ☐ NEW	FROM REST	222-333-4444	REST@integratellcdev.com	4/23/2011 4:33 PM	System Account	4
Moore ☐ NEW	Demi	555-666-8888	Demi.Moore@hollywood.com	4/23/2011 11:07 AM	Balaji Kithiganahalli	4
Taylor ☐ NEW	Elizabeth	222-333-4444	ETaylor@movies.com	4/23/2011 11:05 AM	Balaji Kithiganahalli	4

How it works...

The code is self-explanatory. As indicated before, when Visual Studio adds the service reference, it creates all the necessary `proxy` code to use the service APIs. In here, we made use of the method `AddContact`. Similarly, there are methods to add attachments to a list, and so on.

There's more...

In case you want to update or delete a contact from our contacts list, similar to `AddContact`, there are methods like `UpdateObject` and `DeleteObject`.

Both methods take only one parameter, and are of type object. You can pass in your `ContactItem` to this method to update or delete the item. The following code is for updating the contact:

```
string URL = "http://intsp1/_vti_bin/ListData.svc";
ServiceReference1.DevelopmentPortalDataContext context = new Developme
ntPortalDataContext(new Uri(URL));
context.Credentials = System.Net.CredentialCache.DefaultCredentials;
ContactsItem item = context.Contacts.Where(i => i.LastName ==
"Kithiganahalli").FirstOrDefault();
 //Make changes to item and then do the update.
  context.UpdateObject(item);
  context.SaveChanges();
```

See also

- ► *Creating a custom SharePoint WCF service* recipe
- ► *LINQ Quickly by* N. Satheesh Kumar *from the Packt Publishing website*

Creating a custom SharePoint WCF service

So far, we have made use of the out-of-the-box web services provided in the SharePoint. There are situations where SharePoint could be acting as a data store providing your business data to external applications. These applications requesting data may need to provide information on having a valid subscription or license before accessing the data. The out-of-the-box web services will not provide you a way to verify this information before allowing access. There may also be a scenario where you may want to strip out confidential information from the list before passing the data to these external applications. In these scenarios, you can create your own custom web service which could validate the credentials, or strip out the confidential data before passing the information to these external applications.

In this recipe, we will create a custom SharePoint WCF service which returns us the ubiquitous string *Hello World*.

Getting ready

For this exercise, make sure your SharePoint website is enabled for anonymous access. To enable anonymous access go to **IIS Manager** and enable it for your SharePoint web application.

How to do it...

In order to create a custom SharePoint WCF service, adhere to the following steps:

1. Open Visual Studio 2010 and create an empty SharePoint project.

2. Name the project **CustomWCF**. Deploy the solution as the farm solution.

3. Add a SharePoint mapped folder for ISAPI. In this folder, create a folder named **CustomWCF**.

4. Add an empty text file named CustomWCF.svc to the CustomWCF folder underneath ISAPI.

5. Add a new item to the project and select the **WCF Service** template in the Visual Studio as shown in the following screenshot:

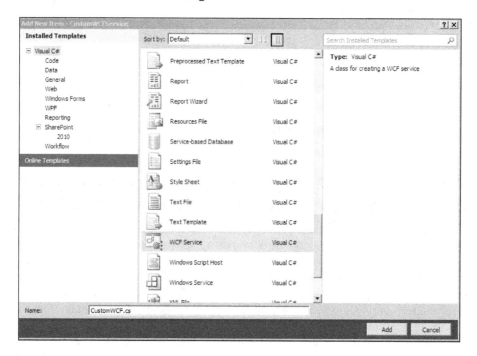

6. This will add three files to your project namely: CustomWCF.cs, ICustomWCF.cs, and app.config.

7. Move the app.config file from the root folder to the ISAPI\CustomWCF folder in the project and rename it web.config.

8. Build your project.

9. Open the Visual Studio command prompt and navigate to the `bin\debug` directory of your project and execute the following command to get the public key token of the assembly:

```
Sn -T CustomWCF.dll
```

10. Add the following line to the `CustomWCF.svc` file and add the public key token obtained from the previous step:

```
<%@ ServiceHost Debug="true" Language="C#" Service="CustomWCF.
CustomWCF, CustomWCF, Version=1.0.0.0, Culture=neutral, PublicKeyT
oken=2832c7898c525539" CodeBehind="CustomWCF.cs" %>
```

11. The default `DoWork` method the Visual Studio added to `ICustomWCF.cs` returns `void`. Change that to `string`.

12. Make the same change in the `CustomWCF.cs` file as well. This is the file where the interface is implemented. Add the following line of code as shown in the `DoWork()` method:

```
return "Hello World from Custom WCF";
```

13. Add the `AspNetComaptibility` attribute to the class that is implementing the interface. So your `CustomWCF.cs` class should look as follows:

```
using System.ServiceModel.Activation;
namespace CustomWCF
{
    // NOTE: You can use the "Rename" command on the "Refactor"
menu to change the class name "CustomWCF" in both code and config
file together.
    [AspNetCompatibilityRequirements(RequirementsMode =
AspNetCompatibilityRequirementsMode.Required)]
    public class CustomWCF : ICustomWCF
    {
        public string DoWork()
        {
            return "Hello World from Custom WCF";
        }
    }
}
```

14. Build and deploy the application. You should now be able to access this WCF service from the browser by typing in the URL: `http://yourservername/_vti_bin/CustomWCF/CustomWCF.svc`.

15. You should see a screenshot similar to the following:

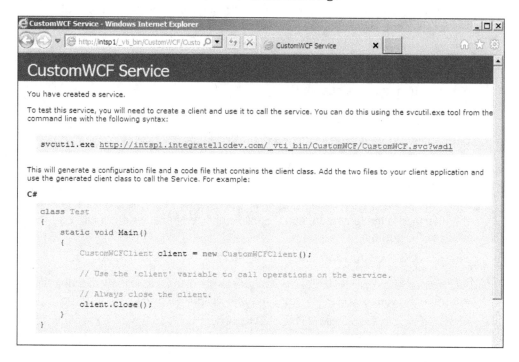

How it works...

The code is basically self-explanatory. From the previous recipes, we know that SharePoint stores all its services in the ISAPI folder. Hence we added this reference and created a subfolder to store our SVC file. There is no need to create a subfolder in the ISAPI folder for the service to work. It is just a good coding practice. The SVC file is indicating, that it is a service host and the service that it is representing is contained in the assembly. It also provides information on the class name that the service should use for the method invoking purpose.

Whenever a client consumes a service, it should know what parameters it needs to pass to the methods it exposes and in what format the result is returned. This is called **Contract** between client and service. Contract is the heart of the service. The service agrees to perform the services that it has specified in its contract. Service exposes the methods and its signatures. Clients do not need to know how these methods are implemented. Let us take an example of a service that returns listings of all movie theatres for a particular zip code. The client needs to know that it needs to pass the ZIP code information as string and the results are returned as an array of strings that contain theatre names. It does not need to know whether the method internally goes to a database to retrieve this information or calls another web service to get the data.

This contract in WCF is implemented as an interface and is decorated with an attribute `[ServiceContract]`. This is the reason we have the `ICustomWCF.cs` file. In this file we define all the methods and its signature that we want to expose in our service. Each of the method will be decorated with an attribute `[OperationContract]` indicating that the service can expose this method as one of the operations that it provides in its contract to the client.

The `CustomWCF.cs` is the code file that implements the preceding interface. In this file we will define the internal implementation of how our method works. This is where we may go to the database to get all the theatres for a particular ZIP code or call another service to get that data.

Apart from this information, the client also needs to know how to discover the service. This is where the address information comes in. Address information in our case is the URL for the service like `http://intsp1/_vti_bin/CustomWCF`. The binding information is the protocol that is used to talk to the service. In our case it is HTTP.

All these three pieces contract, address, and binding information together make up the **EndPoint** of the service. This is one of the pieces of information defined in the `web.config` file.

The configuration file `web.config` contains information about end points, serviceBehavior information, and so on.

In the top part of the `web.config`, Visual Studio dynamically created the Behavior information as shown in the following code:

```
<serviceBehaviors>
    <behavior name="CustomWCF.CustomWCFBehavior">
    <serviceMetadata httpGetEnabled="true" />
    <serviceDebug includeExceptionDetailInFaults="false" />
    </behavior>
    </serviceBehaviors>
```

The serviceBehavior information contains the unique name for the Behavior and provides information on whether the **Metadata exchange** is enabled or not. Clients can use the service metadata information to create the proxy. WSDL that is used to create the proxy classes. This is important because once your service is deployed, clients can create these WSDL files and create the proxy once instead of creating it every time it connects to the service.

In the bottom part of the `web.config`, Visual Studio also added an entry that binds the service to the behavior as follows:

```
<service behaviorConfiguration="CustomWCF.CustomWCFBehavior"
                 name="CustomWCF.CustomWCF">
   <endpoint address="" binding="wsHttpBinding" contract="CustomWCF.
   ICustomWCF">
```

```
                <identity>
                        <dns value="localhost" />
                </identity>
         </endpoint>
         <endpoint address="mex" binding="mexHttpBinding" contract="IMetada
taExchange" />
                      <host>
                          <baseAddresses>
                              <add baseAddress="http://localhost:8732/
Design_Time_Addresses/CustomWCF/CustomWCF/" />
                          </baseAddresses>
                      </host>
              </service>
```

The service element has two end points, one for ICustomWCF and other for mex. ICustomWCF is understandable, what is the mex end point? This is the **Metadata exchange** that can be used by the clients to create proxies dynamically.

The service identity element in the `ICustomWCF` end point defines the security piece. This value is propagated to the client through **Web Services Definition Language** (**WSDL**) and is used to authenticate the service. This way the client knows that they are talking to the right service. This helps as a protection against phishing. For more information on different identity configurations refer to MSDN at: `http://msdn.microsoft.com/en-us/library/ms733130.aspx`.

There's more...

The community kit for SharePoint offers many more templates in Visual Studio 2010 that you can make use of to simplify the development process. One of the templates provided simplifies the development of WCF services for SharePoint. Check out the CKS toolkit at: `http://cksdev.codeplex.com/`.

Creating a client application to consume the custom WCF service

In the previous recipes, we have shown how to create a client application to consume the service. You use the same approach to develop a client application for the custom service we developed in this recipe.

You can also use command-line to create the `proxy`, instead of going through the wizard that Visual Studio offers. It is shown as follows:

1. Open the Visual Studio command prompt and execute the following command:

   ```
   Svcutil.exe http://yourservername/_vti_bin/CustomWCF/CustomWCF.
   svc?wsdl
   ```

2. This will create the `proxy` and the `config` files. Add these two files to your client application and make sure to add a reference to `System.ServiceModel` and `System.Runtime.Serialization`.

3. Add the following lines of code. Make sure to change the address to refer to your server information.

```
EndpointAddress ea = new EndpointAddress("http://intsp1/_vti_bin/
CustomWCF/CustomWCF.svc");
    CustomWCFClient client = new CustomWCFClient(new
WSHttpBinding(), ea);
  // Use the 'client' variable to call operations on the service.
  client.DoWork();
  // Always close the client.
    client.Close();
```

4. The following screenshot shows the end result of the console application:

See also

▶ *Creating a list using Client Object Model* recipe in *Chapter 7*.

7
Working with Client Object Model

In this chapter, we will cover:

- ▸ Creating a list using a Client Object Model
- ▸ Handling exceptions
- ▸ Calling Object Model asynchronously
- ▸ Using JavaScript Object Model
- ▸ Using Silverlight Object Model

Introduction

In the previous chapters, we learnt how to extend the SharePoint server functionality by creating event receivers, web parts, workflows, content types, and so on. We also wrote client applications (that are not running on the same machine as the SharePoint server) that can use SharePoint as the data source. In order to use SharePoint as the data source, we made use of web services that SharePoint provides out-of-the-box. We also learnt how to create custom web services if out-of-the-box web service did not meet the business requirements.

Since out-of-the-box web services does not provide the full functionality that the server model exposes, developers always end up creating custom web services for use with client applications. But there are situations where deploying custom web services may not be feasible. For example, if your company is hosting SharePoint solutions in a cloud environment where access to the root folder is not permitted. In such cases, developing client applications with **new Client Object Model (OM)** will become a very attractive proposition.

SharePoint exposes three OMs which are as follows:

- ▸ Managed
- ▸ Silverlight
- ▸ JavaScript (ECMAScript)

Each of these OMs provide object interface to functionality exposed in `Microsoft.SharePoint` namespace. While none of the object models expose the full functionality that the server-side object exposes, the understanding of server Object Models will easily translate for a developer to develop applications using an OM. A managed OM is used to develop custom .NET managed applications (service, WPF, or console applications). You can also use the OM for ASP.NET applications that are not running in the SharePoint context as well. A Silverlight OM is used by Silverlight client applications. A JavaScript OM is only available to applications that are hosted inside the SharePoint applications like web part pages or application pages.

Even though each of the OMs mentioned previously provide different programming interfaces to build applications, behind the scenes, they all call a service called `Client.svc` to talk to SharePoint. This `Client.svc` file resides in the `ISAPI` folder. The service calls are wrapped around with an Object Model that developers can use to make calls to SharePoint server. This way, developers make calls to an OM and the calls are all batched together in XML format to send it to the server. The response is always received in JSON format which is then parsed and associated with the right objects. The basic architectural representation of the client interaction with the SharePoint server is as shown in the following image:

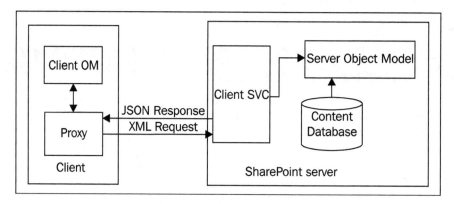

The three Object Models come in separate assemblies. The following table provides the locations and names of the assemblies:

Object OM	Location	Names
Managed	ISAPI folder	`Microsoft.SharePoint.Client.dll`
		`Microsoft.SharePoint.Client.Runtime.dll`
Silverlight	Layouts\ClientBin	`Microsoft.SharePoint.Client.Silverlight.dll`
		`Microsoft.SharePoint.Client.Silverlight.Runtime.dll`
JavaScript	Layouts	`SP.js`

 The Client Object Model can be downloaded as a redistributable package from the Microsoft download center at: `http://www.microsoft.com/downloads/en/details.aspx?FamilyID=b4579045-b183-4ed4-bf61-dc2f0deabe47`.

OM functionality focuses on objects at the site collection and below. The main reason being that it will be used to enhance the end-user interaction. Hence the OM is a smaller subset of what is available through the server Object Model. In all three Object Models, main object names are kept the same, and hence the knowledge from one OM is easily portable to another. As indicated earlier, knowledge of server Object Models easily transfer development using client OM The following table shows some of the major objects in the OM and their equivalent names in the server OM:

Client OM	Server OM
`ClientContext`	`SPContext`
`Site`	`SPSite`
`Web`	`SPWeb`
`List`	`SPList`
`ListItem`	`SPListItem`
`Field`	`SPField`

Creating a list using a Managed OM

In this recipe, we will learn how to create a list using a Managed Object Model. We will also add a new column to the list and insert about 10 rows of data to the list. For this recipe, we will create a console application that makes use of a generic list template.

Getting ready

You can copy the DLLs mentioned earlier to your development machine. Your development machine need not have the SharePoint server installed. But you should be able to access one with proper permission. You also need Visual Studio 2010 IDE installed on the development machine.

How to do it...

In order to create a list using a Managed OM, adhere to the following steps:

1. Launch your Visual Studio 2010 IDE as an administrator (right-click the shortcut and select **Run as administrator**).

2. Select **File | New | Project**. The new project wizard dialog box will be displayed (make sure to select **.NET Framework 3.5** in the top drop-down box).

3. Select Windows Console application under the **Visual C# | Windows | Console Application** node from **Installed Templates** section on the left-hand side.

4. Name the project **OMClientApplication** and provide a directory location where you want to save the project and click on **OK** to create the console application template.

5. To add a references to `Microsoft.SharePoint.Client.dll` and `Microsoft.SharePoint.Client.Runtime.dll`, go to the menu **Project | Add Reference** and navigate to the location where you copied the DLLs and select them as shown In the following screenshot:

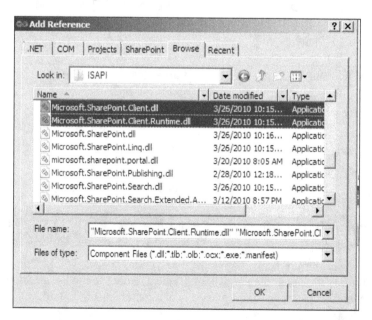

6. Now add the code necessary to create a list. A description field will also be added to our list. Your code should look like the following (make sure to change the URL passed to the `ClientContext` constructor to your environment):

```
using Microsoft.SharePoint.Client;

namespace OMClientApplication
{
    class Program
    {
        static void Main(string[] args)
        {
            using (ClientContext clientCtx = new
ClientContext("http://intsp1"))
            {

                Web site = clientCtx.Web;

                // Create a list.
                ListCreationInformation listCreationInfo = new
ListCreationInformation();
                listCreationInfo.Title = "OM Client Application
List";
                listCreationInfo.TemplateType =
(int)ListTemplateType.GenericList;
                listCreationInfo.QuickLaunchOption =
QuickLaunchOptions.On;
                List list = site.Lists.Add(listCreationInfo);
                string DescriptionFieldSchema = "<Field
Type='Note' DisplayName='Item Description' Name='Description'
Required='True' MaxLength='500' NumLines='10'  />";
                list.Fields.AddFieldAsXml(DescriptionFieldSchema,
true, AddFieldOptions.AddToDefaultContentType);

// Insert 10 rows of data - Concat loop Id with "Item Number"
string.
                for (int i = 1; i < 11; ++i)
                {
                    ListItemCreationInformation
listItemCreationInfo = new ListItemCreationInformation();
                    ListItem li = list.AddItem(listItemCreationInf
o);
                    li["Title"] = string.Format("Item number
{0}",i);
                    li["Item_x0020_Description"] = string.
Format("Item number {0} from client Object Model", i);
```

```
                li.Update();
            }
            clientCtx.ExecuteQuery();
            Console.WriteLine("List creation completed");
            Console.Read();
        }
    }
}
```

7. Build and execute the solution by pressing *F5* or from the menu **Debug | Start Debugging**. This should bring up the command window with a message indicating that the `List creation completed` as shown in the following screenshot. Press *Enter* and close the command window.

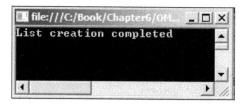

8. Navigate to your site to verify that the list has been created. The following screenshot shows the list with the new field and ten items inserted:

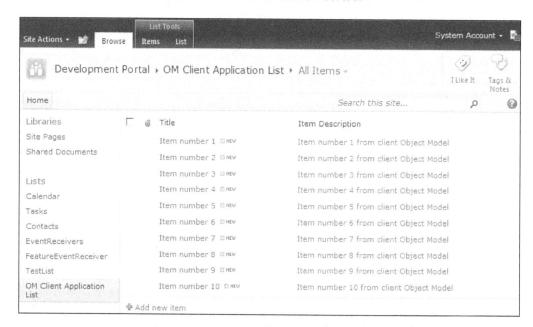

How it works...

The first line of the code in the `Main` method is to create an instance of `ClientContext` class. The `ClientContext` instance provides information about the SharePoint server context in which we will be working. This is also the proxy for the server we will be working with. We passed the URL information to the context to get the entry point to that location. When you have access to the context instance, you can browse the site, web, and list objects of that location. You can access all the properties like **Name**, **Title**, **Description**, and so on.

The `ClientContext` class implements the `IDisposable` interface, and hence you need to use the `using` statement. Without that you have to explicitly dispose the object. If you do not do so, your application will have memory leaks. For more information on disposing objects refer to MSDN at: `http://msdn.microsoft.com/en-us/library/ee557362.aspx`.

From the context we were able to obtain access to our site object on which we wanted to create the list. We provided list properties for our new list through the `ListCreationInformation` instance.

Through the instance of `ListCreationInformation`, we set the values to list properties like name, the templates we want to use, whether the list should be shown in the quick launch bar or not, and so on.

We added a new field to the field collection of the list by providing the field schema. Each of the `ListItems` are created by providing `ListItemCreationInformation`.

The `ListItemCreationInformation` is similar to `ListCreationInformation` where you would provide information regarding the list item like whether it belongs to a document library or not, and so on. For more information on `ListCreationInformation` and `ListItemCreationInformation` members refer to MSDN at: `http://msdn.microsoft.com/en-us/library/ee536774.aspx`.

All of this information is structured as an XML and batched together to send it to the server. In our case, we created a list and added a new field and about ten list items. Each of these would have an equivalent server-side call, and hence, all these multiple calls were batched together to send it to the server. The request is only sent to the server when we issue an `ExecuteQuery` or `ExecuteQueryAsync` method in the client context.

The `ExecuteQuery` method creates an XML request and passes that to `Client.svc`. The application waits until the batch process on the server is completed and then returns back with the JSON response. `Client.svc` makes the server Object Model call to execute our request.

There's more...

By default, `ClientContext` instance uses windows authentication. It makes use of the windows identity of the person executing the application. Hence, the person running the application should have proper authorization on the site to execute the commands. Exceptions will be thrown if proper permissions are not available for the user executing the application. We will learn about handling exceptions in the next recipe.

It also supports **Anonymous** and **FBA** (**ASP.Net** form based authentication) authentication. The following is the code for passing FBA credentials if your site supports it:

```
using (ClientContext clientCtx = new ClientContext("http://intsp1"))
{
clientCtx.AuthenticationMode = ClientAuthenticationMode.
FormsAuthentication;
FormsAuthenticationLoginInfo fba = new FormsAuthenticationLoginInfo("u
sername", "password");
clientCtx.FormsAuthenticationLoginInfo = fba;
//Business Logic
}
```

Impersonation

In order to impersonate you can pass in credential information to the `ClientContext` as shown in the following code:

```
clientCtx.Credentials = new NetworkCredential("username", "password",
"domainname");
```

Passing credential information this way is supported only in Managed OM.

See also

> ▸ *Handling* exceptions recipe
> ▸ *Calling Object Model asynchronously* recipe

Handling exceptions

In the previous recipe, we created a list with a custom field and some data. If all of these calls are batched together and sent to the server, how do we handle exceptions? In this recipe, we will create a console application to see how to handle exceptions.

Getting ready

You should complete the previous recipe successfully to follow this one.

How to do it...

In order to handle exceptions, adhere to the following steps:

1. Launch your Visual Studio 2010 IDE as an administrator (right-click the shortcut and select **Run as administrator)**.

2. Select **File | New | Project**. The new project wizard dialog box will be displayed (make sure to select **.NET Framework 3.5** in the top drop-down box).

3. Select Windows console application under the **Visual C# | Windows | Console Application** node from **Installed Templates** section on the left-hand side.

4. Name the project **HandleErrors** and provide a directory location where you want to save the project and click on **OK** to create the console application template.

5. Add references to `Microsoft.SharePoint.Client.dll` and `Microsoft.SharePoint.Client.Runtime.dll`.

6. Add the code to retrieve a non-existent list called **Standard Method** list and try to add an item to this list. Your code in `Program.cs` should look like the following block:

```
using System;
using System.Collections.Generic;
using System.Linq;
using System.Text;
using Microsoft.SharePoint.Client;

namespace HandleError
{
    class Program
    {
        static void Main(string[] args)
        {
            CreateListAndAddItemStandard("http://intsp1",
"Standard Method List", "Add Item By Standard Method");
        }
        public static void CreateListAndAddItemStandard(string
siteUrl, string listName, string itemTitle)
        {
            using (ClientContext clientCtx = new
ClientContext(siteUrl))
            {
                Web site = clientCtx.Web;
                try
```

```
            {
                //Get the list
                List list = site.Lists.GetByTitle(listName);
                ListItemCreationInformation
listItemCreationInfo = new ListItemCreationInformation();
                ListItem li = list.AddItem(listItemCreationInfo);
                li["Title"] = itemTitle;
                li.Update();
                list.Update();
                clientCtx.ExecuteQuery();
            }
            catch (ServerException)
            {
                // Create a list.
                ListCreationInformation listCreationInfo = new
ListCreationInformation();
                listCreationInfo.Title = listName;
                listCreationInfo.TemplateType =
(int)ListTemplateType.GenericList;
                listCreationInfo.QuickLaunchOption =
QuickLaunchOptions.On;
                List list = site.Lists.Add(listCreationInfo);
                ListItemCreationInformation
listItemCreationInfo = new ListItemCreationInformation();
                ListItem li = list.AddItem(listItemCreationInfo);
                li["Title"] = itemTitle;
                li.Update();
                list.Update();
                clientCtx.ExecuteQuery();
                Console.WriteLine("List Created");
                Console.Read();
            }
        }
    }
}
```

7. The list will be created from the `catch` block and an item will be added as shown in the following screenshot:

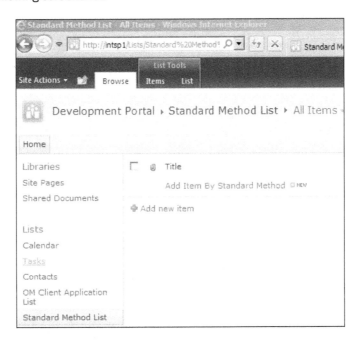

How it works...

In the previous recipe, we indicated to you that the batch processing would not send the request to the server until you issue an `ExecuteQuery` call. In the preceding program too, the batch request is issued as a `ExecuteQuery` method. `Client.svc` uses the server Object Model to get the list and fails, and hence throws the error.

In the catch block, we are creating the list and adding the item. We are also issuing another `ExecuteQuery` command to send the batch request to perform the required actions.

This is typical .NET programming, where we make decisions based on exceptions. If the exception caught was due to the list not found, then we will create a new one and continue with our business logic.

The flaw in this case is calling `ExecuteQuery` method twice. This is inefficient coding. Round trips to server should be reduced as much as possible for better user interactions.

Fortunately, an OM provides a way to batch our exception scopes without multiple trips to the server. The same code that we ran in the recipe can be rewritten with exception scope as follows:

```
public static void CreateListAndAddItem(string siteUrl, string
listName, string itemTitle)
    {
        using (var clientContext = new ClientContext(siteUrl))
        {
            var ehScope = new ExceptionHandlingScope
            (clientContext);

            List list;
            using (ehScope.StartScope())
            {
                using (ehScope.StartTry())
                {
                    list = clientContext.Web.Lists.
GetByTitle(listName);
                    clientContext.Load(list);

                }
                using (ehScope.StartCatch())
                {
                    var listCreationInformation = new
                    ListCreationInformation();
                    listCreationInformation.Title = listName;
                    listCreationInformation.TemplateType =
                    (int)ListTemplateType.GenericList;

                    list = clientContext.Web.Lists.Add
                    (listCreationInformation);

                }
                using (ehScope.StartFinally())
                {
                    ListItemCreationInformation
listItemCreationInfo = new ListItemCreationInformation();
                    ListItem li = list.AddItem(listItemCreationInfo);
                    li["Title"] = itemTitle;
                    li.Update();
                    list.Update();

                }
```

```
        }
        clientContext.ExecuteQuery();
}
```

The exception block in OM programming starts with an instance of `ExceptionHandlingScope`. This scope defines the scope of the exception that it needs to tackle in case the server raises an exception.

`ExceptionHandlingScope` always starts with the `StartScope()` method which should contain `StartTry()` and `StartCatch()` methods respectively in that order. `StartFinally()` in the end if provided, will always execute.

Apart from these methods, `ExceptionHandlingScope` also provides useful properties like `ErrorMessage`, `ServerStackTrace`, `ServerErrorValue`, `ServerErrorCode`, and `HasException` for you to understand what exactly went wrong on the server. The following is the **Fiddler** output of the JSON response for our recipe. If you look closely, it does indicate `HasException`, `ErrorMessage`, `ServerErrorCode`, and `ServerErrorValue`.

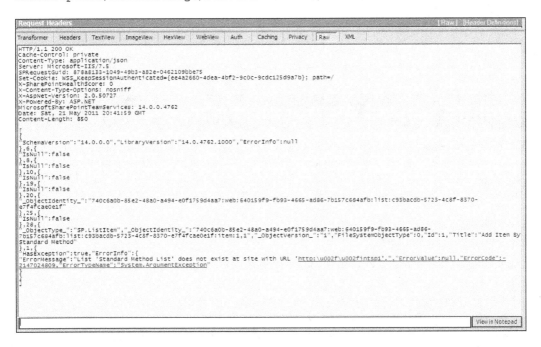

For more information on `ExceptionHandlingScope` refer to MSDN at: `http://msdn.microsoft.com/en-us/library/ee541237.aspx`.

There's more...

By default, to improve performance and reduce the network traffic, certain properties are not retrieved. In case you try to access such a property you will get a `PropertyOrFieldNotInitializedException` exception. The properties that are retrieved are based on the object type that is used in the `Load` method. For example, on `ListItem`, properties like `DisplayName`, `RoleAssignments`, `EffectiveBasePermissions`, and `HasUniqueRoleAssignments` are not retrieved by default. Use the `IsPropertyAvailable` method to check if that property is retrieved or not. You can also specify the properties that you want to retrieve in the client context `Load` method as follows:

```
clientContext.Load(listItems, li => li.Include(i => i["WorkPhone"], i
=> i["EMail"]));
clientContext.Load(web, w => w.Id, w => w.Title,w => w.Created);
```

See also

- ▸ *Creating a list using a Client Object Model* recipe
- ▸ *Calling Object Model asynchronously* recipe

Calling Object Model asynchronously

The previous recipes all included calling object model synchronously. There are times when the execution is a long running process, it makes sense to call the method asynchronously and provide a visual cue to the users about the progress of the execution. In this recipe, we will create a console application that calls the Object Model asynchronously.

Getting ready

You should have successfully completed the previous two recipes to follow this.

How to do it...

In order to call the Object Model asynchronously, adhere to the following steps:

1. Launch your Visual Studio 2010 IDE as an administrator (right-click the shortcut and select **Run as administrator).**
2. Select **File | New | Project**. The new project wizard dialog box will be displayed (make sure to select .NET Framework 3.5 in the top drop-down box).
3. Select Windows console application under the **Visual C# | Windows | Console Application** node from the **Installed Templates** section on the left-hand side.

4. Name the project **OMClientAsynch** and provide a directory location where you want to save the project and click on **OK** to create the console application template.

5. Add references to `Microsoft.SharePoint.Client.dll` and `Microsoft.SharePoint.Client.Runtime.dll`.

6. Add the code to change the site title and retrieve the names of all the lists in the site. Your code in `Program.cs` should look like the following:

```
using System;
using System.Collections.Generic;
using System.Linq;
using System.Text;
using Microsoft.SharePoint.Client;

namespace OMClientAsynch
{
    class Program
    {
        static void Main(string[] args)
        {
            OMClientAsynch asynch = new OMClientAsynch();
            asynch.RunAsynchronously();
        }
    }

    class OMClientAsynch
    {
        delegate void ExecuteAsynchQuery();
        Microsoft.SharePoint.Client.Web site;
        Microsoft.SharePoint.Client.ClientContext context;
        public void RunAsynchronously()
        {
            context = new ClientContext("http://intsp1");
            site = context.Web;
            ListCollection listcol = context.Web.Lists;
            context.Load(site, s => s.Title);
            context.Load(listcol);
            ExecuteAsynchQuery executeQueryAsync = new ExecuteAsynchQuery(context.ExecuteQuery);
            executeQueryAsync.BeginInvoke(AsynchCallback, null);
            Console.WriteLine("This will be the first line that
             will be displayed in the console");
            Console.WriteLine("Asynchronous method is already
            invoked. But the results will show up now");
            Console.Read();
```

```
                }
                private void AsynchCallback(IAsyncResult arg)
                {
                    Console.WriteLine("Aynchronous Callback!");
                    Console.WriteLine("Let us change the site title");
                    Console.WriteLine("Title before changing: {0}", site.
                    Title);

                    site.Title = site.Title + " From Aysnchronous client
                    application";
                    site.Update();

                    Console.WriteLine("Listings of all the lists from the
                    site!");
                    foreach (Microsoft.SharePoint.Client.List list in site.
                    Lists)
                    {
                        Console.WriteLine(list.Title);
                    }
                    context.ExecuteQuery();
                    Console.WriteLine("Query completed!");
                }
            }
        }
```

7. The following screenshot shows the output of the program:

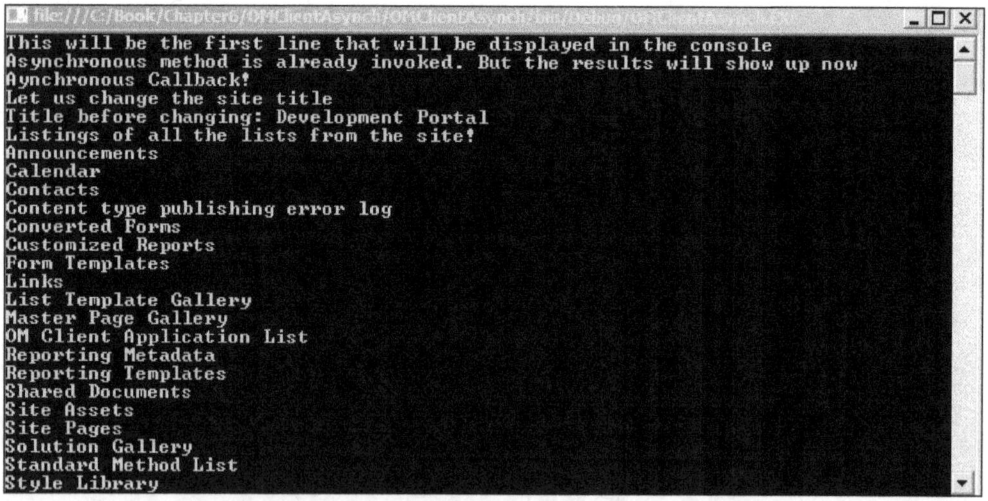

8. The change of the site title is shown as follows:

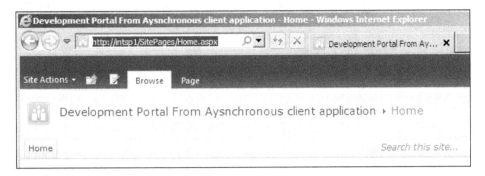

How it works...

The `ExecuteQueryAsynch` method is used by both Silverlight and JavaScript Object Models to make asynchronous calls. This method is not supported in the Managed OM. We have to use the standard .NET techniques to invoke the `ExecuteQuery` method asynchronously. For that purpose, we use delegate. When we execute a method asynchronously, we need to provide a `callback` method that can be invoked when the asynchronous call completes and is ready with the response. Our `callback` method in the code is `AsynchCallback`.

A delegate is a type that references a method. You can associate a delegate with any method as long as they have the compatible signature. We defined a delegate named `ExecuteAsynchQuery`. In our declaration of delegates, we did not define any parameters because `ExecuteQuery` does not have any either. We associated our delegate instance with `ExecuteQuery` and invoked it asynchronously by using the method `BeginInvoke`. The .NET runtime automatically defines the `BeginInvoke` and `EndInvoke` methods on the delegate with appropriate signatures. The method signature of `BeginInvoke` is `BeginInvoke(callback, object[]params);`.

The first parameter takes the callback method delegate. The second parameter is the user defined values that can be passed to the `callback` method. In our case, we are not passing in any and hence null. The `BeginInvoke` executes the method described in the delegate asynchronously. Once the method completes its execution, it invokes the `callback` method indicated. For more information on calling synchronous methods asynchronously, refer to MSDN at: `http://msdn.microsoft.com/en-US/library/2e08f6yc(v=VS.80).aspx`.

See also

► *Using JavaScript Object Model* recipe

Using JavaScript Object Model

So far we have only used the Managed Object Model. IIn this recipe we will use JavaScript OM and list first five items of our contacts list.

Getting ready

You should complete the previous recipe successfully to follow this one.

How to do it...

In order to use the JavaScript Object Model, adhere to the following steps:

1. If you have closed your Visual Studio IDE, launch it now as an administrator and create a new project of type **Empty SharePoint Project.** Name the project **JavaScriptOM**.

2. By default, Visual Studio selects the SharePoint site available on the machine. Select **Deploy as Farm Solution** and click on **Next** to proceed to the next step in the wizard.

3. Now add a new item and choose **Application Page**. Name this page **JavaScriptOM. aspx**.

4. Visual Studio automatically creates a `Layouts` folder and a subfolder underneath it called **JavaScriptOM**. Inside this folder you should see your ASPX page.

5. In this page, add the code and get the items from the contacts list. Your application page should have the JavaScript code as follows:

```
<asp:Content ID="Main" ContentPlaceHolderID="PlaceHolderMain"
runat="server">
<script type="text/javascript">
    var clientContext = null;
    var web = null;
    ExecuteOrDelayUntilScriptLoaded(Initialize, "sp.js");
    function Initialize() {
        clientContext = new SP.ClientContext.get_current();
        web = clientContext.get_web();
        var list = web.get_lists().getByTitle("Contacts");
        var query = new SP.CamlQuery();
        var rowLimit = '<View><RowLimit>5</RowLimit></View>';
        query.set_viewXml(rowLimit);
        this.listItems = list.getItems(query);
        clientContext.load(listItems, 'Include(DisplayName,Id)');
        clientContext.executeQueryAsync(Function.
createDelegate(this, this.onSuccessDelegate),
Function.createDelegate(this, this.onFailDelegate));
```

```
        }
        function onSuccessDelegate(sender, args) {
            var listItemEnumerator = this.listItems.getEnumerator();
            //iterate though all of the items
            while (listItemEnumerator.moveNext()) {
                var item = listItemEnumerator.get_current();
                var title = item.get_displayName();
                var id = item.get_id();
                AddItem(title, id);
            }
        }

        function onFailDelegate(sender, args) {
            alert('request failed ' + args.get_message() + '\n' +
args.get_stackTrace());
        }

        function AddItem(Text, Value) {
            // Create an Option object
            var opt = document.createElement("option");

            // Add an Option object to Drop Down/List Box
            document.getElementById("showItems").options.add(opt);
// Assign text and value to Option object
            opt.text = Text;
            opt.value = Value;

        }
        </script>

    <h1> Contacts Items From JavaScript OM </h1>
        <select id="showItems" size="5">
        </select>
</asp:Content>
```

6. Build and execute the solution by pressing *F5* or from menu **Debug | Start Debugging**. This should bring up the default browser with the local site that you provided in the project creation wizard.

7. Browse to: `http://yourservername/_layouts/JavaScriptOM/`
`JavaScriptOM.aspx`. Make sure to substitute your server name in the link. You should be able to see the application page with contacts loaded from the contacts list as follows:

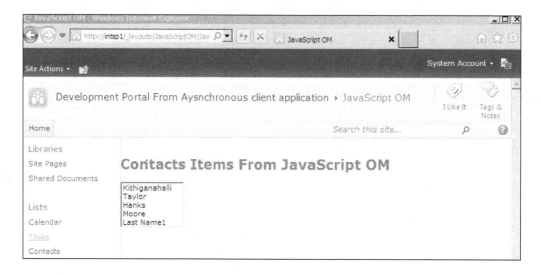

How it works...

The ASPX page that uses the JavaScript OM should register `Microsoft.SharePoint.WebControls` before it can make use of the OM. The reason is that the web controls provide support for adding the script reference and form digest controls for security authorizations. When we develop pages using Visual Studio 2010 SharePoint projects, `Microsoft.SharePoint.WebControls` and `SP.js` registrations are already handled. `SP.js` is already defined in the default master page, and hence we did not register the script. If you are not using the default master page and if you are unsure of the reference to this script file, you can use `<SharePoint:ScriptLink ID="JavaOMScriptLink" runat="server" LoadAfterUI="true" Name="sp.js" />`.

The method calls in the JavaScript OM use the JavaScript notation instead of dot notation used in .Net programming. Also due to the difference in data value types between .NET and JavaScript, collections like `StringCollection` will be treated as `string[]` (string array) in JavaScript. For all the differences between .NET and JavaScript OM refer to MSDN at: `http://msdn.microsoft.com/en-us/library/ee539429.aspx`.

As in the Managed OM, you will have to create the context by calling a `SP.CreateContext` method. In a JavaScript OM, there is no need to provide the URL of the server we will be working with. It uses the current context in which the page is running, and hence the use of `get_current()`. This is different from the Managed OM applications, as these are not executed in the SharePoint context.

As in the Managed OM, we can get the site object and web object from the context. You can see that, the properties are obtained using the `get_` method names. This is a JavaScript convention for properties. The `executeQueryAsync` method executes asynchronously and based on the response, invokes the callback delegates `onSuccessDelegate` or `onFailureDelegate` based on success or failure of the execution. In our sample, on successful execution of the code, items will be added to the list and in case of error, an alert with the error message is shown.

There's more...

The error handling is similar to the Managed OM. You can define the `ExceptionHandlingScope`. The following code shows the `try catch` block with the `ExceptionHandlingScope`:

```
<script type="text/javascript">
    var clientContext = null;
    var web = null;
    var list = null;

    ExecuteOrDelayUntilScriptLoaded(Initialize, "sp.js");
    function Initialize() {
        clientContext = new SP.ClientContext;
        web = clientContext.get_web();

        var ehScope = new SP.ExceptionHandlingScope(clientContext);
        var scopeStart = ehScope.startScope();
        var myTry = ehScope.startTry();

            list = web.get_lists().getByTitle("JavaOMList");
            list.set_description("Change description in Try block");
            list.update();
            myTry.dispose();

        var myCatch = ehScope.startCatch();
          //  list = null;
         var catchListCreationInfo = new SP.ListCreationInformation();
            catchListCreationInfo.set_title("JavaOMList");
            catchListCreationInfo.set_templateType(104);
            catchListCreationInfo.set_quickLaunchOption
            (SP.QuickLaunchOptions.on);

            list = web.get_lists().add(catchListCreationInfo);

            myCatch.dispose();
```

```
        var myFinal = ehScope.startFinally();

        var itemCreateInfo = new SP.ListItemCreationInformation();
        this.oListItem = list.addItem(itemCreateInfo);
        oListItem.set_item('Title', 'Item Created from JavascriptOM
Finally Block ');

        oListItem.update();

        list.update();

        myFinal.dispose();

        scopeStart.dispose();


        clientContext.executeQueryAsync(Function.createDelegate(this,
this.onSuccessDelegate),
Function.createDelegate(this, this.onFailDelegate));
    }
    function onSuccessDelegate(sender, args) {
        alert('Request success');
    }

    function onFailDelegate(sender, args) {
        alert('Request failed: ' + args.get_message() + '\n Stack
Trace: ' + args.get_stackTrace());
    }
</script>
```

The preceding code checks for the list and tries to update the description. Since the list is non-existent, it will fail and the catch block will be executed. In here, we will create the list and finally we will add an item to the list. The following screenshot shows the outcome of the preceding code:

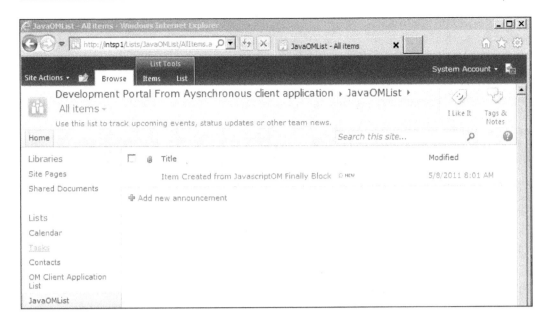

You can also see the format of the request that is sent to the server for the preceding code through **Fiddler** below:

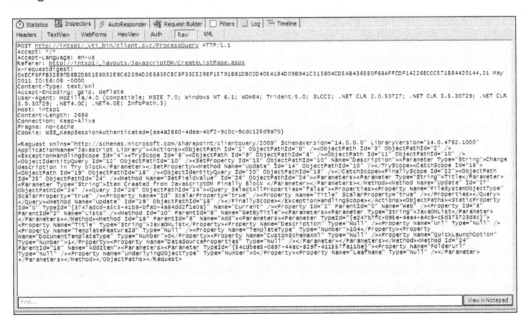

See also

> ▸ *Creating a list using a Client Object Model* recipe.
>
> ▸ *Handling exceptions* recipe
>
> ▸ *Using a Silverlight Object Model* recipe

Using a Silverlight Object Model

Silverlight is a development platform to develop rich internet applications that are cross-browser and cross-platform compatible. Silverlight applications are executed through a browser plug-in that means it runs inside the Internet Explorer on the client machines. By using Silverlight and SharePoint as the data source you can develop visually appealing clients for your users.

In this recipe, we will create a Silverlight application using the Silverlight Object Model. The application like the previous recipes, will display list items from the contacts list.

Getting ready

The previous recipes should be completed successfully. Additionally, create a new document library on your site using SharePoint UI and name it **XAPFiles**.

How to do it...

In order to use Silverlight Object Model, adhere to the following steps:

1. If you have closed Visual Studio IDE, launch it as an administrator.

2. Create a new **Empty SharePoint Project** called **SilverlightOM.** Take defaults on the next steps of the wizard.

3. To this solution add a new Silverlight application project and name it **ContactsListSilverlight**.

4. Now to your **Empty SharePoint Project**, add a new module and name it **XAPFiles**.

5. Delete the `Sample.txt` file it adds to the module. The `Elements.xml` file will be automatically updated by VS 2010.

6. In the properties window for this module, click on the **ellipsis** of the **Project Output References** as shown follows:

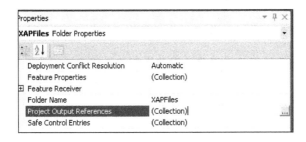

7. This should bring up the **Project Output References** collection window. Click on the **Add** button and add the **ContactsListSilverlight** project as a member project and set the **Deployment Type** to **ElementFile** as shown in the following screenshot:

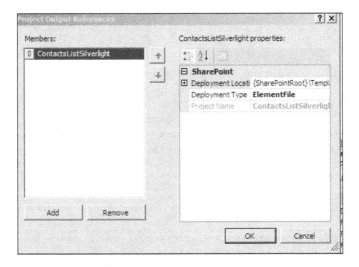

8. Visual Studio automatically updates your elements file in the module with the XAP files. Open the `Elements.xml` file from the module and add a URL attribute to the `Module` element and set the value to the document library name. In our case it is **XAPFiles**. Also add `Type` attribute to the file element and set the value to `GhostableInLibrary`. Your `Elements.xml` file in the XAP files module should appear as follows:

```xml
<?xml version="1.0" encoding="utf-8"?>
<Elements xmlns="http://schemas.microsoft.com/sharepoint/">
  <Module Name="XAPFiles" Url="XAPFiles">
  <File Path="XAPFiles\ContactsListSilverlight.xap" Url="XAPFiles/
ContactsListSilverlight.xap" Type="GhostableInLibrary" />
  </Module>
</Elements>
```

9. Add references to Silverlight client object model assemblies to your **ContactsListSilverlight** project.

10. Add a datagrid and a button to your `MainPage.xaml` and your XAML file should appears as follows:

```xml
<UserControl x:Class="ContactsListSilverlight.MainPage"
    xmlns="http://schemas.microsoft.com/winfx/2006/xaml/
presentation"
    xmlns:x="http://schemas.microsoft.com/winfx/2006/xaml"
    xmlns:d="http://schemas.microsoft.com/expression/blend/2008"
    xmlns:mc="http://schemas.openxmlformats.org/markup-
compatibility/2006"
    mc:Ignorable="d"
    d:DesignHeight="290" d:DesignWidth="508" xmlns:data="clr-
namespace:System.Windows.Controls;assembly=System.Windows.
Controls.Data">

    <Grid x:Name="LayoutRoot" Background="#B4ECFFE6" Height="264"
Width="466">
        <Button Content="Get Data" Height="23" HorizontalAlignment
="Left" Margin="268,12,0,0" Name="button1" VerticalAlignment="Top"
Width="105" Click="button1_Click" />
        <data:DataGrid AutoGenerateColumns="True" Height="200"
HorizontalAlignment="Left" Margin="12,52,0,0" Name="dataGrid1"
VerticalAlignment="Top" Width="420" />
    </Grid>
</UserControl>
```

11. Add the code to retrieve contacts from the contacts list that we have used in the previous chapters and recipes. Your code in `MainPage.xaml.cs` should look like the following:

```csharp
namespace ContactsListSilverlight
{
    public class MyContacts
    {
        public string LastName { get; set; }
        public string FirstName { get; set; }
        public string BusinessPhone { get; set; }
        public string EmailAddress { get; set; }
    }
    public partial class MainPage : UserControl
    {
        private Microsoft.SharePoint.Client.Web _web;
        private Microsoft.SharePoint.Client.List _list;
        private ListItemCollection _listItemCol;
        public MainPage()
```

```csharp
{
    InitializeComponent();
}

private void button1_Click(object sender,
 RoutedEventArgs e)
{
    ClientContext context = new ClientContext
    (ApplicationContext.Current.Url);
    _web = context.Web;
    context.Load(_web);
    _list = _web.Lists.GetByTitle("Contacts");
    var query = new CamlQuery();
    var rowLimit = "<View><RowLimit>5</RowLimit></View>";
    query.ViewXml = rowLimit;
    _listItemCol = _list.GetItems(query);
    context.Load(_listItemCol);
    context.Load(_list);
    context.ExecuteQueryAsync(new ClientRequestSucceededEv
entHandler(OnSuccessRequest), new ClientRequestFailedEventHandler(
OnFailedRequest));
}

private void OnSuccessRequest(Object sender,
ClientRequestSucceededEventArgs args)
{
    Dispatcher.BeginInvoke(FillGrid);
}

private void OnFailedRequest(Object sender,
ClientRequestFailedEventArgs args)
{
    MessageBox.Show("Request Failed: " + args.Message + ",
Stack Trace:" + args.StackTrace);
}

private void FillGrid()
{
    List<MyContacts> _myContacts = new List<MyContacts>();
    foreach(ListItem item in _listItemCol)
    {
        _myContacts.Add(new MyContacts
        {
            LastName = item["Title"].ToString(),
            FirstName = item["FirstName"].ToString(),
```

```
                                    BusinessPhone = item["WorkPhone"].ToString(),
                                    EmailAddress = item["Email"].ToString()
                               });
                          }
                          dataGrid1.ItemsSource = _myContacts;
                     }
                }
           }
```

12. Build and run the project by pressing *F5.* You should see the XAP file deployed to your documents folder **XAPFiles** created before the beginning of this recipe.

13. Add the Silverlight web part for your page and provide the **URL** of the XAP file as shown in the following screenshot:

14. The output of the Silverlight web part is as shown in the following screenshot:

How it works...

The classes and methods in the Silverlight Object Model are similar to the Managed and JavaScript Object Models. The programming in Silverlight uses asynchronous execution like in JavaScript. The code is very similar to the one we did in JavaScript recipe.

Similar to JavaScript OM, we defined the event handlers for a `SuccessRequest` and a `FailedRequest`. We also had a callback method to fill in the gird with contacts. You will follow this procedure whenever you create a Silverlight application using the Client Object Model.

There's more...

Error handling in Silverlight applications follows the same pattern as in the other two models. You can use the `ExceptionScopeHandling` with modified `try` and `catch` blocks.

See also

▶ _Creating a list using_ a _Client Object Model_ recipe

▶ _Handling exceptions_ recipe

▶ _Using_ a _JavaScript Object Model_ recipe

Index

Thank you for buying
Microsoft SharePoint 2010 Development with Visual Studio 2010: Expert Cookbook

About Packt Publishing

Packt, pronounced 'packed', published its first book "*Mastering phpMyAdmin for Effective MySQL Management*" in April 2004 and subsequently continued to specialize in publishing highly focused books on specific technologies and solutions.

Our books and publications share the experiences of your fellow IT professionals in adapting and customizing today's systems, applications, and frameworks. Our solution-based books give you the knowledge and power to customize the software and technologies you're using to get the job done. Packt books are more specific and less general than the IT books you have seen in the past. Our unique business model allows us to bring you more focused information, giving you more of what you need to know, and less of what you don't.

Packt is a modern, yet unique publishing company, which focuses on producing quality, cutting-edge books for communities of developers, administrators, and newbies alike. For more information, please visit our website: www.PacktPub.com.

About Packt Enterprise

In 2010, Packt launched two new brands, Packt Enterprise and Packt Open Source, in order to continue its focus on specialization. This book is part of the Packt Enterprise brand, home to books published on enterprise software – software created by major vendors, including (but not limited to) IBM, Microsoft and Oracle, often for use in other corporations. Its titles will offer information relevant to a range of users of this software, including administrators, developers, architects, and end users.

Writing for Packt

We welcome all inquiries from people who are interested in authoring. Book proposals should be sent to author@packtpub.com. If your book idea is still at an early stage and you would like to discuss it first before writing a formal book proposal, contact us; one of our commissioning editors will get in touch with you.

We're not just looking for published authors; if you have strong technical skills but no writing experience, our experienced editors can help you develop a writing career, or simply get some additional reward for your expertise.

Microsoft SharePoint 2010 End User Guide: Business Performance Enhancement

ISBN: 978-1-84968-066-0   Paperback: 424 pages

Taking the basics to the business with no-coding solutions for the SharePoint 2010

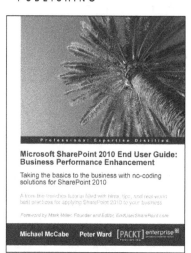

1. Designed to offer applicable, no-coding solutions to dramatically enhance the performance of your business

2. Excel at SharePoint intranet functionality to have the most impact on you and your team

3. Drastically enhance your End user SharePoint functionality experience

Microsoft SharePoint 2010 Power User Cookbook: SharePoint Applied

ISBN: 978-1-84968-288-6   Paperback: 350 pages

Over 90 advanced recipes for expert-level End Users to unlock the real value of SharePoint in your business

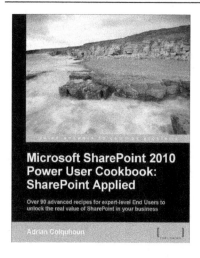

1. Discover how to apply SharePoint far beyond basic functionality

2. Explore the Business Intelligence capabilities of SharePoint with KPIs and custom dashboards

3. Take a deep dive into document management, data integration, electronic forms, and workflow scenarios

Please check **www.PacktPub.com** for information on our titles

Microsoft SharePoint 2010 Enterprise Applications on Windows Phone 7

ISBN: 978-1-84968-258-9   Paperback: 252 pages

Create enterprise-ready websites and applications that access Microsoft SharePoint on Windows Phone 7

1. Provides step-by-step instructions for integrating Windows Phone 7-capable web pages into SharePoint websites

2. Provides an overview of creating Windows Phone 7 applications that integrate with SharePoint services

3. Examines Windows Phone 7's enterprise capabilities

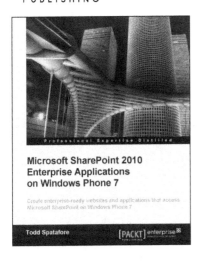

Microsoft SharePoint 2010
Enterprise Applications
on Windows Phone 7

Create enterprise-ready websites and applications that access
Microsoft SharePoint on Windows Phone 7

Todd Spatafore

Microsoft Silverlight 4 and SharePoint 2010 Integration

ISBN: 978-1-849680-06-6   Paperback: 336 pages

Techniques, practical tips, hints, and tricks for Silverlight interactions with SharePoint

1. Develop Silverlight RIAs that interact with SharePoint 2010 data and services

2. Explore the diverse alternatives for hosting a Silverlight RIA in a SharePoint 2010 Page

3. Work with the new SharePoint Silverlight Client Object Model to interact with elements in a SharePoint Site

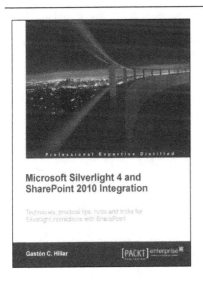

Microsoft Silverlight 4 and
SharePoint 2010 Integration

Techniques, practical tips, hints and tricks for
Silverlight interactions with SharePoint

Gastón C. Hillar

Please check **www.PacktPub.com** for information on our titles